An Alternative Assembly Book

Linda Hoy   Mike Hoy

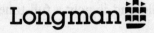

LONGMAN GROUP LIMITED
*Longman House, Burnt Mill, Harlow, Essex CM20 2JE, England
and Associated Companies throughout the World*

First published in 1985

ISBN 0 582 36124 9

Set in 12/13pt Plantin, Linotron 202

*Printed in Great Britain
by Butler and Tanner Ltd; Frome*

Linda Hoy taught English for nine years at a comprehensive school in Sheffield and is now a full-time writer.

Mike Hoy is deputy headteacher at Birley Middle School in Sheffield.

Contents

Introduction

If school assemblies take it for granted that everyone present believes in a white male Christian god in heaven, many of the participants are made to feel like football supporters accidentally finding themselves on the opponents' side of the ground. They might slip their scarves discreetly inside their pockets and mouth token support for the other team but, when the final whistle goes, they just can't get away fast enough.

So, what should we teach in school assemblies? That chewing gum must not be placed on the underside of school desks? That pupils should queue for lunch in an orderly manner and always have their names on their gym shoes? In a society in which few people go to church and the majority find traditional dogma hard to accept, it's tempting to leave religion conveniently out of schools and their assemblies. If we do that though, how can we expect young people to make up their own minds about religion when they know next to nothing about it? And how can we expect them to acquire principles like honesty and consideration for others when we give them no framework to base those principles on?

If we do give up religion, it should not mean that we also give up believing in peace, justice, freedom and love. Much of this book is based on secular material; atheists and agnostics should feel able to use it just as comfortably as Anglicans, Jews or anyone else. There are traditional religious readings as well, but the approach of the book is to accept the participants' right to doubt and question dogma and to bring those doubts into the service rather than forcing them outside it.

Any book of this sort is bound to reflect the attitude of its writer. In childhood I was an Anglican, an atheist in my teens and twenties and then became a Quaker, 'by convincement', as they say, in my thirties.

The principles on which this book are based are:
- that all people are valuable and should be respected regardless of race, sex, class – that we should relate to 'that of God in every man'.

- religious worship should be the way we live our lives and conduct our affairs rather than merely following some weekly ritual – 'letting our lives speak'.
- honesty is important – in our dealings with others and in understanding ourselves.
- we should seek to discover the causes of social unrest and injustice and work towards a better and fairer order of society.
- religion is not there to help us escape from the depressing realities of life but to give us the strength to come to terms with them and, where necessary, struggle against them.
- the most important issue facing the world today is the threat of its annihilation. We cannot claim to care about others or to respect life on this planet without taking account of this threat and playing our part in helping to prevent it becoming reality.

Well-meaning principles, however, will not by themselves make religion attractive. The main complaint pupils make about assembly is that it's boring. The more exciting things in life are wrapped up and packaged well: the best records do have exciting sleeves and many good books have lurid covers. We may live with the assumption that religion is more like a good old-fashioned medicine – if you have faith that it's good for you, it hardly needs packaging at all. But the majority of our pupils nowadays do not have that faith. Without it, they won't willingly suffer boredom in assemblies.

When taking assemblies myself, I chose material that was absorbing, entertaining and, through my concerns as an English teacher, of high literary quality. Reading extracts in assembly helps stimulate a demand for reading the whole book and teachers would be well advised to make sure the novels they read in assembly are available in the school library, bookshop or the classroom.

For the majority of pupils and teachers who never go to church, the school assembly will be their main or only contact with religion. This places an awesome responsibility on teachers taking assemblies to make them interesting, entertaining and valuable. This book tries to help.

Linda Hoy

1 Honesty

Day 1

Autocover Insurance (1)

Introduction

One of the ten commandments which was given to Moses was 'Thou shalt not bear false witness', which is another way of saying that we should always speak the truth.

The following statements are real examples taken from insurance forms where drivers have tried to explain what has happened in an accident. In these cases the drivers have made very poor witnesses. Many of them made themselves sound ridiculous by trying to make it appear that the accident was somebody else's fault:

— 'My car was legally parked as it backed into the other vehicle.'

— 'An invisible car came out of nowhere, struck my car and vanished.'

'I told the police I was not injured but, on removing my hat, found I had a fractured skull.'

— 'Coming home I drove into the wrong house and collided with a tree I don't have.'

— 'The other car collided with mine without giving warning of its intention.'

— 'A pedestrian hit me and went under my car.'

'I thought my window was down, but I found out it was up when I put my head through it.'

— 'I collided with a stationary truck coming the other way.'

'In an attempt to kill a fly, I drove into a telephone pole.'

— 'I had been driving for forty years when I fell asleep at the wheel and had an accident.'

— 'The guy was all over the road. I had to swerve a number of times before I hit him.'

Conclusion

The people who wrote these accounts were probably not telling deliberate lies. They wanted to give a good impression of themselves but, in distorting the truth, finished up making themselves look ridiculous.

Prayer

When we are asked to bear witness to something we have seen or heard, may we try to do so honestly and accurately. May we never fall into the temptation of blaming other people for things we are responsible for ourselves.

Amen

Day 2

The Fib (1)

Introduction

The following extract is taken from a collection of short stories about the northern working-class childhood of the writer, George Layton. We're going to hear the first part of a story called 'The Fib' which mentions two footballers who were very famous when George Layton was a boy. Most of you will have heard of them.

Gordon Banks was a brilliant goalkeeper for England until a tragic accident in 1972 when he lost the sight of his right eye and was never able to return to first class English football.

Bobby Charlton was one of the few survivors of the Munich air crash which killed most of Manchester United's football squad. He was one of England's leading footballers between 1957 and 1970.

'Are you up? I've called you three times already.'
'Yes, Mum, 'course I am.'
I knew it was a lie, but I just wanted to have a few more minutes in bed. It was so cosy.
'You'd better be, because I'm not telling you again.'
That was another lie. She was always telling me again.

'Just you be quick, young man, and frame yourself, or you'll be late for school.'

Ooh school! If only I didn't have to go . . . today was Monday and Mondays was football, and I hate blooming football. It wouldn't be so bad if I had proper kit, but I had to play in these old-fashioned shorts and boots that my mum had got from my Uncle Kevin. They were huge. Miles too big for me. Gordon Barraclough's mum and dad had bought him a Bobby Charlton strip and Bobby Charlton boots. No wonder he's a better player than me. My mum said she couldn't see what was wrong with my kit. She couldn't understand that I felt silly, and all the other lads laughed at me – even Tony, and he's my best friend. She just said she wasn't going to waste good money on new boots and shorts, when I had a perfectly good set already.

'But Mum, they all laugh at me – especially Gordon Barraclough.'

'Well laugh back at them. You're big enough aren't you? Don't be such a jessie.'

She just didn't understand.

'You tell them your Uncle Kevin played in those boots when he was a lad, and he scored thousands of goals.'

Blimey, that shows you how old my kit is! My Uncle Kevin's 29! I snuggled down the bed a bit more, and pulled the pillow under the blankets with me.

'I'm coming upstairs and if I find you not up, there'll be trouble. I'm not telling you again.'

Oh 'eck! I forced myself out of bed on to the freezing lino and got into my underpants. Ooh, they were cold! Blooming daft this. Getting dressed, going to school, and getting undressed again to play rotten football. I looked out of the window . . . and started wondering how I could get out of going to football . . . I know, I'd tell my mum I wasn't feeling well. I'd tell her I'd got a cold. No, a sore throat. No, she'd look. Swollen glands. Yes, that's what I'd tell her, swollen glands. No, she'd feel. What could I say was wrong with me? Earache, yes, earache, and I'd ask her to write me a note. I'd ask her after breakfast. Well, it was only a fib wasn't it?

'You're very quiet. Didn't you enjoy your breakfast?'

'Err . . . well . . . I don't feel very well, Mum. I think I've got earache.'

'You *think* you've got earache?'

'I mean I *have* got earache – definitely – in my ear.'

'Which ear?'

'What?'

'You going deaf as well? I said, which ear?'

'Err . . . my right ear. Perhaps you'd better write me a note to get me off football. . .'

'No, love, it'll be good for you to go to football, get some fresh air. I'll write to Mr Melrose and ask him to let you go in goal, so you don't have to run around too much.'

She'd write a note to *ask* if I could go in . . . ! Melrose didn't need a note from me to go in goal. I was *always* shoved in goal. Me and Norbert Lightowler were always in goal 'cos we were the worst players.

Norbert didn't care. He was never bothered when people shouted at him. He just told them to get lost. He never even changed for football. He just stuffed his trousers into his socks and said it was a track suit. He nearly looked as daft as me in my Uncle Kevin's old kit.

'Mum, don't bother writing me a note. I'll be all right.'

'I'm only thinking of you. If you've got earache I don't want you to run around too much . . .'

Do you know, I don't think my mum believed I'd got earache. I know I was fibbing, but even if I had got earache, I don't think she'd have believed me . . . How could my mum know that when I was in goal I ran around twice as much, anyway? Every time the other team scored, I had to belt halfway across the playing field to fetch the ball back.

'Well, finish your Rice Krispies. Tony'll be here in a minute.'

Conclusion

George Layton's story is called 'The Fib'. It's a temptation sometimes to tell a fib if we think it might get us out of an awkward situation – like the writer pretending to have earache to get out of playing football. Later in the story, the writer tells a fib which lands him in a very embarrassing situation.

Prayer

May we strive to be honest in all our dealings so that other people come to feel that they can trust us.

Amen

The Fib (2)

Tony called for me every morning. I was never ready. I was just finishing my toast when I heard my mum let him in. He came through to the kitchen.

'Aw, come on. You're never ready.'

'I won't be a minute.'

'We'll be late, we'll miss the football bus.'

We didn't have any playing fields at our school, so we had a special bus to Bankfield Top, about two miles away.

My mum came in with my kit.

'Yes, hurry up or you'll miss your bus for football.'

'We won't miss our rotten bus for rotten football.'

She gave me a clout on the back of my head. Tony laughed.

'And you can stop laughing, Tony Wainwright,' and she gave him a clout, as well. 'Now go on, both of you.'

We ran to school and got there in plenty of time. I knew we would.

Everybody was getting on the bus. We didn't have to go to assembly when it was football. Gordon Barraclough was on the top deck with his head out of the window. He saw me coming.

'Hey, Gordon Banks . . .'

He always called me that, 'cos he thinks Gordon Banks was the best goalie ever. He reckons he was called Gordon after Gordon Banks.

'Hey, Gordon Banks – how many goals are you going to let in today?'

Tony nudged me.

'Don't take any notice.'

'Come on, Gordon Banks, how many goals am I going to get against you . . . ?'

Tony nudged me again.

'Ignore him.'

'. . . or am I going to be lumbered with you on my side, eh?'

'He's only egging you on. Ignore him.'

Yes, I'll ignore him. That's the best thing. I'll ignore him.

'If you're on my side, Gordon Banks, you'd better not let any goals in, or I'll do you.'

Just ignore him, that's the best thing.

'Get lost, Barraclough, you rotten big-head.'

I couldn't ignore him. Tony was shaking his head.

'I told you to ignore him.'

. . . Gordon still had his head out of the window.

'I'm coming down to get you.'

And he would've done too, if it hadn't been for Norbert. Just as Gordon was going back into the bus, Nobert wound the window up, so Gordon's head was stuck. It must've hurt him – well, it could have choked him.

'You're a maniac, Lightowler. You could have choked me.'

Norbert just laughed, and Gordon thumped him, right in the neck, and they started fighting. Tony and me ran up the stairs to watch. They were rolling in the aisle. Norbert got on top of Gordon and put his knees on his shoulders. Everybody was watching now and shouting: 'Fight! Fight!' . . . I really wanted him to do Gordon.

'Go on Norbert, do him.'

Just then, somebody clouted me on the back of my head, right where my mum had hit me that morning. I turned round to belt whoever it was.

'Who do you think you're thumping. . . ? Oh, morning Mr Melrose.'

He pushed me away, and went over to where Norbert and Gordon were still fighting. He grabbed them both by their jackets and pulled them apart. He used to be in the Commandos did Mr Melrose.

'Animals! You're a pair of animals! What are you?'

Neither of them said anything. He was still holding them by their jackets. He shook them.

'What are you? Lightowler?'

'A pair of animals.'

'Gordon?'

'A pair of animals, sir. It wasn't my fault, sir. He started it, sir. He wound up that window, sir and I got my head stuck. He could have choked me, sir.'

Ooh, he was a right tell-tale was Barraclough.

'Why was your head out of the window in the first place?'

'I was just telling someone to hurry up, sir.'

He's a liar as well, but he knew he was all right with Melrose 'cos he's his favourite.

'And then Lightowler wound up the window, for no reason, sir. He could've choked me . . .'

Prayer

May we try to be honest in all the things we say and do. When we have to deal with people who are not as straightforward with us as we would like, may we still maintain our own integrity and relate to them with fairness and honesty.

Amen

Day 4

The Fib (3)

When we got to Bankfield Top, Melrose told us we had three minutes to get changed. Everybody ran to the temporary changing room. It's always been called the 'temporary changing room' ever since anyone can remember. We're supposed to be getting a proper place sometime with hot and cold showers and things, but I don't reckon we ever will.

The temporary changing room's just a shed. It's got one shower that just runs cold water, but even that doesn't work properly. I started getting into my football togs. I tried to make the shorts as short as I could by turning the waist-band over a few times, but they still came down to my knees. And the boots were great big heavy things. Not like Gordon Barraclough's Bobby Charlton ones. I could've worn mine on either foot – it wouldn't have made any difference.

Gordon was changed first, and started jumping up and down and doing all sorts of exercises. He even had a Manchester United track suit top on.

'Come on Gordon Banks, get out onto the park.'

Get out onto the park! Just 'cos his dad took him over to see Manchester United every other Saturday, he thought he knew it all.

The next hour and a half was the same as usual – rotten. Gordon and Curly Emmott picked sides – as usual. I went in goal – as usual. I nearly froze to death – as usual, and I let in fifteen goals – as usual. Most of the time all you could hear was Melrose shouting: 'Well done, Gordon', 'Go round him, Gordon', 'Good deception, Gordon', . . . 'Shoot, Gordon', 'Hard luck, Gordon'.

. . . I thought Melrose was never going to blow the final whistle. When he did, we all trudged back to the temporary changing room. Even on the way back Gordon was jumping up and down and doing all sorts of funny exercises. He was only showing off to Melrose.

'That's it Gordon, keep the muscles supple. Well played, lad. We'll see you get a trial for United yet.'

Back in the changing room, Gordon started going on about my football kit. He egged everybody else on.

'Listen Barraclough, this strip belonged to my uncle and he scored thousands of goals.'

Gordon just laughed.

'Your uncle? Your auntie more like. You look like a big girl.'

'Listen Barraclough, you don't know who my uncle is.'

I was sick of Gordon Barraclough. I was sick of his bullying and his shouting, and his crawling round Melrose. And I was sick of him being a good footballer.

'My uncle is Bobby Charlton.'

That was the fib.

For a split second I think Gordon believed me, then he burst out laughing. So did everyone else. Even Tony laughed.

'Bobby Charlton – your uncle? You don't expect us to believe that do you?'

'Believe what you like – it's the truth.'

'Course they didn't believe me. That's why the fib became a lie.

'Cross my heart and hope to die.'

I spat on my left hand. They all went quiet. Gordon put his face close to mine.

'You're a liar.'

I was.

'I'm not. Cross my heart and hope to die.'

I spat on my hand again. If I'd dropped dead on the spot, I wouldn't have been surprised. Thank goodness Melrose came in, and made us hurry on to the bus.

Gordon and me didn't talk to each other much for the rest of the day. All afternoon I could see him looking at me. He was so sure I was a liar, but he just couldn't be certain.

Why had I been so daft as to tell such a stupid lie? Well, it was only a fib really, and at least it shut Gordon Barraclough up for an afternoon.

After school, Tony and me went into town to watch the lights being switched on. Norbert tagged along as well. . . . There was a crowd at the bottom of the Town Hall steps, and we managed to get right to the front. Gordon was there already . . . When the Lord Mayor came out we all clapped. He had his chain on and he made a speech about the Christmas appeal.

Then it came to switching on the lights.

'. . . and as you know, ladies and gentlemen, boys and girls, we always try to get someone special to switch on our Chamber of Commerce Christmas lights, and this year is no exception. Let's give a warm welcome to Mr Bobby Charlton . . .'

I couldn't believe it. I nearly fainted. I couldn't move for a few minutes. Everybody was asking for his autograph. When it was Gordon's turn, I saw him pointing at me. I could feel myself going red. Then, I saw him waving me over. Not Gordon. Bobby Charlton!

I went. Tony and Norbert followed. Gordon was grinning at me.

'You've had it now. You're for it now. I told him you said he's your uncle.'

I looked up at Bobby Charlton. He looked down at me. I could feel my face going even redder. . .

Conclusion

You will have to read this story for yourself to find out what happens next.

The writer calls this story 'The Fib'. When we think lies are fairly harmless we call them 'fibs' or 'little white lies' and try to persuade ourselves that they're not important because they are not really hurting anyone.

We can never judge, however, what the consequences of a lie will be – we can never be sure how many people will believe us and how seriously they might take what we say. What seems like a tiny fib, like an exaggerated bit of scandal or gossip, can cause terribly upsetting rumours in a school.

When we judge whether an action is right or not, we have to look at the action itself – not just what we think will be the consequences of it. If we think dishonesty is wrong, we can't then start saying that it's all right sometimes but not at others – we can't say that some lies are all right and some aren't.

Prayer

May we use our imagination for writing and telling stories that no one ever supposes to be true. May we have the cour-

age to own up straightaway when we have done something
wrong and never lie to try and cover our mistakes.

Amen

Day 5 **Autocover Insurance (2)**

Our final assembly on the theme of Honesty contains more
statements sent in by car drivers to the Autocover Insurance
company.

'I pulled away from the side of the road, glanced at my
mother-in-law, and headed over the embankment.'

'I had been shopping for plants all day and was on my way
home. As I reached an intersection a hedge sprang up, obscuring my vision and I did not see the other car.'

'The pedestrian had no idea which way to run, so I ran
over him.'

'I was on my way to the doctor with rear end trouble when
my universal joint gave way causing me to have an accident.'

'The indirect cause of the accident was a little guy in a
small car with a big mouth.'

— 'As I approached the intersection a sign suddenly appeared
in a place where no stop sign had ever appeared before. I was
unable to stop in time to avoid the accident.'

— 'I was sure the old fellow would never make it to the other
side of the road when I struck him.'

'I was thrown from my car as it left the road. I was later
found in a field by some stray cows.'

'I saw a slow-moving, sad-faced old gentleman as he
bounced off the roof of my car.'

Prayer

May we learn to think first, before we speak, to try and ensure that what we say is true. May we not fall into the temptation of distorting the truth to try and make ourselves look
better than we really are.

Amen

2 | Who Is My Neighbour?

Day 1   The Good Samaritan

In a well-known passage from St Luke's Gospel, a lawyer asks Jesus the question: 'Who is my neighbour?'

Jesus answers him in the form of a story or parable and he takes as his subject racial prejudice.

There was a certain group of people called the Samaritans who, for no particular reason, were held in contempt by many Jews. Jews would make long detours to avoid having to travel through the Samaritans' area; Jesus had already made his feelings about this known by making a point of travelling through Samaria himself.

For the setting of his story, Jesus chose the road from Jerusalem to Jericho which was notorious for its thieves and highwaymen. His audience would have already heard many accounts of travellers being stopped on this road and robbed.

'A certain man,' said Jesus, 'was on the way from Jerusalem to Jericho when he was set upon and mugged by a group of robbers. They beat him up and left him on the roadside taking all his belongings and even his clothes with them when they went.

'The man had been left in agony for quite some time when he heard more footsteps on the road. He thought at first that it might be one of the robbers coming back but was relieved to see instead that it was a priest.

'Now priests, as we all know, are busy men. They have many duties to perform and they have standards to keep up. It wouldn't do for a priest to arrive at an appointment two hours late or turn up with his best clothes covered in blood and grime. For all the priest knew, anyway, the robbers might still have been lurking round; so he did what he thought was the only sensible thing – he hurried by on the other side of the road.

'Later on another man approached. He was a Levite and, as we all know, Levites are fellow-Jews – the sort of people we'd expect to help us when we're in trouble.'

The audience nodded approvingly and Jesus went on.

'Well, maybe this Levite was in a hurry or perhaps he just felt embarrassed at seeing a filthy naked body lying in the roadside and just didn't know what to do. Anyway, he felt it was no concern of his how the man had got into such a state – he thought it more polite to just ignore him – pretend he hadn't seen him and pass by.

'It was some time later before the third man came along.' Jesus paused a while here and looked at the crowd, waiting for their reaction. 'He was a Samaritan,' he said. The people in the crowd exchanged glances – some raised their eyebrows – others just smiled knowingly. All of them knew what Samaritans were like although none had ever come into contact with one.

'The Samaritan,' Jesus went on, 'saw the injured man lying by the roadside and straightaway he went across. He wasn't an expert in first aid but he did what he could to cover up his wounds and stop the bleeding. Then he put some of his own clothes on the man, lifted him onto his donkey and took him along to the nearest hotel. When he got there, he paid the man's board and lodgings for the next few days and told the landlord that he'd call in and pay for any extra expenses the man had incurred the next time he was passing.

'Which of these three?' asked Jesus, 'do you think was the best neighbour to the injured man?'

Conclusion

It's nearly two thousand years since Jesus told the story of the Good Samaritan but human nature hasn't changed. Police stations have many files of cases where people have had accidents or they've been viciously attacked in the street – they've shouted repeatedly for help but people round about have just pretended that they haven't heard.

An experiment showed this recently on television. An actor stood in a very busy subway and pretended to have a heart attack. He moaned and writhed about as if he was in great pain and eventually fell to the ground. Hardly anybody stopped even to ask him what was wrong.

We wouldn't have expected any of those people to do what the Samaritan did – nurse the man themselves, pick him up and take him to a hotel and then pay in advance for his board and lodgings. They could only be expected to talk to the injured man and find him a doctor or an ambulance.

One reason people may be reluctant to help is because they feel shy and self-conscious. We don't normally speak to strangers in the street. Even if someone seems to be in trouble, it's not always easy to think of what to say to them and we do not want to make ourselves look foolish.

If any of us were hurt in an accident, though, we'd feel angry if people ignored us just because they were feeling shy. There are occasions when we have to overcome our own self-consciousness because other people's needs are more important.

Prayer

May we learn to be good neighbours – to help all those we come into contact with who need our help. May it never be said that we are the ones who pass by on the other side of the road.

Amen

Day 2 | **The Samaritans**

Every year 200,000 people in the British Isles try to kill themselves. Many of these people don't really want to die. They just don't want to go on living with the way things are. Often they are desperately lonely and need somebody to talk to.

At least one person kills himself, or herself, every two hours. Suicide is one of the top ten causes of death and, what is more worrying, is that suicide is the second most common cause of death amongst young people under the age of 25.

The Reverend Chad Varah was a clergyman working in the City of London in 1953. When he read in a magazine that there were three suicides a day in Greater London, he thought of the idea of having an emergency telephone number for people who were contemplating suicide. He publicised the idea, asking anyone feeling suicidal to telephone MAN 9000, the number of his church, St Stephen Walbrook. The movement which came to be known as the Samaritans was thus started and eventually developed into a nation-wide and now a world-wide organisation.

Although started by a priest, the Samaritans are not a Christian organisation. Volunteers can be of any religion or of no religion at all and it does not make any difference whether the people who contact them have any religion or not. They have taken their name from Jesus's parable of the Samaritan, the anonymous man who stopped to help someone lying by the wayside.

Samaritans are simply friends to people who are feeling desperate, lonely or suicidal.

None of them is paid for their work and they come from every age group, social background and walk of life.

You can tell a Samaritan volunteer exactly how you feel and why everything is so bad. They will listen and try to help you sort things out. You can speak to them in confidence knowing that they will never tell anyone the things you've said to them.

You don't even have to tell them your name. You can just talk to them on the telephone, write, or meet one of the volunteers face to face. You do not have to wait until your problems get so bad that you are thinking about suicide; no problems are too big or small to talk to them about.

Since the Samaritans started their work, the suicide rate in this country has come down by about a third. Evidence suggests that the work of the Samaritans is one of the main reasons for this.

Even though you may be too young to be a Samaritan volunteer yourself, there are ways in which you can help them. If you know someone who is feeling really depressed and who has problems you can't help with, you could try and persuade him or her to phone the Samaritans. Don't put it off and assume it isn't serious, especially if the person talks about suicide. You could help to save a person's life.

Samaritans are desperately in need of money – to pay their telephone bills and to keep their offices open. You could become a Friend of the local Samaritans, helping to raise money for the group that works in your area.

Once you have reached the age of 17, you might think about becoming a Samaritan yourself. You won't be paid any money, but you would find it rewarding to think that you might have helped to save somebody's life. To be a Samaritan you don't have to be an expert, just an ordinary person who is a good listener who understands how other people feel and wants to help them as a friend.

Prayer

People need to love and to be loved; they need to communicate and be listened to, especially when faced with a crisis. May we learn to be good listeners, showing sympathy and compassion when our friends and neighbours are in trouble.

Amen

Day 3 | ## Run for Your Life

Introduction

When Jesus said that one of the greatest commandments was to 'love thy neighbour', someone asked him, 'Who is my neighbour?' Jesus then reminded his followers that neighbours are not just people who live next door to each other; neighbours are the ordinary people we encounter in our daily lives, some of whom may need our help.

Today's reading is about a boy who took the trouble to stop and help somebody in need. It is taken from the first chapter of a book called *Run for Your Life* by David Line.

It was a rainy day in November when I met him first, and about a regiment of them seemed to be bashing him. He was a little dark skinny kid down on his knees in a puddle and that's where they were bashing him.

As far as I could see, he was letting them. He wasn't struggling or yelling or anything. He was just kneeling there sobbing, and doing that pretty quietly.

I said, 'All right, break it up.'

'Get lost', one of then said, uncertainly.

'Yeah, vanish.'

They let go of him all the same.

I could see they were younger than me and smaller, which was all right except one of them had some kind of cosh in his hand, a piece of hosepipe or something. I said to the kid, 'Get up.'

'You leave him alone, the kid with the cosh said. 'He started it. He hit one of us.'

'Yeah, he was throwing things.'

'Were you throwing things?' I said to the kid.

He just shook his head, still sobbing.

'Yes, you did, you rotten little liar! He caught Harris, didn't he, Harris?'

'Right here,' Harris said, pointing to his temple. 'I've still got a headache.'

I said, 'What did he throw?'

'He threw a ball. He threw it flipping hard too. We was in the timber yard and he run away before we could see who done it.'

'How do you know it was him, then?'

'He told us,' Harris said triumphantly. 'He came up and laughed and told us right out, didn't he?'

'I only asked for my ball back,' the kid said. It was the first time he'd spoken and I looked at him twice because it was with a foreign accent. 'I saw them playing with it and I came up and apologised and asked for it back. It was only an accident. I didn't mean to hit anybody. It went over the wall by mistake.'

'Yeah, you rotten little liar, you threw it.'

'No, please, I didn't.'

I said, 'Give him his ball back.'

'You take a jump.'

'Give him it back, quick.'

One of them pulled a ball out of his pocket and dropped it on the ground, and the kid picked it up.

'My brother'll murder you,' one of the kids said.

'Give him his satchel too.'

'He'll jump about on you. He'll tear you in little pieces. He'll give you such a crunching. . .'

I said, 'If those are your bikes jump on them quick.'

Their bikes were leaning up against the alley wall and they got on them and pushed them off.

'I wouldn't like to be you,' the kid with the brother said.

He said something else too, but I didn't catch it. They were all laughing as they rode off.

I said to the little kid, 'You're a bit of a case, aren't you? What did you want to tell them you did it for?'

'They had my ball,' the kid said, still sobbing. 'I thought they might hit me, but they ought to give it back.'

'Give it back! Look, you want to keep away from that lot,'

I said. 'They'd do you up just for fun. Risk a good hiding for a rotten old ball you can buy anywhere for ninepence?'

'I haven't got ninepence,' the kid said. 'I only get three pence a week. My mother can't afford any more.'

I said, 'All right, then, come on,' a bit embarrassed, and hoping he'd dry up now.

He didn't dry up. He started telling me his life story.

I said, 'Look, you don't have to tell me all this.'

'That's all right. I like to tell you.'

He said he was Hungarian and his family had had to run away from there. His father had died about a year ago and his mother was having a hard time earning money. He was still going on about it when we got to the end of the street.

I said, 'You'd better tidy up a bit, hadn't you, before you go in?'

'Yes. Thank you.'

He was pushing something in my hand. He said shyly, 'It's a present. I want you to have it.'

I looked in my hand and saw three pennies and nearly went up the wall. I said, 'Here, I don't want it.'

'Please. It's for you.'

'I don't want it.'

I tried to give it back, but his hand wasn't there and the pennies went rolling in the gutter. He gave a sort of gulp and turned away, and just then I remembered it was all his spending money and he'd given it to me. So I got down and found it.

'Here. Put it in your pocket.'

'It's for you.'

'Come on.' I forced it in his pocket.

'I'm sorry,' he said. 'I don't know how you do things. I haven't any friends here . . . Forgive me.'

He looked so weird I said, 'All right, forget it. What's your name, anyway?' 'Szolda,' he said. 'Istvan Szolda.'

It sounded like Soldier the way he said it, so I said, 'Okay, Soldier – see you again.'

His face came whipping round, smiling all over as if I'd given him the best present he could think of.

'Oh, yes, please. Thank you,' he said.

I suppose I was hooked from then on.

Prayer

May we be good neighbours to everyone we meet. May we have the courage to help those in trouble even if it means putting ourselves at risk. May we learn to make real friends through caring for each other.

Amen

Day 4   ## The Stranger

Introduction

In yesterday's reading, Woolcott looks after a boy called Soldier when some older boys are threatening him.

Soldier is younger than Woolcott; he comes from another country and he doesn't speak English very well. In spite of the fact that the two boys are quite different, they become very good friends and, later on in the book, they have some amazing adventures.

Our reading today is about someone who, unlike Woolcott, is completely intolerant of a person different from himself. It's a Victorian poem called 'The Stranger' by Wallace Bruce.

An aged man came late to Abraham's tent:
The sky was dark, and all the plain was bare.
He asked for bread; his strength was nearly spent,
His haggard look implored the tenderest care.
The food was brought. He sat with thankful eyes,
But spoke no grace, nor bowed he towards the east.
Safe sheltered here from dark and angry skies,
The bounteous table seemed a royal feast.

Before his hand had touched the tempting fare,
Old Abraham rose and, leaning on his rod,
'Stranger,' he said, 'do you not bow in prayer?
Do you not fear? Do you not worship God?'
He answered, 'No.' The patriarch sadly said,
'You have my pity. Go! Eat not my bread.'

Another came that wild and fearful night:
The fierce winds raged, and darker grew the sky;
But all the tent was filled with wondrous light,
And Abraham knew the Lord his God was nigh.
'Where is that aged man,' the Presence said,
'That asked for shelter from the driving storm?
Who made *thee* master of *thy* Master's bread?
What right had you to shower him with scorn?'

'Forgive me, Lord,' Old Abraham answered low,
With downcast look, with bowed and trembling knee.
'The stranger might have stayed with me, I know,
But, oh my God, he would not worship Thee.'
'I've borne him long,' God said, 'and still *I* wait;
Couldst thou not lodge him *one* night in thy gate?

(adapted)

Prayer

Let us remember that there is something good in everyone
– in people of different religions from ourselves and in people
of no religion at all.

May we learn to be tolerant and to seek out the goodness in
everyone. May we treat with consideration and respect even
those people we find it difficult to like.

Amen

| Day 5 | **A Peace Movement Called Steve** |

I know a one-man peace movement called Steve.
He doesn't get worked up about the Bomb.
He doesn't march, wear badges – none of that.
He only makes me talk when we're alone.

'Come on then, Abdul, *talk*! Give us some more
About what things are like in Pakistan . . .
That desert where the sand's all silver-black . . .
That 'sort-of-Christmas' when you kill a goat. . .
That holy man with crocodiles for pets. . .
That raft your dad made with a bullock's hide. . .

And then, when I'm not there, he tells the lads.
He tells them like I can't, and they say 'Cor!'
And then they come and ask me questions too.

Last week we met some yobbos in Brick Lane.
I tried to turn down Grimsby Street, but Steve
Said, 'Don't be stupid! Let me handle this.'
Then, grinning at the biggest, shouted: 'Here,
It's him that I was tellin' you about.
He has to learn a blinkin' book by heart –
In Arabic, all written back to front.'

'Cor, poor old Pakky! Better him than me.'

Next week, Steve says, I've got to get my mum
To make 'them crispy things that burn your mouth,'
And bring a bag to school, and hand them round.

There's nobody but me who understands
Just what Steve's doing. If they really knew
I think he'd have to get the Nobel Prize.

Denis Shaw

Prayer

Let us think today of ways in which we can be helpful to our
neighbours – to our family and friends or other people we
come into contact with.

May we try to make other people happier for having
known us.

Amen

3 The Great Gilly Hopkins
Katherine Paterson

Day 1   **A Fresh Start**

Introduction

Today's reading is the first part of an American novel called
The Great Gilly Hopkins written by Katherine Paterson.

Gilly gets off to a bad start in life by having a mother who
deserts her when she is only three years old but her problems
since then are all of her own making. You could say that
Gilly is her own worst enemy. She seems all the more ob-
jectionable because so many people have been falling over
themselves to help her.

The story starts with Gilly being taken by her social
worker to a new foster home . . . .

'Gilly,' said Miss Ellis with a shake of her long blonde hair
toward the passenger in the back seat. 'I need to feel that you
are willing to make some effort.'

Galadriel Hopkins shifted her bubble gum to the front of
her mouth and began to blow gently. She blew until she
could barely see the shape of the social worker's head
through the pink bubble.

'This will be your third home in less than three years. I
would be the last person to say that it was all your fault. The
Dixons' move to Florida, for example. Just one of those un-
fortunate things. And Mrs Richmond having to go into the
hospital' – it seemed to Gilly that there was a long, thoughtful
pause before the caseworker went on – 'for her nerves.'

Pop!

Miss Ellis flinched and glanced in the rear view mirror but
continued to talk in her calm, professional voice while Gilly

picked at the bits of gum stuck in her straggly hair and on her cheeks and chin. 'We should have been more alert to her condition before placing any foster child there. *I* should have been more alert.'

Cripes, thought Gilly. The woman was getting sincere. What a pain.

'I'm not trying to *blame* you, Gilly. It's just that I need, we all need, your co-operation if any kind of arrangement is to work out.' Another pause. 'I can't imagine you *enjoy* all this moving around. Will you do me a favour, Gilly? Try to get off on the right foot?'

Gilly had a vision of herself sailing around the living room of the foster home on her right foot like an ice skater. With her uplifted left foot she was shoving the next foster mother square in the mouth. She smacked her new supply of gum in satisfaction.

'Do me another favour, will you? Get rid of that bubble gum before we get there?'

Gilly obligingly took the gum out of her mouth while Miss Ellis's eyes were still in the mirror. Then when the social worker turned her attention back to the traffic, Gilly carefully spread the gum under the handle of the left-hand door as a sticky surprise for the next person who might try to open it.

Two traffic lights further on Miss Ellis handed back a towelette. 'Here,' she said, 'see what you can do about that gunk on your face before we get there.'

Gilly swiped the little wet paper across her mouth and dropped it on the floor.

'Gilly – ' Miss Ellis sighed . . . .

'My name,' Gilly said between her teeth, 'is Galadriel.'

Miss Ellis appeared not to have heard. 'Gilly, give Maime Trotter half a chance, OK? She's really a nice person.'

That cans it, thought Gilly. The Newman family, who couldn't keep a five-year-old who wet her bed, had been 'nice'. Well, I'm eleven now, folks, and, in case you hadn't heard, I don't wet my bed anymore. But I am not nice. I am brilliant. I am famous across this entire country. Nobody wants to tangle with the great Galadriel Hopkins. I am too clever and too hard to manage. Gruesome Gilly, they call me. She leaned back comfortably. Here I come, Maime baby, ready or not.'

They had reached a neighbourhood of huge trees and old houses. The social worker slowed and stopped beside a dirty white fence. The house it penned was old and brown with a porch that gave it a sort of potbelly.

'Hey, there, I thought I heard y'all pull up.' The door had opened, and a huge hippopotamus of a woman was filling the doorway. 'Welcome to Thompson Park, Gilly, honey.'

'Galadriel,' muttered Gilly, not that she expected this bale of blubber to manage her real name. Jeez, they didn't have to put her in with a freak.

Half a small face, topped with muddy brown hair and masked with thick metal-rimmed glasses, jutted out from behind Mrs Trotter's mammoth hip.

The woman looked down. 'You want to meet your new sister, don't you? Gilly, this is William Ernest Teague.'

The head immediately disappeared behind Mrs Trotter's bulk. She didn't seem bothered. 'Come on, come in. You belong here now.' Gilly could feel Miss Ellis's fingers on her backbone gently prodding her through the doorway and into the house.

Prayer

All of us feel sometimes that life is treating us unfairly. Let us make sure that we do not direct our anger and frustration onto people who are only trying to help us. May we use our anger in a productive way to try and change things for the better.

Amen

Day 2 | ## Being Gentle with Ourselves

Introduction

Teenage magazines often have stories about girls who fall in love with handsome, exciting young men who don't care for them at all while ignoring the nice, but rather ordinary, boy-next-door who thinks the world of them. The stories often have a happy ending where the girl finally realises what a wonderful husband or boy-friend the boy-next-door could be.

Gilly Hopkins idolises her mother who, as you may guess, doesn't really care about Gilly at all. In today's extract, Gilly spoils all her chances of having a happy and permanent relationship with Maime Trotter – someone who, unlike Gilly's mother, is prepared to be completely kind, affectionate and forgiving.

The extract starts where Gilly has just received a postcard from her mother.

It was a postcard showing sunset on the ocean. Slowly she turned it over.

My dearest Galadriel,
The agency wrote me that you had moved.
I wish it were to here. I miss you.

All my love, Courtney.

That was all. Gilly read it again. And then a third time. No. That was not all. Up on the address side, in the left-hand corner. The letters were squeezed together so you could hardly read them. An address. Her mother's address.

She could go there. She could hitch-hike across the country to California. She would knock on the door, and her mother would open it. And Courtney would throw her arms around her and kiss her all over her face and never let her go. 'I wish it were to here. I miss you.' See, Courtney wanted her to come. 'All my love.'

Inside her head, Gilly packed the brown suitcase and crept down the stairs. It was the middle of the night. Out into the darkness. She'd steal some food. Maybe a little money. People picked up hitch-hikers all the time. She'd get to California in a few days. Probably less than a week. People were always picking up hitch-hikers. And beating them up. And killing them. And pitching their dead bodies into the woods. All because she didn't have the money to buy a plane ticket or even a bus ticket.

Oh, why did it have to be so hard? Other kids could be with their mothers all the time. Dumb, stupid kids who didn't even like their mothers much. While she –

She put her head down and began to cry. She didn't mean to, but it was so unfair. She hadn't even seen her mother since she was three years old. Her beautiful mother who missed her so much and sent her all her love.

'You all right, honey?' Tap, tap, tap. 'You all right?'

Gilly sat up straight. Couldn't anyone have any privacy around this dump? She stuffed the postcard under her pillow and then smoothed the covers that she'd refused to straighten before school.

'Can I come in?'

'No!' shrieked Gilly, then snatched open the door. 'Can't you leave me alone for one stupid minute?'

Trotter's eyelids flapped on her face like shutters on a vacant house. 'You OK honey?' she repeated.

'I will be as soon as you get your fat self outta here.'

'OK.' Trotter backed up slowly towards the stairs. 'Call me, if you want anything.' As an afterthought she said, 'It ain't a shameful thing to need help, you know.'

'I don't need any help.' Gilly slammed the door, then yanked it open – 'from anybody!' She slammed it shut once more.

'I miss you. All my love.' I don't need help from anybody except you. If I wrote you – if I asked, would you come and get me? You're the only one in the world I need, I'd be good for you. You'd see. I'd change into a whole new person. I'd turn from gruesome Gilly into gorgeous, gracious, good, glorious Galadriel. And grateful. Oh, Courtney – oh, mother, I'd be so grateful.

Later, Gilly ripped out a sheet of paper through the rings of her notebook, lay down on the bed, and pressing on her maths book wrote:

> 1408 Aspen Ave:
> Thompson Park, MD.

Dear Courtney Rutherford Hopkins,

I received your card. I am sorry to bother you with my problems, but as my real mother, I feel you have a right to know about your daughter's situation.

At the present time, it is very desperate, or I would not bother you. The foster mother is a religious fanatic. Besides that she can hardly read and write and has a very dirty house and weird friends.

There is another kid here who is probably mentally retarded.

I am expected to do most of the work including taking care of him (the mentally retarded boy) which is very hard with all my school-work too.

She wrote 'Love' then changed it to:

> Yours sincerely,
> your daughter,
> Galadriel Hopkins

P.S. I have checked the cost of a bus ticket to San Francisco. It is exactly 136 dollars 60 one way. I will get a job and pay you back as soon as possible.

She listened at the top of the stairs until she heard Trotter go into the downstairs bathroom. Then she crept into the kitchen, stole an envelope and a stamp from the kitchen drawer, and ran to the corner to mail her letter before she could change her mind.

Conclusion

It's hard to accept that the people we care for may not feel the same way about us. One-sided relationships, however, can be not only hurtful but can spoil our chances of building up friendships with people who might care for us much more.

Prayer

We often pray in Assembly that we may be gentle and kind with other people. Let us pray today that we may be gentle with ourselves, guarding ourselves from relationships that might exploit us or be hurtful. Let us strive for relationships that are mutual and be careful not to impose ourselves on people who don't want or need us.

Amen

Day 3   ## Theft

Introduction

Gilly's foster mother, Maime Trotter, has befriended an elderly, blind neighbour called Mr Randolph. After Mr Randolph has eaten a meal with the Trotter household, Gilly is sent round to his house to collect a book for reading aloud to him.

Gilly dragged a heavy stuffed chair backward to the shelf and climbed up on the very top of its back. On tiptoe, leaning against the rickety lower shelves to keep from toppling, she could barely reach the book. She pulled at it with the tip of her fingers, catching it as it fell. Something fluttered to the floor as she did so.

Money. She half-fell, half-jumped off the chair, and

snatched it up. Two five-dollar bills had fallen out from behind the encyclopedia just when she was needing money so badly. Here they'd come floating down. Like magic. Ten dollars wouldn't get her very far, but there might be more where these came from. She climbed up again, stretching almost to the point of falling. Although she could just about reach the top shelf with her fingertips, she was very unsteady.

Heavy footsteps thudded across the front porch. The front door opened. 'You all right, Gilly, honey?'

Gilly nearly tripped over herself, leaping down and grabbing up 'Sarsaparilla to Sorcery' from the chair seat, stretching her guts out to tip the book into its place on the shelf as Trotter appeared at the door.

'You was taking so long,' she said. 'Then Mr Randolph remembered that maybe the bulbs was all burned out. He tends to forget since they really don't help him much.'

'There's a light here,' Gilly snapped. 'If there hadn't been, I'd have come back. I'm not retarded.'

'I believe you mentioned that before,' said Trotter dryly. 'Well, you find anything you wanted to read to Mr Randolph?'

'It's a bunch of junk.'

'One man's trash is another man's treasure,' Totter said in a maddeningly calm voice, wandering over to a lower shelf as she did so. She pulled out a squat leather-bound volume and blew the dust off the top. 'He's got a yen for poetry, Mr Randolph.' She handed the book up to Gilly, who was still perched on the chair. 'This is one I used to try to read to him last year, but' – her voice sounded almost shy – 'I ain't too hot a reader myself, as you can probably guess. Ready to come along?'

'Yeah, yeah,' she replied impatiently. Holding her neck straight to keep from looking up at 'Sarsaparilla', she followed Trotter's bulk back to her house.

'What did you bring?' Mr Randolph's face looked like a child's before a wrapped-up present. He was sitting right at the edge of the big brown chair.

'*The Oxford Book of English Verse*,' Gilly mumbled.

He cocked his head. 'I beg your pardon?'

'The poems we was reading last year, Mr Randolph.' Trotter had raised her voice as she always did speaking to the old man.

'Oh, good, good,' he said, sliding back into the chair until his short legs no longer touched the worn rug.

Gilly opened the book. She read:

'Our birth is but a sleep and a forgetting:
The soul that rises with us, our life's Star,
Hath had elsewhere its setting,
And cometh from afar:
Not in entire forgetfulness,
And not in utter nakedness
But trailing clouds of glory do we come
From God who is our home . . .'

'Can I go now?' Gilly's voice was sharp like the jagged edge of a tin-can top.

'I do appreciate more than you know – ' but Gilly didn't wait to hear Mr Randolph's appreciation. She ran up the stairs into her room. Behind the closed door, she pulled the two bills from her pocket, and lying on the bed, smoothed out the wrinkles. She would hide them beneath her underwear until she could figure out a better place. 'I'm coming, Courtney,' she whispered. 'Trailing clouds of glory as I come.'

It was only a matter of getting back into Mr Randolph's house and getting the rest of the money. There was sure to be more.

Conclusion

Taking money from an elderly blind person is obviously wrong, but Gilly felt that her need was greater than Mr Randolph's and also assumed that she wouldn't get found out.

Many people try to justify stealing like that. If someone is given too much change in a supermarket, for instance, they might keep the money claiming that they need it much more than the supermarket does and, anyway, nobody would find out.

If we think that stealing is wrong, then it's just as wrong whether we are likely to be found out or not. It's wrong for us to steal from someone who seems to be richer than we are just as it's wrong for someone to steal from us if they think their need is greater than ours.

Prayer

May we give careful thought to questions of what is right and what is wrong and try to live according to our beliefs. May we not fall into the temptation of thinking something is right just because we can get away with it. May we come to respect ourselves for sticking to our principles and living our lives with honesty and integrity.

Amen

Running Away

Introduction

Gilly finds an excuse for going back to Mr Randolph's house and she manages to steal the rest of his money, but there is still not enough to pay for her ticket to San Franciso. Then she sees Trotter's purse lying open with the money she has cashed from the county welfare. Gilly takes the money and plans her departure . . . .

She crept down, keeping her suitcase under her right arm to conceal it as best she could with her body. Crossing the short, bright strip before the door, she glanced in. Neither head turned. She was safely to the front door. She took her jacket off the hook and poked it above the suitcase, so that she had a free hand . . .

'Where you going?' She jumped around at William Ernest's whisper. In the dark hallway his glasses flashed.

'Just out,' she whispered back. Oh, god, make him shut up.

He did shut up and stood silently, looking first at her, then at the suitcase, then back at her.

'Don't go.' His little face squeezed up at her like his tiny voice.

'I got to,' she said through her teeth. Opening the door, pulling it shut behind her, shifting the suitcase and jacket to either hand, and running, running, running, down the hill, the pulse in her forehead pounding as hard as her sneakered feet pounded the sidewalk.

She got to the bus station, stood up straight and went out to the ticket counter.

The man didn't even look up.

'I want a ticket to California, please.' As soon as the words were out, she heard her mistake.

'California where?' He glanced up now, looking at her through half-open lids.

'Uh – San Francisco. San Francisco, California.'

'One-way or round trip?'

Whatever happened to Lady Cool? 'One – one-way.'

He punched some buttons and a ticket magically emerged. 'One thirty six sixty including tax.'

She had it. She had enough. With trembling hands, she took the wad of bills from her pocket and began to count it out.

The man watched lazily. 'Your mother know where you are, kid?'

Come on, Gilly. You can't fall apart now. She pulled herself straight and directed into his sleepy eyes the look she usually reserved for teachers and principals. 'I'm going to see my mother. She lives in San Francisco.'

'OK,' he said, taking her money and recounting it before he handed her the ticket. 'Bus leaves at eight thirty.'

'Eight thirty?'

He nodded to the seats across the waiting room. 'Just sit down over there. I'll call you.'

Gilly didn't even see the policeman until she felt his hand on her arm.

She snatched her arm back as she looked to see who had touched her.

'Where you headed, little girl?' He spoke quietly as though not to disturb anyone.

'To see my mother,' said Gilly tightly. Oh god, make him go away.

'All the way to San Francisco by yourself?' She knew then the clerk had called him. Damn!

'Yes.'

'I see,' he said with a quick look at the clerk, who was now staring at them with both eyes well open.

'I haven't done anything wrong.'

'Nobody's charging you with anything.' The policeman pulled his cap straight and said in a very careful, very patient voice, 'Who you been staying with here in the area?'

She didn't have to answer him. It was none of his business.

'Look. Somebody's going to be worried about you.' Like hell.

He cleared his throat. 'What about giving me your telephone number? So I can just check things out?'

She glared at him.

He coughed and cleared his throat again and looked up at the clerk. She might have gotten away in that instant – except for the money. Where could she go without the money? 'I think,' the policeman was saying, 'I'd better take her in for a little talk.'

The clerk nodded. He seemed to be enjoying himself.

'Here's the money she brought in.' He held up a manila envelope. The policeman took her gently by the arm and walked her over to the counter. The clerk handed him the envelope.

'That's my money,' Gilly protested.

'I'll just bet it is, kid,' the clerk said with a fake smile.

If she had known what to do, she would have done it. She tried to make her brain tell her, but it lay frozen in her skull like a woolly mammoth deep in a glacier. All the way to the station she asked it, Shall I jump out of the car at the next light and run? Should I just forget about the damn money? But the woolly mammoth slept on, refusing to stir a limb on her behalf.

Conclusion

Many young people run away from home rather than face up to their problems. They often think it might demonstrate to their parents how dissatisfied they are without having to talk about it and explain.

Running away brings far more problems than it solves. Parents feel betrayed because their children have caused them so much worry and, later on, children often feel guilty for upsetting their parents so much. You can cope with parents so much better if you feel that you've tried your best with them and you don't feel guilty because you've hurt them.

If life at home ever does become unbearable, there are older relatives, school cousellors, Samaritans and social workers who can sometimes, as a last resort, find you somewhere else to live. The best solution to dealing with problems at home, however, is just to talk things out calmly and honestly and try to reach a compromise.

Prayer

May we learn to face up to our problems and try to sort them out instead of pretending that they don't exist or trying to

run away from them. May we be patient with people who
find it hard to understand us.

Amen

Day 5   **Living with Mistakes**

Introduction

Gilly is taken to the police station and confesses to stealing
the money for her fare to San Francisco. Maime Trotter says
she doesn't want to press any charges so Gilly is allowed
to go back home with her.

During the next few months, Gilly starts to become very
fond of her new foster family. She helps William Ernest with
his reading and encourages him to stick up for himself at
school. She hardly spares a thought for the letter she wrote
to her mother complaining about her foster home and asking
to be moved . . . .

Trotter was at the door, opening it before they reached the
porch. Gilly went cold. You could tell something was badly
wrong by the way the woman's smile twisted and her body
sagged.

Sure enough, Miss Ellis was sitting on the brown chair.
Gilly's heart gave a little spurt and flopped over like a dud
rocket. She sat down quickly on the couch and hugged herself to keep from shaking.

Suddenly Miss Ellis began to speak, her voice bright and
fake like a laxative commercial. 'Well, I've got some rather
astounding news for you, Gilly.' Gilly hugged herself tighter.
The announcement of 'news' had never meant anything in
her life except a new move. 'Your mother . . .'

'My mother's coming?' She was sorry immediately for the
outburst. Miss Ellis' eyebrows launched into the twitchy
dance they always seemed to at the mention of the words,
'my mother.'

'No.' Twitch, twitch. 'Your mother is still in California.
But your grandmother. . . .'

'What have I to do with her?'

'. . . your mother's mother called the office this morning
and then drove up all the way from Virginia to see me. She
and your mother' – twitch – 'want you to go with her.'

'With who?'

'With your grandmother. *Permanently.*' The social worker seemed to be dangling that last word before Gilly's nose, as if expecting her to jump up on her hind legs and dance for it.

Gilly leaned back. What did they take her for? 'I don't want to live with her,' she said.

'Gilly, you've been saying ever since you were old enough to talk . . . .'

'I never said I wanted to live with *her*! I said I wanted to live with my *mother*. She's not my mother. I don't even know her!'

'You don't know your mother, either.'

'I do, too! I remember her! Don't tell me what I remember and what I don't!

Miss Ellis suddenly looked tired. 'Your mother wants you to go to your grandmother's. I talked to her long distance.'

'Didn't she tell you she wanted me to come to California like she wrote me?'

'No, she said she wanted you to go to your grandmother's house.'

'They can't make me go there.'

Gently. 'Yes, Gilly, they can.'

She felt as though the walls were squeezing in on her; she looked around wildly for some way to escape. She fixed on Trotter. 'Trotter won't let them take me, will you Trotter?'

Trotter flinched but kept on looking wooden-faced.

'Trotter! Look at me! You said you'd never let me go. I heard you.' She was yelling now. 'Never! Never! That's what you said!' She was on her feet stamping and screaming. The two women watched her, but numbly as though she were behind glass and there was no way they could reach in to her.

It was William Ernest who broke through. He slid from under Trotter's big hand and ran to Gilly, snatched the band of her jacket, and pulled on it until she stopped screaming and stood still. She looked down into his little near-sighted eyes, full of tears behind the thick lenses.

'Don't cry, Gilly.'

'I'm not crying' – she jerked her jacket out of his hands – 'I'm yelling!' He froze, his hands up as though the jacket were still between his fingers.

Trotter shuddered to her feet like an old circus elephant. 'You tell the child what's got to be done. C'mon William Ernest, honey.' She stuck out her big hand. 'We ain't helping here.' When he hesitated, she reached down and gently pulled him to his feet. They closed the door behind them, leaving Gilly cold and alone.

'So you goofed it, right?' – Gilly didn't answer. What did it matter? 'I'd really like to know what you wrote that fool letter for?'

'You wouldn't understand.'

'You bet I wouldn't. I don't understand why a smart girl like you goes around booby-trapping herself. You could have stayed here indefinitely, you know. They're both crazy about you.' Miss Ellis shook her long blonde hair back off her shoulders. 'Well, it's done now. Your grandmother will come to pick you up at my office tomorrow. I'll come about nine to get you.'

'Tomorrow?'

'Gilly, believe me, it's better. Waiting around is no good in these situations.'

'But I got school' –

'They'll send your records on.' Miss Ellis stood up and began to button her coat. 'I must admit that last month when you ran away, I thought, Uh – oh, here we go again, but I was wrong, Gilly. You've done well here. I'm very pleased.'

'Then let me stay.' Galadriel Hopkins had rarely come so close to begging.

'I can't,' Miss Ellis said simply. 'It's out of my hands.'

Conclusion

The story of Gilly Hopkins is very sad: Gilly has the opportunity to gain everything she's always wanted – someone who cares about her and forgives her and is willing to provide her with a loving home, but Gilly throws all this away simply by writing a letter when she's feeling very upset.

The hardest lesson for Gilly to learn is that she and nobody else is responsible for her own actions and that she has to live with her own mistakes.

Prayer

Let us remember that we are in charge of our own destiny. No matter how many things seem to be working against us we are, ultimately, responsible for our successes and our failures, our sadness and our joy. May we learn to accept responsibility for our own actions and inactions and for our mistakes as well as for our success.

Amen

4 Possessions

See also The Enchanted Shirt on page 223

See also The Enchanted Shirt on page 223

Day 1   Treasure on Earth

Do not store up for yourselves treasure on earth, where it grows rusty and moth-eaten, and thieves break in to steal it. Store up treasure in heaven, where there is no moth and no rust to spoil it, no thieves to break in and steal. For where your treasure is, there will your heart be also.

Therefore I bid you to put away anxious thoughts about food and drink to keep you alive, and clothes to cover your body. Surely life is more than food, the body more than clothes. Look at the birds of the air; they do not sow and reap and store in barns, yet your heavenly Father feeds them. You are worth more than the birds! And why be anxious about clothes? Consider how the lilies grow in the fields; they do not work, they do not spin, and yet, I tell you, even Solomon in all his splendour was not attired like one of these. But if that is how God clothes the grass in the fields, which is there today, and tomorrow is thrown on the stove, will he not all the more clothe you? How little faith you have! No, do not ask anxiously, 'What are we to eat? What are we to drink? What shall we wear?' All these things are for the heathen to run after, not for you, because your heavenly Father knows that you need them all. Set your mind on God's kingdom and his justice before everything else and all the rest will come to you as well.

So do not be anxious about tomorrow; tomorrow will look after itself. Each day has troubles enough of its own.

Matthew 6: 19–34   New English Bible

Conclusion

If someone were ill with starvation, it would be cruel and thoughtless to advise them to look after their spiritual life and not worry about where their next meal was coming from.

None of us is starving, however, and we all have more than enough clothes to wear, but we still spend a large part of our lives worrying about our material needs – what should we eat? What should we wear? What should we buy. . .?

Advertisers keep telling us that if only we were to buy all the right things, wear the right clothes, be seen at the right places, then we could be happy and popular and successful.

You might have noticed however, that people can spend small fortunes on themselves, go out to all the trendy places and stand around admiring themselves in their fashionable clothes but find that no one thinks any better of them for it.

Wearing fashionable clothes might give us more confidence, but we can gain that through thousands of other more important things. We musn't make buying things a substitute for developing the skills that will give us real and lasting confidence in ourselves.

Prayer

May we learn to recognise those things that are of lasting importance to us. In our life-long quest for true fulfilment and for happiness may we not be too often diverted by striving for things which are worldly and too easily discarded.

Amen

Day 2 | **Howard Hughes**

Most people wish they were rich. It is the main reason for filling in football coupons and entering all kinds of competitions. It is one of the reasons behind ambition to get a 'good' job. Almost everyone would like to have more money and many people daydream of being millionaires.

In 1976 one of the richest men in the world died. He was called Howard Hughes and had lived what appeared to be a glamorous, exciting life. By the age of 19 he controlled a company he had inherited from his father. He was interested in aeroplanes and became an aviator. He not only designed and tested his own planes but, for a time, held most of the air speed records as well as the land speed record. He founded an airline and eventually controlled the American company, TWA. Hughes also bought a top Hollywood film company and produced many successful films with stars such as John Wayne, Bette Davis, Jane Russell, Ingrid Bergman, Katherine Hepburn, Ava Gardner and Ginger Rogers. Hughes had a constant supply of glamorous female companions. Yet, in spite of his wealth and success, he died isolated and friendless, feeding on fantasy and drugs.

Howard Hughes hardly ever had a close friend. He felt upset if anyone touched him. He had a brilliant technical mind but found little time for people. He could remember minute details of planes he had helped to design but not the names of people with whom he worked. He married twice but lived apart from both wives most of the time. From 1940 until his death, he never owned a home because that would mean paying state taxation. He wanted to control the lives of everyone around him, dictating even what food they should eat. He was gripped by obsessions. He became completely obsessed about germs, eventually sealing himself in a hotel room with masking tape over the doors and windows and paper towels over the bed and chairs. Anything handed to him had to be wrapped in Kleenex tissues. His money had not brought happiness and perhaps it had contributed to his strange sense of values. His desire to be always in absolute control made it impossible for him to seek the medical and psychological help he needed and he had no close friends to persuade him.

Howard Hughes suffered a total breakdown. Towards the end of his life, he had to be surrounded by bodyguards to protect him from germs and from contact with reality. Emaciated, naked, hair and nails uncut for many months, addicted to drugs and tranquilisers, reduced to almost infantile dependency, the man who had wished to control everything, died controlling nothing. He had been a recluse, completely isolated from the world, for the last ten years.

Conclusion

It is easy to believe that owning money brings happiness. Wealth can make life easier, but the things that really make us happy, like friendship, love and the feeling that we are doing something worthwhile, are things that money cannot buy.

Prayer

Let us pray that we may find the contentment which comes from living our lives to the full and being concerned and thoughtful in our dealings with others. May we find an inner peace and happiness which is beyond the price of money.

Amen

The Secret Diary of Adrian Mole Aged 13¾

Introduction

Today's reading is an extract from a book called *The Secret Diary of Adrian Mole Aged 13¾* by Sue Townsend. Adrian is envious of his schoolfriend, Nigel, whose parents seem to have much more money than Adrian's.

Monday, January 5th
Nigel came round today. He has got a tan from his Christmas holiday. I think Nigel will be ill soon from the shock of the cold in England. I think Nigel's parents were wrong to take him abroad.

He hasn't got a single spot yet.

Wednesday, January 7th
Nigel came round on his new bike this morning. It has got a water bottle, a milometer, a speedometer, a yellow saddle, and very thin racing wheels. It's wasted on Nigel. He only goes to the shops and back on it. If I had it, I would go all over the country and have an experience.

My spot or boil has reached its peak. Surely it can't get any bigger!

Friday, April 10th
Nigel asked me if I wanted to stay the weekend. His parents are going to a wedding in Croydon. My father said I could. He looked quite pleased. I am going round to Nigel's in the morning.

Saturday, April 11th
Nigel is dead lucky. His house is absolutely fantastic! Everything is modern. I don't know what he must think of our house, some of our furniture is over a hundred years old!

His bedroom is massive and he has got a stereo, a *colour* television, a tapedeck, a Scalextric track, an electric guitar and amplifier. Spotlights over his bed. Black walls and a white carpet and a racing car continental quilt. He has got loads of back issues of *Big and Bouncy* so we looked through them, then Nigel had a cold shower while I cooked the soup and cut the French loaf.

I had a go on Nigel's racing bike. I now want one more than anything in the world.

We went to the chip shop and had the works. Fish, chips, pickled onions, gherkins, sloppy peas. Nothing was too expensive for Nigel, he gets loads of pocket money. We walked round for a bit then we came back and watched *The Bug-Eyed Monster Strikes Back* on the television. I said the bug-eyed monster reminded me of Mr Scruton the headmaster. Nigel had hysterics. I think I have got quite a talent to amuse people. I might change my mind about becoming a vet and try writing situation comedy for television.

When the film finished Nigel said, 'How about a nightcap?' He went to the bar in the corner of the lounge and he poured us both a stiff whisky and soda. I hadn't actually tasted whisky before and I never will again. How people can drink it for pleasure I don't know. If it was in a medicine bottle they would pour it down the sink!

Don't remember going to bed, but I must have done because I am sitting up in Nigel's parents' bed writing my diary.

Sunday, April 12th   Palm Sunday
This weekend with Nigel has really opened my eyes! Without knowing it I have been living in poverty for the past 14 years. I have had to put up with inferior accommodation, lousy food and paltry pocket money. If my father can't provide a decent standard of living for me on his present salary, then he will just have to start looking for another job. He is always complaining about having to flog electric storage heaters anyway. Nigel's father has worked like a slave to create a modern environment for *his* family. Perhaps if *my* father had built a formica cocktail bar in the corner of *our* lounge my mother would still be living with us. But oh no. My father actually boasts about our hundred-year-old furniture.

Yes! Instead of being ashamed of our antiques, he is proud of the old rubbish!

Conclusion

Adrian probably knows lots of boys whose standard of living is lower than his own. Instead of comparing himself with them and feeling satisfied, he compares himself with a boy who's much better off financially. In doing that he makes himself miserable. Even people we think of as being extremely rich will often grumble because they compare themselves with those who earn even more money than they do.

In the American state of California, people have a life-style which most of us would envy. Many own luxury homes with swimming pools and no end of household gadgets. But California has what is probably the highest suicide rate in the world. So wealth doesn't make the people happy.

Prayer

May we reserve our admiration for the qualities people have rather than for what they own. May we respect those who give of their time, their friendship and their talents rather than those who strive always to gain more for themselves

Amen

| Day 4 | **The Fox and the Grapes** |

One summer's day a fox was passing through
A vineyard; faint he was and hungry too.
When suddenly his keen eye chanced to fall
Upon a bunch of grapes above the wall.
'Ha! Just the thing!' he said. 'Who could resist it!'
He eyed the purple cluster – jumped – and missed it.
'Ahem!' he coughed. 'I'll take more careful aim,'
And sprang again. Results were much the same,
Although his leaps were desperate and high.
At length he paused to wipe a tearful eye,
And shrug a shoulder. 'I am not so dry,
And lunch is bound to come within the hour. . .
Besides,' he said, 'I'm sure those grapes are sour.'

The moral is: We seem to want the peach
That always dangles just beyond our reach.
Yet, like the fox, we must not be upset
When sometimes things are just too hard to get.

Joseph Lauren

Conclusion

One of the commandments which was given to Moses was:
'Thou shalt not covet' which means, 'You must not be
envious.'

The Commandment says: Thou shalt not covet thy neighbour's house, thou shalt not covet thy neighbour's wife, nor
his manservant, nor his maidservant, nor his ox, nor his ass,
nor anything that is thy neighbour's.'

Most of our neighbours have neither manservants nor
maidservants, let alone oxen or assess – but the principle of
the Commandment still applies. There will always be people
who own more than us as well as plenty who own less than
us. Spending our lives in jealousy and envy can only isolate
us from other people and make us unhappy.

Prayer

May we not waste our lives in jealousy and greed, but play
our part in working towards a more just and equitable future
where resources can be divided equally between all the
peoples of the world.

Amen

| Day 5 | **Speak to Us of Giving**

Introduction

Today's reading is written by the famous poet, philosopher
and artist, Kahlil Gibran.

Gibran was born near Mount Lebanon in 1883. He wrote
his prose poems originally in Arabic and they have now been
translated into more than 20 other languages. His draw-
ings and paintings have been exhibited all over the world.
He is one of the few writers whose books are read and loved

by people in the East and the West. He died in 1931 in Greenwich Village, New York.

Then a rich man said, Speak to us of Giving.
    And he answered:
You give but little when you give of your possessions.
    It is when you give of yourself that you truly give.
    For what are your possessions but things you keep and guard for fear you may need them tomorrow?
    . . . And what is fear of need but need itself?
    Is not dread of thirst when your well is full, the thirst that is unquenchable?
    There are those who give little of the much which they have – and they give it for recognition and their hidden desire makes their gift unwholesome.
    And there are those who have little and give it all.
    These are the believers in life and the bounty of life and their coffer is never empty.
    There are those who give with joy, and that joy is their reward.

Prayer

May we learn to experience the joy of giving. Even if we have few possessions or little wealth to give away, may we seek out opportunities to give of our time, our skills and our concern to those who need us.

Amen

5 United Nations Week

Day 1 | **Swords into Plowshares**

Many people throughout history have dreamed of a world without war.

One of the earliest men we know of to have such a dream was the Old Testament prophet, Micah. This is what he wrote:

And he shall judge among many people and rebuke strong nations afar off; and they shall beat their swords into plowshares and their spears into pruning hooks; nation shall not lift up a sword against nation, neither shall they learn war any more.

But they shall sit every man under his vine and under his fig tree and none shall make them afraid, for the mouth of the Lord of hosts hath spoken it.

For all people will walk every one in the name of his god and we will walk in the name of the Lord our God for ever and ever.

Micah 4: 3–5 Authorised version

Conclusion

Although Micah's words were first heard thousands of years ago, you can find them today inscribed on a very modern building:

On the island of Manhatten in the middle of New York amidst all the noise and the traffic and the bustle, there's a huge stone wall on which Micah's words have been written.

The wall stands outside the building of the United Nations – an organisation founded after the end of the last world war to try and bring about peace between all the different countries of the world. October 24th is United Nations Day.

Recommended music: Last Night I had the Strangest Dream.

Prayer

Let us give thanks for the many people throughout history who have dedicated their lives to working for peace and justice.

May we try by our own example to show that a world of peace and compassion can be more than just a hopeful dream.

Amen

Day 2

The Work of the United Nations

The United Nations Organisation was set up in 1945, just after the second world war, with the aim of keeping peace throughout the world.

All member states of the United Nations have pledged that they will settle their international disputes by peaceful means and will refrain from the threat or use of force against any other state.

The United Nations body responsible for maintaining peace and security is the Security Council. When there is a dispute between nations that could bring a threat to peace, the Security Council listens first to all sides of the argument. It will probably make its own investigations into the conflict as well.

It may then mediate in the dispute – rather like a referee at a football match – trying to keep the sides apart and probably insisting on a 'cease-fire' until a peaceful settlement can be negotiated.

If the cease-fire is not respected, the United Nations can call on its own peace-keeping force. This is an army of soldiers from many different nations who can be brought into a country to preserve law and order and to stop two opposing sides from attacking each other. Such peace-keeping forces from the United Nations are, at the moment, situated in several different areas of tension throughout the world.

The United Nations General Assembly has been called the nearest thing to a world parliament. All member nations who wish to be represented are allowed to have one vote – no matter how large or small the nations are.

The Assembly exists to discuss and make recommendations on all matters within the scope of the United Nations charter. Unlike the Security Council, it has no power to force any government to act on its recommendations but, because those recommendations carry the weight of world opinion behind them, they are usually acted upon.

The General Assembly has stressed the need for what it calls a new economic order. The gap must be narrowed between the rich countries of the world and the poorer countries where 70 per cent of the world's people live on only 30 per cent of its income. The General Assembly has asked the richer countries to give one per cent of their annual budget to try and wipe out poverty in the third world.

Today's prayer is one that has been specially written for United Nations Day – October 24th.

Prayer

O God, give your grace to the United Nations Organisation in all its manifold work; in its work for the children who suffer so much from the injustices of our society, in education and in health, in the relief of poverty and hunger, and in its work for peace. So guide the United Nations that by word and deed it may promote your glory and establish peace and goodwill among the peoples of the world.

Amen

| Day 3 | **The Beatitudes** |

And seeing the multitudes, he went up into a mountain and when he was set, his disciples came unto him.

And he opened his mouth and taught them, saying,

Blessed are the poor in spirit: for theirs is the kingdom of heaven.

Blessed are they that mourn: for they shall be comforted.

Blessed are the meek: for they shall inherit the earth.

Blessed are they which do hunger and thirst after right-eousness: for they shall be filled.

Blessed are the merciful: for they shall obtain mercy.

Blessed are the pure in heart: for they shall see God.

Blessed are the peacemakers: for they shall be called the children of God.

Blessed are they which are persecuted for righteousness' sake: for theirs is the kingdom of heaven.

Matthew 5: 1–10 Authorised version

Conclusion

Today's prayer is one which was offered throughout the world with special focus on the Special Session on Disarm-ament held at the United Nations General Assembly in 1982. People all over the world were asked to offer this prayer for one minute each day at midday so that there would be a continuous vigil of prayer for peace throughout the earth.

Lead me from Death
to Life, from Falsehood to Truth.
Lead me from Despair
to Hope, from Fear to Trust.
Lead me from Hate
to Love, from War to Peace.
Let Peace fill our Heart,
our World, our Universe.

Amen

| Day 4 |

The Mouse and the Plum Cake

UNICEF, the United Nations Children's Relief organisation works in 112 countries to help those children in the world who are suffering most. In 1981 it had a total income of 171 million pounds for the whole year. This sounds a great deal of money but was the same amount that the world spent on weapons in four hours and ten minutes.

Each child born in the industrialised world consumes be-tween 20 and 40 times as much as a child living in one of the poorer countries.

Our reading today is about sharing.

A mouse found a beautiful piece of plum cake,
The richest and sweetest that bakers could make;
It was heavy with lemon and fragrant with spice,
And covered with sugar as sparkling as ice.

'My stars!' cried the mouse, while his eye beamed with
    glee,
'Here's a treasure I've found; what a feast it will be!
But, oh dear, there's a noise; it's my brothers at play;
So I'll hide with the cake, lest they wander this way.

'Not a bit shall they have, for I know I can eat
Every morsel myself, and I'll have such a treat.'
So off went the mouse, as he held the cake fast,
While his hungry young brothers went scampering past.

He nibbled, and nibbled, and panted, but still
He kept gulping it down till he made himself ill;
Yet he swallowed it all, and it's easy to guess
He was soon so unwell that he groaned with distress.

His family heard him, and as he grew worse,
They sent for the doctor, who made him rehearse
How he'd eaten the cake to the very last crumb,
Without giving his playmates and relatives some.

'Ah me!' cried the doctor, 'advice is too late,
You must die before long, so prepare for your fate;
If you had but divided the cake with your brothers,
T'would have done you no harm, and been good for the
    others.

'Had you shared it, the treat had been wholesome enough;
But eaten by one, it was dangerous stuff;
So prepare for the worst;' and the word had scarce fled,
When the doctor turned round, and the patient was dead.

Now all little people the lesson may take,
And some large ones may learn from the mouse and the
    cake;
Not to be over-selfish with what we may gain,
Or the best of our pleasures may turn into pain.

Eliza Cook

Conclusion

Many of the diseases from which people suffer in Western society are caused by over-eating. People who are over-weight are more likely to have heart attacks; there is also a link between certain forms of cancer and people eating too much stodgy food.

Like the mouse in the poem, when we consume more than our fair share of the earth's resources, we not only force our brothers and sisters in other countries to go without, but we damage ourselves as well.

Prayer

Let us give special thought today to those people who have devoted their lives to helping the poor and needy in impoverished parts of the world.

May we try to play some part in making their task easier.

Amen

Day 5

A Cup of Water

Today's readings are taken from a book called *A Cup of Water* written by Janet Lacey who has devoted many years of her life to working for Christian Aid.

In his foreword to the book, Professor Sir Robert Birley says of Janet Lacey: 'One meets energetic people and unorthodox people and efficient people, but it is rare to meet them making up one person . . . add to that the power to speak forcefully and clearly . . . she was the first woman to preach in St Paul's and Liverpool Cathedral and St George's Cathedral in Jerusalem . . . she is also exceedingly good company . . .

'She has played a vital part in some of the most important movements and problems of the last 25 years, the ecumenical movement, the problem of refugees, the problems of world poverty and hunger, the problem of race relations. She has inspired thousands of people to work to solve them and she has organised their efforts.'

Janet Lacey says: 'We live in a world where, in many places, social injustice is the order of the day, where 15,000 people die of hunger each day, where racial discrimination is practised unnoticed on our doorsteps and where political action is disappointing . . . In the West although we are only 20 per cent of the world's 3,000 million we have 90 per cent of the world's income, 90 per cent of its gold reserves, 95 per cent of its scientific knowledge, 70 per cent of its meat and 80 per cent of its protein.'

In her chapter, 'What do you know about hunger?' Janet Lacey quotes an African proverb: *The pot is boiling because somebody makes it boil. . . .*

On a dark and icy cold morning in January 1946 I flew in an RAF plane from Berlin to Kiel and then drove in a jeep to a British Army Church House a few miles outside the city. We passed through what had been the city centre but now the main street was a narrow, bumpy lane and the sides piled up with rubble. All round us were stark-naked ruins and such people as there were about were white-faced and grim. A man was searching in the filth for cigarette ends. Outside the city we passed by a refugee camp where white-faced, unsmiling boys and girls gazed at us through the railings. The next morning I looked out of the window of my warm bedroom into the backyard and saw a child enter the open gate from the garden, look cautiously round, lift the lid from an over-flowing garbage can and quickly and efficiently pick out the scraps of bread and other left-overs from our supper tables the previous night. She ran off with breakfast for her respectable middle-class family. I have never forgotten that little girl. This was what war had done to innocent children, not only had it starved them of food but reduced them to be scavengers.

I thought of her in 1955 when I was in Kenya at the height of the Mau Mau and saw hungry children huddled in corners of African huts. They were afraid of us until we managed to reassure them. Their parents had been taken off to detainee camps, and they were lonely and desolate. She came into my mind when a woman in the slums of West Kingston, Jamaica, with a child at her breast and another three hanging around her skirts followed me around for two hours repeating, 'Some milk would be better than nothing.'

She was there again when I helped in a feeding centre in Seoul in Korea, when the people came from broken down shacks once a day to get soup and rice. Walking about at night in the streets of Calcutta and of necessity stepping over emaciated bodies too lethargic to move, or visiting refugee shacks in beautiful Hong Kong, or standing helplessly in the filthy slums of Kampala, always the same agony and anger assailed me as it did on that cold morning in Kiel. I asked myself each time, Why can't I make the pot boil? It is easy for a well-fed English-woman like myself to shake with anger about the futility of war, to protest about the iniquity of racial prejudice and to deplore the helplessness of little people in the face of vast political forces fighting for power. It is less easy to take a full share of the blame and almost impossible to understand the feelings and aspirations of the legions of hungry people in the world.

I know nothing about hunger. I thought of that little girl last week when I nibbled some chocolates at a London theatre. The price of those chocolates would have paid for food for an Indian family for a whole day.

Conclusion

It's possible to give some help to the poor and needy of the world without having to give the dedication that Janet Lacey did.

Christmas cards and other gifts can be bought from organisations such as Oxfam, UNICEF and Christian Aid. These organisations also have charity shops where people give unwanted goods. Young people are often the best-equipped for giving to shops like this. They grow out of their clothes very quickly or they have clothes which they think are no longer fashionable. They often have expensive toys they've grown out of or they've records and tapes they do not listen to anymore.

If you give items like this, you not only help alleviate poverty and hunger overseas, but you help the less wealthy people in your area who can buy cheap clothes or toys for their children.

Prayer

Let us resolve that we will give something during the coming months, even if it is only something that we no longer need, to help those who are hungry and in desperate need. May we play our small part in helping to alleviate the poverty and suffering of the world.

Amen

6 Assemblies for Remembrance Week

Teachers of younger pupils may consider the assemblies on Days Three, Four and Five too disturbing.
Alternative readings are Love Your Enemies, page 157; and War, page 247.

Day 1 **The Eighteenth Emergency**

Introduction

Today's reading, from *The Eighteenth Emergency* by Betsy Byars, is about a boy called Mouse Fawley. Mouse gets his nickname because he is small and weedy.

In this extract, Mouse knows that the biggest, toughest boy in the school, Marv Hammerman, is looking for a fight with him. Mouse talks about it with his friend, Ezzie . . . .

'You ever been hit before, Mouse? I mean, hard?'

Mouse sighed. The conversation had now passed beyond whether Hammerman would attack. It was now a matter of whether he, Mouse Fawley, could survive the attack. He said thickly, remembering, 'Four times.'

'Four times in one fight? I mean, you stood up for four hits, Mouse?' There was grudging admiration in his voice.

Mouse shook his head. 'Four hits – four fights.'

'You went down each time? I mean POW and you went down, POW and you went down, POW and you went – '

'Yes!'

'Where did you take these hits?' Ezzie asked, straightening suddenly. Ezzie had never taken a single direct blow in his life because he was a good dodger. Sometimes his mother chased him through the apartment, striking at him while he dodged and ducked, crying, 'Look out Mom, look out now! You're going to hit me!'

He asked again, 'Where were you hit?'

Mouse said, 'In the stomach.'

'All four times?'

'Yeah.' Mouse suddenly thought of his stomach as having a big red circular target on it with HIT THERE printed in the centre.

'Who hit you?'

'Two boys in Cincinnati when I was on vacation, and a boy named Mickey Swearinger and somebody else I don't remember.' He lowered his head because he remembered the fourth person all right, but he didn't want to tell Ezzie about it. If he had added the name of Viola Angotti to the list of those who had hit him in the stomach Ezzie's face would have screwed up with laughter. 'Viola Angotti hit you? No fooling, Viola Angotti?' It was the sort of thing Ezzie could carry on about for hours. 'Viola Angotti. *The* Viola Angotti?'

And Mouse would have had to keep sitting there saying over and over, 'Yes, Viola Angotti hit me in the stomach. Yes, the Viola Angotti.' And he would have to tell Ezzie all about it, every detail, how one recess long ago the boys had decided to put some girls in the school trash cans. It had been one of those suggestions that stuns everyone with its rightness. Someone had said, 'Hey, let's put those girls over there in the trash cans!' and the plan had won immediate acceptance. Nothing could have been more appropriate. The trash cans were big and had just been emptied, and in an instant the boys were off chasing the girls and yelling at the tops of their voices.

It had been wonderful at first, Mouse remembered. Primitive blood had raced through his body. The desire to capture had driven him like a wild man through the school yard, up the sidewalk, everywhere. He understood what had driven the cavemen, and the barbarian, because the same passion was driving him. Putting the girls in the trash cans was the most important challenge of his life. His long screaming charge ended with him red-faced, gasping for breath – and with Viola Angotti pinned against the garbage cans.

His moment of triumph was short. It lasted about two seconds. Then it began to dim as he realised, first, that it was Viola Angotti and, second, that he was not going to get her into the garbage can without a great deal of help.

He cried, 'Hey, you guys, come on, I've got one,' but behind him the school yard was silent. Where was everybody? he had wondered uneasily. As it turned out, the principal had caught the other boys, and they were all being marched back in the front door of the school, but Mouse didn't know that.

He called again, 'Come on, you guys, get the lid off this garbage can, will you?'

And then, when he said that, Viola Angotti had taken two steps forward. She said, 'Nobody's putting me in no garbage can.'

He cried, 'Hey, you guys!' It was a plea. 'Where are you?'

And then Viola Angotti had taken one more step, and with a faint sigh she had socked him in the stomach so hard that he had doubled over and lost his lunch. He hadn't known it was possible to be hit like that outside a boxing ring. It was the hardest blow he had ever taken. Viola Angotti could be heavyweight champion of the world.

As she walked past his crumpled body she had said again, 'Nobody's putting me in no garbage can.' It had sounded like one of the world's basic truths. The sun will rise; the tides will flow. Nobody's putting Viola Angotti in no garbage can.

Conclusion

Mouse had what people call an 'inferiority complex' about being small. Dumping Viola Angotti in the garbage can was a way of re-establishing his pride – of making himself feel big and important.

Mouse underestimated Viola Angotti. He probably thought that, because she was a girl, she must be weaker than him. Obviously, that was not the case but it may be that Viola was so used to people thinking like that about her that she felt a need to assert herself as well. She might have made her point a lot better by picking up Mouse and dumping him in the garbage can – instead she responded with violence that was really out of proportion to Mouse's attack.

This week's assemblies are about war. One of the ways in which wars start is by nations trying to assert themselves by insulting, humiliating and attacking other countries. When this happens they often find that, like Viola Angotti, other countries make a response that is out of proportion in order to rescue their damaged pride. Before anyone knows what's happening, a full-scale war has developed.

Behaving peacefully on a personal level will make life much more pleasant but, by itself, it will not stop war. If everyone can learn to understand, however, how wars can be started so easily, there is a hope that more people might work to prevent them.

Prayer

None of us is perfect. There will always be people stronger, cleverer and more popular than all of us. Let us ensure that we do not try to make ourselves look better than we really are by humiliating others. May we take pride in our achievements and accept our limitations.

Amen

| Day 2 | **For the Fallen** |

Introduction

The poem you're about to hear is one that's recited all over the country on Remembrance Day – the fourth verse, in particular, you'll hear recited on its own or see inscribed on war memorials. The poem wasn't written to give a realistic account of war but to glorify those men who were killed in the war, to give some comfort to their friends and relatives.

> With proud thanksgiving, a mother for her children,
> England mourns for her dead across the sea,
> Flesh of her flesh they were, spirit of her spirit,
> Fallen in the cause of the free.
>
> Solemn the drums thrill: Death august and royal
> Sings sorrow up into immortal spheres,
> There is music in the midst of desolation
> And a glory that shines upon our tears.
>
> They went with songs to the battle, they were young,
> Straight of limb, true of eye, steady and aglow.
> They were staunch to the end against odds uncounted,
> They fell with their faces to the foe.

440:

HYMN

BENEDICTION

VESPER

They shall not grow old as we that are left grow old:
Age shall not weary them, nor the years condemn.
At the going down of the sun and in the morning
We will remember them.

They mingle not with their laughing comrades again;
They sit no more at familiar tables of home;
They have no lot in our labour of the day-time;
They sleep beyond England's foam.

But where our desires are and our hopes profound,
Felt as a well-spring that is hidden from sight,
To the innermost heart of their own land they are known
As the stars are known to the Night.

As the stars that shall be bright when we are dust
Moving in marches upon the heavenly plain,
As the stars that are starry in the time of our darkness,
To the end, to the end, they remain.

Laurence Binyon

Conclusion   WAR AND HISTORY

We have Remembrance Sunday each year in November to
remember the two World Wars and the men [people] who fought in
them. Many people think that is just a waste of time. They
say that, as the wars happened such a long time ago we
should simply forget about them now.

One of the sad things about history is that nations keep
making the same mistakes.

In our own lives, when we look back over things we've
done, we try to learn something from them – if we know
we've done something stupid, we try to make sure that we
don't keep on making the same mistakes over and over again.

That's one of the important reasons why we need to study
history. If we didn't know that terrible things like war had
happened, or why they had happened, it would be so easy
for us as a country to continue with the same policies that
had led to these mistakes in the past.

Prayer

Be silent Let us remember today the suffering and pain that are caused
by war and be mindful of all those throughout the world
today who are caught up in areas of conflict.   over

Let us pray that the leaders of the world will learn from history and not repeat the mistakes of the past.

When they plan out their policies for the future, may they keep the interests of humanity at heart.

Amen

Day 3   **Hiroshima (1)**

Introduction

On 6 August 1945, the first atomic bomb was dropped by the Americans on the town of Hiroshima in Japan.

In 1945 John Hersey, an American journalist, was sent by *The New Yorker* to interview survivors of Hiroshima. The following extract is taken from his account of what happened to a Japanese doctor, Dr Sasaki:

He arrived at the hospital at seven forty and reported to the chief surgeon. A few minutes later he went to a room on the first floor to take a blood test. With the blood specimen in his left hand . . . he started along the main corridor on his way toward the stairs. He was one step beyond an open window when the light' of the bomb was reflected, like a gigantic photographic flash, in the corridor. He ducked down on one knee and said to himself, 'Sasaki, *gambare*! Be brave!' Just then the blast ripped through the hospital. The glasses he was wearing flew off his face; the bottle of blood crashed against one wall . . . .

Dr Sasaki shouted the name of the chief surgeon and rushed around to the man's office and found him terribly cut by glass. The hospital was in horrible confusion: heavy partitions and ceilings had fallen on patients, beds had overturned, windows had blown in and cut people, blood was spattered on the walls and doors, instruments were everywhere, many of the patients were running about screaming, many more lay dead. A colleague working in the laboratory to which Dr Sasaki had been walking was dead; Dr Sasaki's patient whom he had just left was also dead. Dr Sasaki found himself the only doctor in the hospital who was unhurt.

Dr Sasaki, who believed that the enemy had hit only the building he was in, got bandages and began to bind the wounds of those inside the hospital; while outside, all over Hiroshima, maimed and dying citizens turned their unsteady steps toward the Red Cross Hospital to begin an invasion that was to make Dr Sasaki forget his own private nightmares for a long, long time . . . .

By nightfall, ten thousand victims of the explosion had invaded the Red Cross Hospital, and Dr Sasaki, worn out, was moving aimlessly and dully up and down the stinking corridors with wads of bandages and bottles, binding up the worst cuts as he came to them. Other doctors were putting compresses of saline solution on the worst burns. That was all they could do. After dark, they worked by the light of the city's fires and by candles the ten remaining nurses held for them.

Dr Sasaki had not looked outside the hospital all day; the scene inside was so terrible and so compelling that it had not occurred to him to ask any questions about what had happened beyond the windows and doors. Ceilings and partitions had fallen, plaster, dust, blood and vomit were everywhere. Patients were dying by the hundreds, but there was nobody to carry away the corpses. Some of the hospital staff distributed biscuits and rice, but the charnel-house smell was so strong that few were hungry.

By three o'clock the next morning after 19 straight hours of his gruesome work, Dr Sasaki was incapable of dressing another wound. He and some other survivors of the hospital staff got straw mats and went outdoors – thousands of patients and hundreds of dead were on the driveway and in the yard – and hurried around behind the hospital and lay down in hiding to snatch some sleep. But within an hour wounded people had found them; a complaining circle formed around them: 'Doctors! Help us! How can you sleep?'

Dr Sasaki got up and went back to work.

Prayer

On Remembrance Sunday, ministers will be asking their congregations to remember their fellow countrymen who have died in war. Let us also remember the untold thousands in other countries who have died as a result of our bombs, our guns, the lands mines we have planted, the artillery we have fired . . . the ships that we have sunk.

May we use our knowledge of history and our memories of war to strive for a world in which people live together in peace.

Amen

Day 4   **Hiroshima (2)**

Introduction

Today's reading is another account by John Hersey of the effects of the bomb on Hiroshima. He tells the true story of a clergyman, Father Kleinsorge, who was helping to tend the wounded . . . . His description of the injuries caused by the bomb was shocking and horrific.

The morning again was hot. Father Kleinsorge went to fetch water for the wounded in a bottle and a teapot he had borrowed. He had heard that it was possible to get fresh tap water outside Asano Park. Going through the rock gardens, he had to climb over and climb under the trunks of fallen pine trees; he found he was weak. There were many dead in the gardens. At a beautiful moon bridge, he passed a naked living woman who seemed to have been burned from head to toe and was red all over. Near the entrance to the park, an Army doctor was working, but the only medicine he had was iodine, which he painted over cuts, bruises, slimy burns, everything – and by now everything that he had painted had pus on it.

Outside the gate of the park, Father Kleinsorge found a tap that still worked – part of the plumbing of a vanished house – and he filled his vessels and returned. When he had given the wounded the water, he made a second trip. This time the woman by the bridge was dead. On his way back with the water, he got lost on detour around a fallen tree, and as he looked for his way through the woods, he heard a voice ask from the underbrush, 'Have you anything to drink?' He saw a uniform. Thinking there was just one soldier, he approached with the water. When he had penetrated the bushes, he saw there were about 20 men, and they were all in exactly the same nightmarish state: their faces were wholly burned, their eyesockets were hollow. They must have had their faces upturned when the bomb went off;

perhaps they were anti-aircraft personnel. The fluid from their melted eyes had run down their cheeks. Their mouths were mere swollen wounds which they could not bear to stretch enough to admit the spout of the teapot. So Father Kleinsorge got a large piece of grass and drew out the stem so as to make a straw, and gave them all water to drink that way. Father Kleinsorge told them as cheerfully as he could, 'There's a doctor at the entrance to the park. He's busy now, but he'll come soon I hope . . . .'

Conclusion

A hundred thousand people were killed from the effects of the bomb dropped on Hiroshima – many of the casualties were children.

Many more stories could be told of the effects of the bomb – of terrible burns and of people dying slowly from radiation.

Prayer

Let us think for a few moments of the wonderful achievements of the human race – the towns that have been built, the works of art that have been produced – the books, plays, films, pictures, music . . . the progress that has been made in science and technology.

The human mind is vast and boundless. It has the capacity for great creativity, reason and love. It also has the capacity to do more evil than any other species known on earth.

May we nurture the good that lies within us and seek to overcome the seeds of violence and hate.

Amen

Day 5   **Nuclear Weaponry**

In comparison with modern nuclear weapons, the bomb dropped on Hiroshima seems insignificant. By 1958, both the United States and the Soviet Union had carried out test explosions with single bombs at least a thousand times more deadly. If the world's 1984 stockpile of nuclear weapons were compressed into bombs of the size dropped on Hiroshima, it would take 4,600 years to go through them all if they were let off at the rate of one a day.

If all the gunpowder which has ever been used in war throughout the world could be contained on a single train with 50 tons of gunpowder in each freight car, the train would be 50 miles long.

The world's nuclear stockpile now stands at 16 thousand million tons of TNT. To carry that would need a train two and a half million miles long. It would stretch round the equator 97 times or reach to the moon and back five times.

Some of the world's top scientists attended an important conference in 1983, to study the effects of nuclear weapons. They concluded that a conflict involving only 1 per cent of the world's supply of nuclear weapons would produce enough dust to block out the rays of the sun. It would cause a long and harsh 'nuclear winter' with Arctic conditions and continuous darkness. Temperatures would drop below freezing in many parts of the world and, even if the war occurred in summer, many areas would have snowfall for months. Animals would die of cold and thirst, food supplies would soon run out and most of the human survivors would starve or freeze to death. Only insects and grasses might remain.

The English writer, Arthur Koestler, commenting on the magnitude of the destruction in Hiroshima, stated:

'If I were asked to name the most important date in the history of the human race, I would answer without hesitation August 6 1945. From the dawn of consciousness until August 6 1945, man had to live with the prospect of his death as an individual; since the day when the first atomic bomb outshone the sun over Hiroshima, he has had to live with the prospect of his extinction as a species.'

Prayer

Let us give thanks for the progress made in scientific research, for the luxuries and comforts it has given us, for the assistance in curing disease, with storing information and with improving communications. May we play our part in the use of scientific discovery for the benefit of the human race. Let us pray that we may never misuse the knowledge and the skills which have been given to us.

Amen

7 The Child Is Father of the Man

Day 1   Parents Are People Too

Today's reading comes from *Skulker Wheat,* a collection of short stories by John Griffin which tell about a young boy's working-class childhood. The extract is taken from the beginning of a story called 'Gaffer Roberts'.

If my Mam got mad with me for something I'd done – or more often something I hadn't done – she used to make moaning noises and stagger about the house as if she was dying. My Dad used to say, 'Now look what you've done to your mother,' and if I answered back, he would start pelting things at me – plates, cups, his dinner, the carving knife, and once a picture of Jesus floating up to heaven with a lamb tucked under each arm.

When he started his pelting I ran, either to my bedroom upstairs or to the toilet at the bottom of the garden. Both places had latches and as long as I got ten yards' start on him, I could slam the door shut and slip my half clothes-peg under the latch – I always carried a half clothes-peg for the purpose – and no matter how much he blasphemed and kicked at the door he couldn't get in.

One Monday morning I lay in bed looking out of my sky-light window at nothing in particular; there wasn't anything to see except sky because the window was merely a hole in the roof which you could open or shut with a long wooden handle. I had to sleep with it closed because if I left it open the cat would jump in and more likely than not land from ten feet on to my face – a nasty way to wake up. Anyway this particular Monday morning I didn't feel like getting up although my Mam had already shouted: 'If he thinks he's going to have me at his beck and call just to get him his breakfast when he wants, he's got another think coming.' She never addressed me directly when she was mad.

When I eventually got downstairs she said to my Dad, 'Tell him his breakfast's in the oven if he wants it.' I was feeling pretty fed up but I shouldn't have said what I did.

'Tell her to stuff her head in the oven.'

I know it wasn't very witty but it certainly galvanised my Dad.

'Right you great wammock,' he shouted and looked round for something to pelt. I was still a bit sleepy and I hesitated a moment, not knowing whether to run to the bog or the bedroom. The last time I'd made for the bog he'd broken my back when he caught me straight between the shoulder blades with a loaf of bread. If you think that wouldn't hurt, I'd better tell you it was one of Albert Rowe's specials – stale and very crusty.

Anyway that thought decided me to make for the bedroom but I was late starting and had only just reached the top of the stairs when he was half-way up with the big brown tea-pot held in his pelting position. I wasn't going to make it! I couldn't possibly get the peg in the door before he got his foot in it. I turned to face him. He stopped. Neither of us knew what to do. Then he put his head down, growled and took the last few stairs three at a time. Just as he reached the top step I gave him a push – not a hard push, just defensive. He lost his balance and he and the teapot clattered down-stairs. He reached the bottom first and the teapot, a close second, hit him on the head and smashed, spilling luke-warm tea down his navy-blue shirt. He looked up at me with a scowl, a scowl of surprise. I looked down at him in aston-ishment. It was a significant moment. Neither of us spoke. He picked up the broken pot and went away.

After that he still chased me, firing away with wellington boots, sugar bowls and other unlikely weapons. But both of us knew he didn't intend catching me. We both went a bit slower. What used to be a real chase had become a ritual. I had become as strong as my Dad.

Conclusion

Young children often idolise their parents. They think they're wonderful people who can never do anything wrong.

When children are older, they often feel angry that their parents aren't as wonderful as they once thought. They become disillusioned when they realise that their parents have just as many faults as everyone else.

At some stage, children become stronger than their parents; they often become more intelligent, quicker-thinking . . . they may also be better-educated than their parents were and even better-off financially. The roles of parents and children gradually become reversed and children start to look after their parents and worry about them instead of the other way around.

Many parents find this change of role quite difficult. They know that their children are stronger than them in many ways and it is hard for them to come to terms with that and still keep their dignity and self-respect.

Many family arguments are made worse because people are afraid of losing their dignity. It is possible, however, to disagree with people and still treat them with respect.

Prayer

Let us remember that parents are people too. Bringing up children is a difficult job and parents work very hard at it.

May we treat our parents with respect and consideration, even when we disagree with them.

Amen

Day 2

The Rainbow

Introduction

The early Vikings believed that the rainbow was a bridge for the gods to walk over when they wanted to visit the earth.

In the Old Testament, after the Great Flood, we're told that God sent his rainbow as a sign of his agreement or covenant, that he would never again attempt to destroy the peoples of the world. This is what it says in Genesis:

'I do set my bow in the cloud, and it shall be for a token of a covenant between me and the earth.

And it shall come to pass, when I bring a cloud over the earth, that the bow shall be seen in the cloud . . .'

A rainbow seems like a miracle – it appears out of nowhere, it forms a perfect arc – it's made up of beautiful colours, always the same ones in just the same order – and it always mysteriously disappears.

A young child will marvel at a rainbow. In the poem you are about to hear, the famous poet, William Wordsworth tells us that the day we lose the ability to marvel at something as wonderful as a rainbow, we lose something very important.

> My heart leaps up when I behold
> A rainbow in the sky:
> So was it when my life began;
> So is it now I am a man;
> So be it when I shall grow old,
> Or let me die!
> The Child is father of the Man:
> And I could wish my days to be
> Bound each to each by natural piety.

Prayer

Let us give thanks for the beauty of the world.

May our minds never become so tarnished with worries and cares that we fail to find joy and wonder in the world about us.

Amen

Day 3

Suffer the Little Children

And they brought young children to him, that he should touch them: and his disciples rebuked those that brought them.

But when Jesus saw it, he was much displeased, and said unto them, 'Suffer the little children to come unto me, and forbid them not: for of such is the kingdom of God.

Verily I say unto you, Whosoever shall not receive the kingdom of God as a little child, he shall not enter therein.'

And he took them up in his arms, put his hands upon them, and blessed them.

Mark 10: 13–16 Authorised version

As we become older, we often try to appear more sophisticated and, in doing so, we lose much of the sense of wonder and excitement we felt when we were younger.

Those people who have had deep religious experiences often talk about them with a sense of awe – the feeling many of us have had as little children when we've been in the presence of something powerful and magnificent. The key to religious understanding is not cleverness. In order to appreciate something which is above and beyond ourselves we have to rid ourselves for a time of our sophistication and, in the words of Jesus Christ, become as little children again.

Prayer

May we never become so worldly that we close our eyes to the miracle and mystery of life. May we give pleasure to other people by sharing our joy and happiness with them.

Amen

Day 4 ## I Like Youngsters

God says: I like youngsters. I want people to be like them.
   I don't like old people unless they are still children.
   I want only children in my kingdom.
   Youngsters – twisted, humped, wrinkled, white-bearded
      – all kinds of youngsters, but youngsters.
   So, when I gently lean over them, I recognise myself in
      them.
   I like them because they are still growing, they are
      still improving.
   They are on the road, they are on their way.
   But with grown-ups there is nothing to expect any more.
   They will no longer grow, no longer improve.
   They have come to a full stop.
   It is disastrous – grown-ups think they have arrived
   . . . .

   In my heaven, there will be only five-year-old eyes, for
      I know of nothing more beautiful than the pure eyes of
      a child.
   It is not surprising, for I live in children, and it is I who
      look out through their eyes.
   When pure eyes meet yours, it is I who smile at you
      through the flesh.

But on the other hand, I know of nothing sadder than
lifeless eyes in the face of a child.
The windows are open, but the house is empty.
And, saddened, I stand at the door, and wait in the cold
and knock. I am eager to get in.
And he, the child, is alone.
He fattens, he hardens, he dries up, he gets old. Poor old
fellow!

Alleluia! Open, all of you, little old men!
It is I, your God, coming to bring back to life the child
in you.
Hurry! I am ready to give you again the beautiful face of
a child, the beautiful eyes of a child . . .
For I love youngsters, and I want everyone to be like
them.

(abridged) Michel Quoist

Prayer

In the Bible it says:
Behold, I stand at the door and knock: if any man hear my
voice, and open the door, I will come in to him

Revelation 3: 20

May we come to know again the trust and faith of little children. May we not be afraid of opening the door when we feel
aware of God waiting to enter our lives.

Amen

Day 5   ## The Great Lover

Today's reading is a poem written by the British poet,
Rupert Brooke, who was born in Rugby in 1887. He fought in
the first World War and died in the Aegean in 1915 at the age
of 27.

These I have loved:
   White plates and cups, clean-gleaming,
Ringed with blue lines; and feathery, faery dust;
Wet roofs, beneath the lamp-light; the strong crust
Of friendly bread; and many-tasting food;

Rainbows; and the blue bitter smoke of wood;
And radiant raindrops couching in cool flowers;
And flowers themselves, that sway through sunny hours,
Dreaming of moths that drink them under the moon;
Then, the cool kindliness of sheets, that soon
Smooth away trouble; and the rough male kiss
Of blankets; grainy wood; live hair that is
Shining and free; blue-massing clouds; the keen
Unpassioned beauty of a great machine;
The benison of hot water; furs to touch;
The good smell of old clothes; and other such –
The comfortable smell of friendly fingers,
Hair's fragrance, and the musty reek that lingers
About dead leaves and last year's ferns . . . .

. . . .
Firm sands; the little dulling edge of foam
That browns and dwindles as the wave goes home;
And washen stones . . . the cold
Graveness of iron; moist black earthen mould;
Sleep; and high places; footprints in the dew;
And oaks; and brown horse-chestnuts, glossy-new;
And new-peeled sticks; and shining pools on grass; –
All these have been my loves. And these shall pass,

. . . .
This one last gift I give: that after men
Shall know, and later lovers, far-removed,
Praise you, 'All these were lovely'; say, 'He loved.'

Rupert Brooke found pleasure in simple things – most of
which didn't cost anything at all.

The famous American film star, W C Fields, has been
known to earn as much as £1,000 a day and yet he has said
that his greatest thrill in life is the luxury of stretching out
at night between freshly laundered sheets. At one time in his
life, he didn't sleep in a bed for four whole years. He slept
on park benches, in packing boxes, and he even slept in holes
in the ground with a strip of linoleum for a blanket.

Having a comfortable bed to sleep in is a luxury that most
of us take for granted. We tend not to appreciate pleasures
like that unless we have had to manage without them.

All too often we fall into the trap of thinking that the only
really joyful experiences of life are those that we don't have;
we can miss out on so much happiness if we don't appreciate what we have already.

Prayer

Let us remember that life is very short. May we learn to appreciate its beauty and its comforts whilst we still have them to enjoy.

Amen

8 Run Baby Run – the Story of Nicky Cruz

Day 1   Arrival in New York

Introduction

Our readings this week are extracts from a book called *Run Baby Run* which tells the true story of a young man called Nicky Cruz.

Nicky was born on the small island of Puerto Rico close to the United States of America. Nicky's parents found him impossible to look after: he was always picking fights, especially with smaller children; he had a fight with his teacher at school and ran away from home five times in two years. In desperation, Nicky was sent by his parents to New York to stay with his older brother.

Nicky, however, had no intention of even looking for his brother in New York. As soon as his plane touched down in New York airport, he was running away again . . .

A large bus was sitting at the curb, door open, engine throbbing. People were boarding and I elbowed my way into line. The driver grabbed me by the shoulder and asked for my fare. I shrugged my shoulders and answered him in Spanish. He gruffly shoved me out of line, too busy to fool with a silly kid who could barely understand English. As he turned his attention to a woman who was fumbling with her purse, I ducked my head and squeezed behind her through the door and into the crowded bus. Glancing over my shoulder to make sure he hadn't seen me, I jostled my way to the rear and sat down next to a window.

As the bus pulled from the curb, I saw the fat gate-guard and two others puff out the side door of the terminal looking in all directions. I couldn't resist knocking on the window, waving and grinning through the glass. I had made it.

The bus ground its way through the heavy New York traffic toward the middle of the city. Outside there was snow and slush along the streets and sidewalks. I had always pictured snow as clean and beautiful, stretched out over acres of fairyland. But this was dingy, like dirty mush. My breath made fog on the window and I leaned back and ran my finger through it. It was a different world entirely from the one I had just left . . . .

. . . The bus jerked to a stop. Outside, the bright lights and multicoloured signs blinked and gleamed in the cold darkness. The man across the aisle got up to leave. I followed him out the back door. The doors swished shut behind me and the bus pulled away from the curb. I was left alone in the middle of eight million people.

I picked up a handful of dirty snow and brushed the crust off the top. There it was, sparkling white and pure. I wanted to put it to my mouth and eat it but as I watched, small dark spots began to appear on the surface. I suddenly realised the air was filled with soot from the chimneys above and the snow was taking on the appearance of cottage cheese sprinkled with black pepper.

I threw it to one side. It made little difference. I was free.

For two days I wandered through the city. I found an old coat thrown across a garbage can in a back alley. The sleeves drooped over my hands and the hem scraped the sidewalk. The buttons had been ripped off and the pockets torn open, but it kept me warm. That night I slept on the subway, curled up on one of the seats.

By the end of the second day the excitement had worn off. I was hungry . . . and cold. On two occasions, I tried to talk to people and ask for help. The first man simply ignored me. He walked by like I wasn't there. The second man pushed me back against the wall. 'Beat it, Spic. Don't put your greasy hands on me.' I was afraid. I kept trying to keep the panic from bubbling up from my stomach into my throat.

That evening I walked the streets again. The long overcoat dragging the sidewalk, my little suitcase clutched in my hand. People would move around me and look back but no one seemed to care. They just looked and walked on.

That night I spent the ten dollars Papa had given me. I stopped in a little restaurant and ordered a hot dog by pointing at a picture of one that hung over the greasy counter. I gobbled it up and pointed that I wanted another. The man at the counter shook his head and held out his hand. I reached in my pocket and pulled out the wadded up bill. Wiping his hands on a towel, he opened it up, stretched it a couple of times, and then slipped it in the pocket of his dirty apron. He then brought me another hot dog and a bowl of chili. When I finished, I looked for him but he had disappeared into the kitchen. I picked up my bag and went back into the cold street. I'd had my first experience with American enterprise. And how was I to know that American hot dogs didn't cost five dollars each?

Prayer

Let us give thanks for our homes and for our families, for the people who care for us and look after us and for all the comforts we enjoy.

Amen

Day 2 | **Mugging**

Introduction

Our assemblies continue with the true story of Nicky Cruz, the young Puerto Rican boy who is sent to New York by his family and then runs away.

Nicky finds himself in Brooklyn where most of the other Puerto Ricans live. The other teenagers he meets there are mainly criminals – thieves, prostitutes and drug pedlars – and most of them are members of the infamous teenage gangs which sometimes turn the city into a battleground.

Nicky has to find somewhere to live, and for that he needs money . . . .

I knew that if I tried to rob someone and got caught, I'd go to jail. But I was desperate . . . a room was going to cost money and I didn't have a penny. It was almost 10 pm and the winter wind was freezing cold. I shrank back into the shadows of the alley and saw people passing by on the sidewalk. I pulled the switchblade out of my pocket and pressed the button. The blade snapped open with a soft click. I pressed the tip against the palm of my hand. My hand was shaking as I tried to imagine just how I would perform the robbery. Would it be best to pull them into the alley? Should I go ahead and stab them or just scare them? What if they yelled . . . ?

My thoughts were interrupted by two people talking at the entrance of the alley. An old wino had stopped a young man in his late teens who was carrying a huge sack of groceries. The old man was begging him for a dime to buy a cup of coffee. I listened as the young man tried to get away – telling the wino he didn't have any money.

The thought ran through my mind that the old man probably had a pocket full of money he had begged and stolen. He wouldn't dare scream for help if I robbed him. As soon as the boy left I'd pull him into the alley and take it from him.

The young man was putting his grocery sack on the sidewalk. He fished in his pocket until he found a coin. The old man mumbled and shuffled away.

'Damn,' I thought to myself. 'Now what will I do?'

Just then the boy tipped over his sack of groceries. A couple of apples rolled onto the sidewalk. He bent to pick them up and I pulled him into the alley and smashed him up against the wall. Both of us were scared to death but I had the advantage of surprise. He was petrified with fear as I held my knife in front of him.

'I don't want to hurt you, but I need money. I'm desperate. Give it to me. Now! Quick! All you got before I kill you.'

My hand was shaking so badly I was afraid I'd drop the knife.

'Please. Please. Take it all. Don't kill me,' the boy pleaded.

He pulled out his billfold and tried to hand it to me. He dropped it and I kicked it down the alley. 'Take off,' I said. 'Run, man, run! And if you stop running for two blocks, you're a dead man.'

He looked at me, eyes wide with horror, and started to run. He tripped over his groceries and sprawled on the pavement at the mouth of the alley. Scrambling to his feet, he tripped again as he half-crawled, half-ran down the sidewalk. As soon as he turned the corner, I grabbed the wallet and sprinted down the alley. Emerging in the darkness, I vaulted the chain-link fence surrounding the park and ran through the high grass into the trees. Squatting behind an embankment, I paused to catch my breath and let my pounding heart settle down. Opening the wallet I counted out 19 dollars. It felt good to hold the bills in my hand. I tossed the wallet into the high grass and counted the money again before I folded it and put it in my pocket.

Not bad, I thought. The gangs are killing hobos for less than a dollar and I get 19 on my first try. This isn't going to be so bad after all.

But my confidence did not remove all my fear, and I stayed hidden in the high grass until after midnight. By then it was too late to get the room and I walked back to the spot where I had committed the robbery. Someone had already picked up all the spilled groceries with the exception of a crushed box of crackers. I picked up the box and shook it as the crumbs fell out on the pavement. I relived the experience in my mind and grinned. I should have cut him, just to find out what it felt like, I thought. Next time I will.

Conclusion

In the Lord's Prayer we say the words: 'Lead us not into Temptation.' All of us have to face temptation and there are times, as with Nicky in the reading, when the pressures on us to do something wrong are very strong.

We do always, however, have a choice about what we do – nobody forces us to do wrong. Even when other people around us do things we disapprove of, we don't have to follow their example.

Prayer

We know that there is evil in the world. May we struggle against evil with courage and determination. May we draw on God's power to strengthen us when we feel tempted to do wrong.

Amen

Day 3 | **Meeting with a Preacher**

Introduction

Nicky is initiated into a world of robbery and violence. Before very long he becomes the leader of one of the most powerful teenage gangs in Brooklyn. His life is devoted to fights with rival gangs, stabbing, mugging, drinking and taking drugs.

Then he meets a man called David Wilkerson, a preacher, who stands on street corners telling the young people about God.

The skinny man walked over to me and stuck out his hand. 'Nicky, my name is David Wilkerson. I'm a preacher from Pennsylvania.'

I just stared at him and said, 'Go to hell, Preacher.'

'You don't like me, Nicky,' he said, 'but I feel different about you. I love you. And not only that, I've come to tell you about Jesus who loves you, too.'

. . . No one loved me. No one ever had. As I stood there my mind raced back to that time so many years ago when I had heard my mother say, 'I don't love you, Nicky.' I thought, 'If your own mother doesn't love you then no one loves you – or ever will.'

The preacher just stood there, smiling, with his hand stuck out. I always prided myself on not being afraid. But I was afraid. Deeply afraid that this man was going to put me in a cage. He was going to take away my friends. He was going to upset everything and because of this I hated him. 'You come near me, Preacher, and I'll kill you,' I said, shrinking back towards the protection of the crowd.

The fear overwhelmed me. I was close to panic.

I was running, and I knew it. But I couldn't fight this kind of approach. If he had come at me with a knife, I would have fought him. If he had come begging and pleading, I would have laughed at him and kicked him in the teeth. But he came saying, 'I love you.' And I had never come up against this kind of approach before.

Some of the boys followed and we went down into the basement and I turned the phonograph on as loud as it would play. Suddenly, there was a commotion at the door and I looked up and saw the skinny preacher walk in. He seemed so out of place, with his nice suit and white shirt and neat tie, walking into this filthy basement room. He asked one of the boys, 'Where's Nicky?'

The boy pointed across the room where I was sitting with my head in my hands, cigarette dangling out of my mouth.

Wilkerson walked across the room like the place belonged to him. He had a big smile on his face. He stuck out his hand again and said, 'Nicky, I just wanted to shake hands with you and . . . '

Before he could finish, I slapped him in the face – hard. He tried to force his grin . . . he held his ground and the fear once again welled up inside me so that I was sick to my stomach. I did the only thing I knew to retaliate. I spat on him.

'Nicky, they spat on Jesus too, and he prayed, *Father forgive them, for they know not what they do.*'

I screamed at him, cursing, 'Get out, you crazy priest. You don't know what you're talking about. I'll give you 24 hours to get off my turf or I'll kill you.'

Wilkerson backed out the door, still smiling. 'Remember, Nicky, Jesus loves you.' It was more than I could take. I reached down and picked up the empty wine bottle and smashed it to the floor. I had never felt so frustrated, so desperate, so completely undone.

. . . I had never gone to my room this early. It was 10.30 . . . I closed the door behind me and locked it. I was shaking as I crossed the room . . . I took my gun out of the closet and put two bullets in the magazine and laid it on the table beside my bed. I kicked off my shoes and changed clothes. Laying my pack of cigarettes on the table, I lay back on the bed and looked at the ceiling. I could hear those words of David Wilkerson over and over, 'Jesus loves you, Nicky, Jesus loves you.'

I reached up and flipped off the light and lit a cigarette. I was chain smoking again. I couldn't rest. I twisted one way and then another. I couldn't sleep. The hours went by . . . .

The next morning I sat on the front steps with my head in my hands. I heard a car pull up in front of the apartment and heard the door slam shut. A hand clasped me on the shoulder. I lifted my weary head and saw the skinny preacher standing in front of me. He was still smiling and he said, 'Hi, Nicky. Do you remember what I told you last night?'

I jumped to my feet and made a motion for him. Wilkerson looked me straight in the eye and said, 'You could kill me, Nicky. You could cut me in a thousand pieces and lay them out on the street. But every piece would cry out, Jesus loves you. And you'll never be able to run away from that.'

I tried to stare him down but he kept talking. 'Nicky, I'm not scared of you. You talk tough but inside you're just like all the rest of us. You're lonely.'

Something clicked. How did he know that I was lonely?

The gang was always with me. I had any of the girls I wanted. People were afraid of me – they would see me coming and move off the sidewalk and into the street. How could anyone think I was lonely? And now this preacher knew it.

'Nicky, you didn't sleep much last night, did you?' Again I was amazed. How did he know that I hadn't slept?

Wilkerson continued, 'I didn't sleep much last night either, Nicky. I stayed awake most of the night praying for you. But before I did, I talked to some of your boys. They tell me that no one can get close to you. They are all afraid of you. But Nicky, I've come to tell you that somebody does care. Jesus cares. He loves you.' And then he looked me straight in the face, 'One day, soon, Nicky, God's spirit is going to deal with you. One day, Nicky, you are going to stop running and come running to him.'

I said no more. I got to my feet and walked back into the apartment. I climbed the steps to my room and sat on the side of the bed looking out the window. In the east, the sky was beginning to turn a rosy hue. The huge building across the street blocked my view of the horizon. But suddenly, like catching a whiff of the sea when you're still miles up the river, I had a feeling there was more to life than this. More than these towering concrete buildings – these prison walls of glass and stone.

I thought of his words, 'One day you will stop running and come running to Him'. I didn't even know who He was. But I thought, sitting there on the side of my bed looking out over the trash-filled street with the sound of the trucks grinding and roaring down the thoroughfare, that He must be something like the sun rising out of the ocean on a cloudless day. Or maybe something like the morning star that still hung in the dawning sky. Maybe . . . Someday . . . .

The time was closer than I knew.

Prayer

David Wilkerson's message to Nicky was very simple: *Jesus loves you.*

No matter how wasted our lives seem to be, no matter what we do, or how often we turn our backs on Him, God is still there waiting for us whenever we choose to make contact with him. May we have the courage to respond when we sense that He is speaking to us.

Amen

The Offering

Introduction

David Wilkerson organises a huge Christian rally. He invites all the teenage gangs in Brooklyn and provides free transport for them. Nicky Cruz and his gang, the Mau Maus, decide to go along for the ride . . . .

More than 50 Mau Maus crowded onto the bus. The harried men tried to keep order but finally gave up and let us take over. The gang was pulling at each other, shouting obscenities, opening windows, smoking, drinking wine, pulling the bell cord and shouting for the bus to get under way.

When we arrived at the arena, we opened the emergency doors and some even crawled out the windows. Israel and I pushed by the startled and helpless usher and swaggered into the arena dressed in our Mau Mau uniforms. We paraded down the aisle, tapping loudly with our canes and shouting and whistling to the crowd.

Looking out over the crowd, I could see members of rival gangs. The arena was almost full and it had all the makings of a full scale rumble. This might not be so bad after all. The din of noise was deafening. We took our seats and joined in, whistling and shouting and tapping our canes against the floor . . . .

Suddenly the skinny preacher stepped forward. I hadn't seen him since that early morning encounter several weeks before. My heart skipped a beat and the fear came flooding back. It was like a dark foreboding cloud that settled on every aspect of my personality. Israel was on his feet. 'Hey, Dave! Here I am. See, I told you I'd come. And look who's here,' he said, pointing to me.

I knew I had to do something or I was going to crack from the fear. I jumped to my feet and shouted, 'Hey Preacher, watcha gonna do . . . convert us or something?'

The Mau Maus joined in the laughter and I sat back down, feeling better. They still recognised me. Despite the fact that I was petrified with fear, I was still their leader. I was back in control of the situation.

Wilkerson began to speak: 'This is the last night of our city-wide youth crusade. Tonight, we're going to do something different. I'm going to ask my friends, the Mau Maus, to receive the offering.'

Pandemonium broke loose. Gang members all over the audience knew our reputation. For the Mau Maus to take up the offering was like asking Jack the Ripper to baby sit. The people began to laugh and shout.

But I was on my feet in a second. I'd been waiting for some opportunity to show off, to draw attention to myself. I pointed at five others, including Israel. 'You, you, you, . . . let's go.' The six of us walked to the front and lined up in front of the stage. Behind us things got quiet – deathly quiet.

Wilkerson bent down and handed each one of us a big ice cream carton. 'Now,' he said, 'I want you to line up here in front of the platform. The organ will play and I'm going to ask the people to come forward and give their offerings. When it is finished, I want you to come around behind that curtain and up onto the stage.

It was too good to be true. There was no doubt in anyone's mind what we would do. Anyone who didn't take advantage of a situation like this was a fool.

The offering was large. The aisles were full of people who were coming to the front. Many of the adults put in large bills and others put in cheques. Nearly everyone made some kind of a contribution.

When all had come forward, I motioned with my head and we all marched out the right side of the auditorium through the drapes that hung along the wall. Right above our heads was a huge red-lettered sign that said EXIT. It was noticeable to everyone and as we disappeared behind the curtain, the laughter began. It was low at first, then we could hear it rising until the whole auditorium was engulfed in gales of laughter at the poor preacher who had been duped by the Mau Maus.

We gathered behind the curtain. The boys looked at me expectantly. But something inside me was tugging in the other direction. The preacher's trust ignited a spark inside of me. I could do what was expected of me by the crowd, or I could do what he trusted me to do. Instead of flicking my eyes toward the exit door, I shook my head *no*. 'Come on,' I said. The boys couldn't believe me but they had to do what I told them to do . . . .

'Now, let's go,' I said.

We walked single file onto the stage. A lot of kids began to boo. They thought we had made a fool out of the preacher and were sorry we hadn't ducked out the door as they would have done. But it gave a warm, satisfying feeling to know I had done something right. Something honourable. For the first time in all my life I had done right because I wanted to do right. I liked the feeling.

'Here, Priest!' I said, 'this is yours.' I was nervous standing there in front of the crowd. But as I handed him the money the room grew quiet again.

Wilkerson took the cartons from us and looked me straight in the eye. 'Thank you, Nicky. I knew I could count on you.' We turned and filed back to our seats. The auditorium was quiet enough to hear a pin drop.

Conclusion

Nicky responded because, probably for the first time in his life, someone had shown trust in him and had treated him with respect.

Prayer

When we make it obvious that we expect the worst from people, the worst is usually what we get.

May we learn to treat with respect everyone that we come into contact with. May we search consistently for the best in other people.

Amen

| Day 5 | **Conversion**

Introduction

At David Wilkerson's rally, tension increases between the different teenage gangs and, before long, fighting breaks out in the arena.

All of us were on our feet. The room was charged with hatred. I was looking for a way out into the aisle. A full scale riot was building.

Suddenly I had a compelling urge to look at Wilkerson. He was standing calmly on the stage. His head bowed. His hands clasped tightly in front of his chest. I could see his lips moving. I knew he was praying.

Something clutched at my heart. I stopped and looked at

myself. All around me the bedlam continued but I was looking inward. Here was this skinny man, unafraid, in the midst of all this danger. Where did he get his power? Why wasn't he afraid like the rest of us? I felt shame. Embarrassment. Guilt.

I slumped down in my chair. All around me the pandemonium continued. Israel was standing up looking backward. He was shouting, 'Hey! Cool it! Let's hear what the preacher has to say.'

The Mau Maus sat down. The noise died. Like a fog moving in from the sea the silence swept toward the back of the room and then up into the balconies.

Something was happening to me. I was remembering. I remembered my childhood. I remembered the hate for my mother. I remembered the first days in New York when I ran like a wild animal set free from a cage. It was as though I were sitting in a movie and my actions were flashing in front of my eyes. I saw the girls . . . the lust . . . the sex. I saw the stabbings . . . the hurt . . . the hatred. It was almost more than I could stand.

Wilkerson was speaking again. He said something about repenting for your sin. I was under the influence of a power a million times stronger than any drug. It was as though I had been caught in a wild torrent of a rampaging river. I was powerless to resist. I didn't understand what was taking place within me. I only knew the fear was gone.

Beside me I heard Israel blow his nose. Behind me I heard people crying. Something was sweeping through that massive arena like the wind moving through the top of the trees.

Wilkerson was speaking again. 'He's here! He's in this room. He's come especially for you. If you want your life changed, now is the time.' Then he shouted with authority: 'Stand up! Those who will receive Jesus Christ and be changed – stand up! Come forward!'

I felt Israel stand to his feet. 'Boys, I'm going up. Who's with me?'

I was on my feet. I turned to the gang and waved them on with my hand. 'Let's go.' There was a spontaneous movement out of the chairs and toward the front. More than 25 of the Mau Maus responded. Behind us about 30 boys from other gangs followed our example.

We stood around the bottom of the stage looking up at Wilkerson. He dismissed the service and told us to follow him to the back rooms for counselling.

Israel was in front of me, his head bowed, his handkerchief to his face. We went through the door and into a hallway that led to the dressing rooms . . . . Nothing else mattered at the moment except the fact that I wanted to be a follower of Jesus Christ – whoever He was.

A man talked to us about the Christian way of life. Then Wilkerson came in. 'All right, fellows,' he said, 'kneel down right here on the floor.'

I thought he was crazy. I had never knelt down in front of anyone. But an invisible force pressed down on me. I felt my knees buckling. I couldn't remain erect. It was as though a giant hand were pushing me downward until my knees hit the floor.

The touch of the hard floor brought me back to reality. It was summer. It was time for the rumbles. I opened my eyes and thought to myself, 'What're you doing here?' Israel was beside me, weeping, loudly. In the midst of all this tension I giggled.

'Hey, Israel, you're bugging me with that crying.' Israel looked up and smiled through the tears. But as we looked at each other I had a strange sensation. I felt the tears welling up in my eyes and suddenly they spilled over the sides and dripped down my cheeks. I was crying. For the first time since I cried my heart out in Puerto Rico – I was crying.

Israel and I were both on our knees, side by side, with tears streaming down our faces, yet laughing at the same time. It was an indescribably exotic feeling.

Tears and laughter. I was happy, yet I was crying. Something was taking place in my life that I had absolutely no control over . . . and I was happy about it.

Suddenly I felt Wilkerson's hand on my head. He was praying – praying for me. The tears flowed more freely as I bowed my head and the shame and repentance and the wonderful joy of salvation mixed their ingredients in my soul.

'Go on, Nicky,' Wilkerson said, 'Go ahead and cry. Pour it out to God. Call on Him.'

I opened my mouth but the words that came out were not mine. 'O God, if you love me, come into my life. I'm tired of running. Come into my life and change me. Please change me.'

That's all it was. But I felt myself being picked up and swept heavenward.

Marijuana! Sex! Blood! All the sadistic, immoral thrills of

a million lifetimes put together could not begin to equal what I felt. I was literally baptised with love.

After the emotional crisis passed, Wilkerson quoted some Scripture to us. 'If any man be in Christ, he is a new creature: old things are passed away; behold, all things are become new.' (2 Corinthians 5:17)

It made sense. For the first time in my life it made sense. I had become new. I was Nicky and yet I was not Nicky. The old way of life had disappeared. It was as though I had died to the old way – and yet I was alive in a new kind of way.

Happiness. Joy. Gladness. Release. Relief. Freedom. Wonderful, wonderful freedom.

I had stopped running.

Conclusion

Nicky's conversion to Christianity shows that we don't necessarily need to be clever and learned to find God – religion is not like finding out about astronomy or physics.

In the Muslim religion, for instance, the word 'Muslim' means 'one who submits to the will of God.'

What Nicky discovered is that responding to God is an act of submission – of giving in to a force much more powerful than our own.

Prayer

Dear God, we call on you to take our lives over for carrying out your work.

Show us what you want us to do and give us the strength to submit our will to yours.

Amen

9 Christmas

See also The Ballad of the Bread Man, page 153.

| Day 1 | **Carol** |

The Palm Court Lounge is snug and warm
There's Scotch on every table
It's not our fault it's not so hot
Next door in the hotel stable.

The passengers are drunk tonight
The crew have cash to burn
So who will hear the drowning man
We've left ten miles astern?

Let's all go down the Motorway
And see who's first at Chester
Let's forget the scruffy dog
We knocked for six at Leicester.

O we're all right and so is Jack
(He's underneath the table)
It's not our fault it's not so hot
Next door in the hotel stable.

God rest us merry Gentlemen,
This is no time for sorrow
Because ten thousand refugees
Will get no grub tomorrow.

The Landlord smiles and lays the bill
Quite gently on the table
The man who'll pay has just been born
Next door in an ice–cold stable.

Ronald Deadman

Prayer

Let us give thanks for the example of love and compassion
shown to us by the life of Jesus Christ.
    May we use his example to remind us to be caring and
compassionate to everyone this Christmas time.

Amen

Day 2   **Nativity**

It was a terrible time to have Christmas.
He'd only just got right from flu.
The icicles froze on the end of his nose
And Rudolph's red nose had turned blue.

His cheeks they were frozen like fishcakes
as he wearily trudged door to door.
Both his feet in his wellies were squelchin' like jellies
and his knees they were swollen and raw.

He'd got rid of most of the presents
when he suddenly heard a strange sound;
it came from a car near a pub called 'The Star'
on an acre of derelict ground.

So he pulled up the brakes on the reindeer
for the cry of a baby he'd heard;
but the car was in darkness – the engine was off
and so were the wheels, he observed.

Then he reached in his sack for a pressie
but those left were all spoken for.
All he'd got for the mite was a tatty old kite
that he'd used twice for moppin' the floor.

So Santa Claus finished his journey
though the air was so cold, so they say,
dewdrops formed on his nose and they instantly froze
and icicles hung round his sleigh.

They were just about reaching exhaustion
when they found it was time to go back.
And the reindeer fair flew down Artisan View
now the weight had gone out of their sack.

They were all looking forward to supper
with cocoa and rum and mince pies
when Santa Claus thought that he still hadn't brought
a gift for the babe he'd heard cry.

There was quite a big crowd round the car now
for the parties were ending, of course.
There were three Pakistanis with crepe paper crowns
and the front legs of a pantomime horse.

Father Christmas felt guilty and sorry
that all the best pressies had gone
and the kid had a fright when he took out the kite
from a bag that said 'Made in Hong Kong'.

For the kite was all tattered and torn now.
It didn't look much of a toy:
it looked more like a cluster of bats in a duster
than a gift for a new baby boy.

But Santa Claus put down the pressie
next to the small child in the car
then in two minutes flat he was waving his hat
and shooting off home – like a star.

The wind blew all night round the baby;
it howled like a vampire in pain.
All the stuff off the kite blew right out of sight –
and all that was left was the frame.

And there if you went you could see them:
the kite with its cloth torn away; the boy clinging tight to
    his cross all the night –
the sole gift for his first Christmas Day.

Conclusion

Christmas is a celebration of the joy and hope which the birth of Jesus Christ has brought to millions throughout the ages. Contained within that joy is the message of the cross – the symbol of sacrifice and giving.

Prayer

Let us rember that Christmas is a time of giving. As well as giving presents, let us make sure that we also give of our time and attention to those who care about us and our thanks to those who have given to us.

Amen

| Day 3 |

The Magnificat

And in the sixth month the angel Gabriel was sent from God unto a city of Galilee, named Nazareth. To a virgin espoused to a man whose name was Joseph of the house of David; and the virgin's name was Mary.

And the angel came in unto her, and said, 'Hail, thou that art highly favoured, the Lord is with thee: blessed art thou among women.'

And when she saw him, she was troubled at his saying, and cast in her mind what manner of salutation this should be.

And the angel said unto her, 'Fear not, Mary: for thou hast found favour with God.

And behold, thou shalt conceive in thy womb and bring forth a son, and shalt call his name Jesus.

He shall be great, and shall be called the Son of the Highest and the Lord God shall give unto him the throne of his father David. And he shall reign over the house of Jacob for ever and of his kingdom there shall be no end.

And Mary said, 'My soul doth magnify the Lord, and my spirit hath rejoiced in God my Saviour. For he hath regarded the low estate of his handmaiden, for behold, from henceforth all generations shall call me blessed.

For he that is mighty hath done to me great things, and holy is his name. And his mercy is on them that fear him from generation to generation.

He hath showed strength with his arm; he hath scattered the proud in the imagination of their hearts.

He hath put down the mighty from their seats and exalted them of low degree.

He hath filled the hungry with good things and the rich he hath sent empty away.

Luke 1: 26–33, 46–53 Authorised version

Prayer

Mary's poem of thanks is called the Magnificat. Her words are a celebration of the miracle of birth.

In our own celebrations this Christmas, may we join with Mary in giving thanks for the amazing gift of human life.

Amen

Day 4 **The Nativity**

And it came to pass in those days, that there went out a decree from Caesar Augustus that all the world should be taxed. And all went to be taxed, everyone into his own city.

And Joseph also went up from Galilee, out of the city of Nazareth, into Judea, unto the city of David, which is called Bethlehem to be taxed with Mary his espoused wife, being great with child.

And so it was, that while they were there, the days were accomplished that she should be delivered.

And she brought forth her first-born son, and wrapped him in swaddling clothes, and laid him in a manger; because there was no room for them in the inn.

And there were in the same country shepherds abiding in the field, keeping watch over their flocks by night.

And lo, the angel of the Lord came upon them, and the glory of the Lord shone round about them and they were sore afraid.

And the angel said unto them, 'Fear not, for behold I bring you good tidings of great joy, which shall be to all people.

For unto you is born this day in the city of David a Saviour, which is Christ the Lord. And this shall be a sign unto you, Ye shall find the babe wrapped in swaddling clothes, lying in a manger.'

And suddenly there was with the angel a multitude of the heavenly host praising God and saying:

'Glory to God in the highest, and on earth peace, good will toward men.'

And it came to pass, as the angels were gone away from them into heaven, the shepherds said one to another, 'Let us now go even unto Bethlehem, and see this thing which is come to pass, which the Lord hath made known to us.'

And they came with haste, and found Mary, and Joseph, and the babe lying in a manger. And when they had seen it they made known abroad the saying which was told them concerning the child. And all they that heard it wondered at those things which were told them by the shepherds.

But Mary kept all these things, and pondered them in her heart.

Luke 2: 1–19 Authorised version

Conclusion

The significance of the birth of Christ is not the sudden appearance of angels all over the place, but the fact that such an important person was born in the most humble surroundings – in a poor and lowly stable.

Prayer

May we be wary of judging people by their wealth.

Let us remember that it is often the most poor and humble who have the most to teach us.

Amen

Day 5   **The Wise Men**

Now when Jesus was born in Bethlehem of Judea in the days of Herod the king, behold there came wise men from the east to Jerusalem, saying, 'Where is he that is born King of the Jews? For we have seen his star in the east and are come to worship him.'

When Herod the king heard these things, he was troubled and all Jerusalem with him. And when he had gathered all the chief priests and scribes of the people together he demanded of them where Christ should be born.

And they said unto him, 'In Bethlehem of Judea, for thus it is written by the prophet.'

And Herod, when he had privily called the wise men, enquired of them diligently what time the star appeared. And he sent them to Bethlehem and said, 'Go and search diligently for the young child; and when ye have found him, bring me word again, that I may come and worship him also.'

When they had heard the king, they departed; and lo, the star, which they saw in the east, went before them, till it came and stood over where the young child was. And when they saw the star, they rejoiced with exceeding great joy.

And when they were come into the house, they saw the young child with Mary his mother, and fell down and worshipped him; and when they had opened their treasures, they presented unto him gifts: gold and frankincense and myrrh.

And being warned of God in a dream that they should not return to Herod, they departed into their own country another way.

And when they were departed, behold, the angel of the Lord appeareth to Joseph in a dream saying, 'Arise, and take the young child and his mother, and flee into Egypt, and be thou there until I bring thee word, for Herod will seek the young child to destroy him.'

When he arose, he took the young child and his mother by night, and departed into Egypt.

Matthew 2: 1–14 Authorised version

Prayer

Let us give thanks for the example given to us by Jesus Christ. May we find room in our hearts this Christmas for his message of hope and love.

Amen

10 Faith

Day 1 | **God Knows**

Our reading today is the first part of a poem written by Minnie Louise Haskins who died in 1957.

This particular verse, about the New Year, was used by King George VI in his Christmas radio broadcast in 1939. This was the year in which war had just been declared and was a time of great worry and foreboding.

No one, of course, would want to compare the first week of school term with the outbreak of a world war, but we are at the beginning of a New Year and a gateway to the future.

I said to the man
who stood at the gate of the year,
'Give me a light that I may tread safely
into the unknown.'
And he replied, 'Go out into the darkness
and put your hand into the hand of God.
That shall be to you better than light
and safer than a known way!'
So I went forth and,
finding the hand of God,
trod gladly into the night.
And he led me towards the hills
and the breaking of day in the
lone east.

Prayer

At this breaking of day and at this dawning of a new year

may we have the courage to put our hands into the hand of God.

May we allow Him to lead us into the unknown, may we draw our courage from Him and may we place our trust in His loving kindness.

Amen

Day 2

Abou Ben Adhem

Our readings this week are about having faith and trust in God.

Many of us find it difficult to have faith and trust and feel love for someone that we cannot see and often feel that we cannot hear or get close to.

Today's reading is quite a well-known poem about a man who had such a difficulty:

Abou Ben Adhem – may his tribe increase –
Awoke one night from a deep dream of peace,
And saw, within the moonlight in his room,
Making it rich and like a lily in bloom,
An angel writing in a book of gold.
Exceeding peace had made Ben Adhem bold,
And to the presence in the room, he said:
'What writest thou?' The vision raised its head,
and with a look made of all sweet accord,
Answered: 'The names of those who love the Lord.'
'And is mine one?' said Abou. 'Nay, not so,'
Replied the angel. Abou spoke more low,
But cheerily still; and said: 'I pray thee then,
Write me as one that loves his fellow-men.'
The angel wrote, and vanished. The next night
It came again with a great wakening light,
And showed the names whom love of God had blest,
And lo! Ben Adhem's name led all the rest.

Leigh Hunt

Prayer

Ben Adhem said, 'Write me as one that loves his fellow men.' And it was through his caring and concern for other people that Ben showed his love for God.

May we also learn to care for each other and, through our concern and love for other people, come to be blessed by God.

Amen

Day 3

The Lord Is My Shepherd

The Lord is my shepherd; I shall not want.

He maketh me to lie down in green pastures: he leadeth me beside the still waters.

He restoreth my soul: he leadeth me in the paths of righteousness for his name's sake.

Yea, though I walk through the valley of the shadow of death, I will fear no evil: for thou art with me; thy rod and thy staff they comfort me.

Thou preparest a table before me in the presence of mine enemies: thou anointest my head with oil; my cup runneth over.

Surely goodness and mercy shall follow me all the days of my life: and I will dwell in the house of the Lord for ever.

Psalm 23 Authorised version

Prayer

Today's prayer was written by St Richard of Chichester who lived from 1197 to 1253.

O most merciful Redeemer, Friend and Brother,
May we know Thee more clearly,
Love Thee more dearly,
Follow Thee more nearly;
For ever and ever.

Amen

Day 4

Meditation

Recommended music: A useful opening for this assembly would be an extract from one of Beethoven's pieces composed after he had begun to go deaf. The beginning of the third movement of the Ninth Symphony, or the third movement of the Archduke Trio would be appropriate.

Introduction

It's easy for us to keep our religious faith when things are going well for us and we feel successful.

When we're unhappy and nothing seems to be turning out right, it's tempting to despair – to feel as though God is abandoning us.

Today's reading, by Cardinal Newman, gives us the reassurance that there is a purpose in our lives.

God has created me to do Him some definite service. He has committed some work to me which he has not committed to another. I have my mission.

I may never know it in this world but I shall be told it in the next. I am a link in the chain, a bond of connection between persons. He has not created me for nothing. I shall do good. I shall do His work. I shall be an angel of peace – a preacher of truth in my own place, if I do but keep His commandments.

Therefore will I trust Him. Wherever, whatever I am, I can never be thrown away. If I am in sickness, my sickness may serve Him; in perplexity, my perplexity may serve Him; if I am in sorrow, my sorrow may serve Him.

He does nothing in vain. He knows what he is about. He may take away my friends. He may throw me among strangers. He may make me feel desolate, make my spirits sink, hide my future from me . . . still . . . He knows what He is about.

Conclusion

Today's prayer was written by someone who must have experienced the terrible sense of desolation that Cardinal Newman spoke about – it was written by the great composer, Beethoven, at a time when he realised that his deafness was incurable.

Prayer

O God give me the strength to be victorious over myself, for nothing may chain me to this life. Please guide my spirit and raise me up from depths of misery, so that my soul may be carried through your wisdom and may struggle fearlessly upwards in fiery flight. For you alone can understand me and you alone can inspire me.

Amen

Day 5

I Am the Great Sun

Today's reading is a poem based on an inscription found on a Normandy crucifix dated 1632.

It tells how essential God's presence is in making our lives rich and meaningful and bemoans the fact that so many people turn away from him.

I am the great sun, but you do not see me,
    I am your husband, but you turn away.
I am the captive, but you do not free me,
    I am the captain you will not obey.

I am the truth, but you will not believe me,
    I am the city where you will not stay,
I am your wife, your child, but you will leave me,
    I am that God to whom you will not pray.

I am your counsel, but you do not hear me,
    I am the lover whom you will betray,
I am the victor, but you do not cheer me,
    I am the holy dove whom you will slay.

I am your life, but if you will not name me,
Seal up your soul with tears, and never blame me.

Charles Causley

Conclusion

One of the most wonderful things about religion is that it's always there waiting for us. We might turn away from our own particular church – we might go through a period of not knowing what we believe in – we might change from being a Catholic to a Buddhist or from a Jehovah's Witness to an Anglican; but, no matter how many times we reject religion, we know it will never reject us.

Prayer

Today's reading compares God with a great sun – a source of tremendous strength and energy which never goes away.

May we turn our eyes towards this great sun, draw warmth and strength and comfort from it and receive its blessing.

Amen

11 Those Less Fortunate Than Ourselves

Day 1 Anything You Do for Others

When the Son of Man comes in his glory and all the angels with him, he will sit in state on his throne, with all the nations gathered before him. He will separate men into two groups, as a shepherd separates the sheep from the goats, and he will place the sheep on his right hand and the goats on the left.

Then the king will say to those on his right hand, 'You have my Father's blessing; come, enter and possess the kingdom that has been ready for you since the world was made. For when I was hungry, you gave me food; when thirsty, you gave me drink; when I was a stranger you took me into your home, when naked you clothed me; when I was ill you came to my help, when in prison you visited me.'

Then the righteous will reply, 'Lord, when was it that we saw you hungry and fed you, or thirsty and gave you drink, a stranger and took you home, or naked and clothed you? When did we see you ill or in prison, and come to visit you?'

And the king will answer, 'I tell you this: anything you did for one of my brothers here, however humble, you did for me.'

Then he will say to those on his left hand, 'The curse is upon you; go from my sight to the eternal fire that is ready for the devil and his angels. For when I was hungry you gave me nothing to eat, when thirsty nothing to drink; when I was a stranger you gave me no home, when naked you did not clothe me; when I was ill and in prison you did not come to my help.'

And they too will reply, 'Lord, when was it that we saw you hungry or thirsty or a stranger or naked or ill or in prison, and did nothing for you?'

And he will answer, 'I tell you this: anything you did not do for one of these, however humble, you did not do for me.'

Matthew 25: 31–46   New English Bible

Conclusion

It's easy for us to be friendly and kind to people that we think highly of or that we want to impress. But Jesus said, 'anything you did not do for one of these, *however humble*, you did not do for me.'

Prayer

Let us remember that there is something of God in everyone – even people we find it difficult to like.

May we try to do something to make other people's lives happier and easier – even those people who seem to be doing nothing at all to help us.

Amen

Day 2   **Timothy Winters**

Timothy Winters comes to school
With eyes as wide as a football pool,
Ears like bombs and teeth like splinters:
A blitz of a boy is Timothy Winters.

His belly is white, his neck is dark,
And his hair is an exclamation mark.
His clothes are enough to scare a crow
And through his britches the blue winds blow.

When teacher talks he won't hear a word
And he shoots down dead the arithmetic-bird,
He licks the patterns off his plate
And he's not even heard of the Welfare State.

Timothy Winters has bloody feet
And he lives in a house on Suez Street,

He sleeps in a sack on the kitchen floor
And they say there aren't boys like him any more.

Old Man Winters likes his beer
And his missus ran off with a bombadier,
Grandma sits in the grate with a gin
And Timothy's dosed with an aspirin.

The Welfare Worker lies awake
But the law's as tricky as a ten-foot snake,
So Timothy Winters drinks his cup
And slowly goes on growing up.

At Morning Prayers the Master helves
For children less fortunate than ourselves
And the loudest response in the room is when
Timothy Winters roars 'Amen!'

So come one angel, come on ten:
Timothy Winters says 'Amen
Amen amen amen amen.'
Timothy Winters, Lord.

Amen

Charles Causley

Prayer

No matter how sorry we may feel for ourselves at times, there are always people worse off than us.

Let us pray for children who are poor, unloved, lonely and uncared for. May their teachers be kind to them and may they find good friends to help them.

Amen

Day 3 **The Pinballs (1)**

One summer two boys and a girl went to a foster home to live together.

One of the boys was Harvey. He had two broken legs. He got them when he was run over by his father's new Grand Am.

The day of his accident was supposed to be one of the happiest of Harvey's life. He had written an essay on 'Why I Am Proud to Be an American', and he had won third prize. Two dollars. His father had promised to drive him to the meeting and watch him get the award. The winners and their parents were going to have their pictures taken for the newspaper.

When the time came to go, Harvey's father said, 'What are you doing in the car?' Harvey had been sitting there, waiting, for fifteen minutes. He was wearing a tie for the first time in his life. 'Get out, Harvey, I'm late as it is.'

'Get out?'

'Yes, get out.'

Harvey did not move. He sat staring straight ahead. He said, 'But this is the night I get my award. You promised you'd take me.'

'I didn't *promise*. I said I would if I could.'

'No, you promised. You said if I'd quit bugging you about it, you'd take me. You promised.' He still did not look at his father.

'Get out, Harvey.'

'No.'

'I'm telling you for the last time, Harvey. Get out.'

'Drive me to the meeting and I'll get out.'

'You'll get out when I say!' Harvey's father wanted to go to a poker game at the Elks Club, and he was already late. 'And I say you get out *now*.' With that, the father leaned over, opened the door and pushed Harvey out of the car.

Harvey landed on his knees in the grass. He jumped to his feet. He grabbed for the car door. His father locked it.

Now Harvey looked at his father. His father's face was as red as if it had been turned inside out.

Quickly Harvey ran round the front of the car to try and open the other door. When he was directly in front of the car, his father accidentally threw the car into drive instead of reverse. In that wrong gear, he pressed the accelerator, ran over Harvey and broke both his legs.

The court had taken Harvey away from his father and put him in the foster home 'until such time as the father can control his drinking and make a safe home for the boy.'

The girl was Carlie. She was as hard to crack as a coconut. She never said anything polite. When anyone asked how she was, she answered 'What's it to you?' or 'Bug off'. Her main fun was watching television, and she threw things at people who blocked her view. Even the dog had been hit with *TV Guide* when he stepped in front of the set when Sonny and Cher were singing 'I Got You, Babe'.

Carlie had to go to the foster home because she couldn't get along with her stepfather. She had had two stepfathers, but the new one, Russell, was the worst. He was mean to everybody in the family, but especially to Carlie. He resented everything she did.

Once he had hit her so hard when she wouldn't tell him where she'd been that she had had concussion. Even with concussion she had struggled up and hit him with a frying pan. 'Nobody hits me without getting hit back,' she had said before she collapsed.

Carlie was to stay at the foster home 'until the home situation stabilises'.

'Stabilises!' Carlie had said to the social worker in charge of her case. 'What does that mean?'

'It means until your mother and your stepfather work out their problems.'

'Whoo,' Carlie said, 'that means I'll stay until I'm ready for the old folks home.'

The first thing Carlie did when she got to the foster home was pull the plastic footrest up close to the TV: 'Don't talk to me when "Young and Restless" is on,' she warned the foster mother who was standing behind her.

'I just wanted to welcome you,' Mrs Mason said. She put one hand on Carlie's back.

Carlie shook it off. 'Welcome me during the commercials,' she said.

Betsy Byars

Conclusion

The two children in this story have been through very bad experiences. Carlie and Harvey feel bitter and resentful about the way they've been treated. Because of this, they don't find it easy to make friends and are very difficult to get on with.

It's easy to be friendly to nice people. It takes a lot of patience to be friendly towards people who at first seem hostile and resentful.

Prayer

Jesus Christ said: 'Anything you did not do for one of these, however humble, you did not do for me.'

May we be patient with those people whose lives have been difficult and who feel bitter and resentful. May we try to show them by our own example that there is something good in everyone.

Amen

| Day 4 |

The Pinballs (2)

Carlie had been suspicious of people since the day she was born. She swore she could remember being dropped on the floor by the doctor who delivered her.

'You weren't dropped,' her mother had told her.

'All right then, why is my face so flat? Was I *ironed?*'

Carlie also claimed that when she was two months old a baby-sitter had stolen a gold cross from round her neck.

'No baby-sitter stole a gold cross from you,' her mother had told her.

'All right then, where is it?'

Carlie believed everyone was out to do her in, and she had disliked Mrs Mason, the foster mother, as soon as she had seen her standing in the doorway.

'I knew she'd have on an apron,' Carlie said to the social worker. 'She's trying to take off Mrs Walton – unsuccessfully, I might add.'

'Maybe she had on the apron because she was cooking, Carlie.'

'*I* should be the social worker. I'm not fooled by things like aprons.'

She also didn't like the Mason's living room. 'This is right out of "Leave it to Beaver",' she said. She especially distrusted the row of photographs over the fireplace. Seventeen pictures of – Carlie guessed – 17 foster children.

'Well, my picture's not going up there,' she grumbled to herself. 'And nobody had better snap me when I'm not looking.' She sat.

Mrs Mason waited until 'Young and Restless' was over and then she said, 'Carlie?'

'I'm still here.'

'Well, come on and have some lunch. Then afterwards you can help me get the boys' room ready.'

Carlie turned. She looked interested for the first time. 'The boys?' she asked. 'There're going to be some boys here?'

'Yes, two boys are coming this afternoon – Thomas J and Harvey.'

'How old?'

'Eight and thirteen.'

'Oh, boo, too young.' Carlie got up from the footstool. 'What's wrong with them?'

'Wrong with them?'

'Yeah, why do they have to be here? I'm here because I got a bum stepfather. What's their trouble?'

'Well, I guess they'll have to tell you that.'

Carlie lifted her hair up off her neck. 'How about the 13-year-old?' she asked. 'What's he like? Big for his age, I hope.'

'He has two broken legs. That's about all I can tell you.'

'Well,' Carlie said, 'that lets out dancing.'

Carlie was sitting in front of the television when Harvey arrived. He had to be carried in because of his legs. They set the wheelchair down by Carlie's footstool.

She looked round. 'What happened to your legs?' she asked. She was interested in medical matters.

He said, 'Nothing.'

'Well, *something* must have happened. They don't just put plaster casts on your legs for the fun of it.'

There was a long pause. Harvey looked down at his legs. In his mind the shiny Grand Am lunged over him again. He felt sick. He said, 'If you must know, I broke my legs playing football.'

He wished it had happened that way. A boy at school had broken his ankle playing football, and everyone in school had autographed his cast. Girls had even kissed the cast and left their lipstick prints.

Harvey's casts were as white as snow. He wished he had thought to forge some names on them. 'Love and kisses from Linda.' 'Best wishes to a wonderful English student from Miss Howell.'

Carlie was still looking at him, eyeing the casts, his toes sticking out at the end. Then she glanced up at his face.

'What position were you playing?'

Harvey hesitated. 'Quarterback,' he said.

Carlie snorted. 'You're no quarterback. I've seen Joe Namath in person.' She looked him over. 'If you were playing football at all, you were probably the ball.'

Harvey kept looking at his legs.

Carlie decided to give him one more chance. 'So what really happened?'

'I was playing football,' he insisted.

'Listen,' Carlie said. 'This is one of my favourite shows, so if you're going to tell me a bunch of big lies about what happened to your legs, well, I'll just go back to watching my show.'

'Go back to watching it,' Harvey said.

Betsy Byars

Prayer

It's always difficult to be aware of other people's pain when we are hurt ourselves.

Let us pray that we may use our own experiences – our grief, our worries and our disappointments – to help other people cope with their problems. May we seek, as teachers and as pupils, to become sensitive and caring. May the lives of those we meet become richer for having known us.

Amen

| Day 5 | **On the Swag**

His body doubled
    under the pack
    that sprawls untidily
    on his old back
    the cold wet deadbeat
    plods up the track.

The cook peers out:
    'oh curse that old lag
    here again
    with his clumsy swag
    made of a dirty old
    turnip bag.'

'Bring him in, cook,
    from the grey level sleet,
    put silk on his body,
    slippers on his feet,
    give him fire
    and bread and meat,

'Let the fruit be plucked
    and the cake be iced,
    the bed be snug
    and the wine be spiced
    in the old cove's nightcap:
    for this is Christ.'

R A K Mason

Prayer

Let us remember that it's not the popular, attractive people
who need our help most, but the lonely and the unpopular
. . . those it might be easier to laugh at than to be seen helping. Let us learn to treat other people as we would like them
to treat us.

Amen

12 Am I My Brother's Keeper?

Day 1   Cain and Abel

Introduction

Today's reading, about Cain and Abel, is one of the stories from the book of Genesis in the Old Testament.

In the story, Cain and Abel were supposed to be the sons of Adam and Eve. Abel was a shepherd and Cain was a farmer. As was the local custom, they both made sacrifices to God from the products of their labour, Cain sacrificing one of his sheep and Abel some of his vegetables. For some reason, Abel's offering seemed to go down much better with God than his brother's did.

Cain was jealous and upset to think that his brother was more highly favoured with God. When Cain made his feelings known, the only explanation he received was that he had to master his sin before God would be impressed with him. We pick up the story with Cain plotting fiendishly against his brother.

Cain said to Abel his brother, 'Let us go out to the field.' And when they were in the field, Cain rose up against his brother Abel, and killed him.

Then the Lord said to Cain, 'Where is Abel your brother?'

He said, 'I do not know; am I my brother's keeper?'

And the Lord said, 'What have you done? The voice of your brother's blood is crying to me from the ground.

'And now you are cursed from the ground which has opened its mouth to receive your brother's blood from your hand.

'When you till the ground, it shall no longer yield to you its strength; you shall be a fugitive and a wanderer on the earth.'

Cain said to the Lord, 'My punishment is greater than I can bear.

'Behold, thou hast driven me this day away from the ground; and from thy face I shall be hidden; and I shall be a fugitive and a wanderer on the earth and whoever finds me will slay me.'

Then the Lord said to him, 'Not so! If anyone slays Cain, vengeance shall be taken on him sevenfold.' And the Lord put a mark on Cain, lest any who came upon him should kill him.

Then Cain went away from the presence of the Lord and dwelt in the Land of Nod, east of Eden.

Genesis 4: 8–16 Revised Standard version

Conclusion

When Cain asked, 'Am I my brother's keeper?' he was trying to say that he was not responsible for his brother. And, of course, that wasn't true. Cain had killed his brother because he was jealous of the fact that Abel seemed to be the one that was favoured by God.

The question: 'Am I my brother's keeper?' is one that we often hear quoted. When we use the words, 'brothers' and 'sisters' we usually mean the people in our immediate families, but it can also mean other people in the world who might be in need of our help.

Prayer

May we learn to be caring and considerate and come to look upon everyone in the world as our brothers and sisters – people whose lives might be improved through something we can offer.

Amen

Day 2   ## No Man Is an Island

Today's reading was written nearly 400 years ago by a poet

called John Donne who was a clergyman, the Dean of St Paul's Cathedral in 1621.

The poem mentions the tolling of a bell; we say that a bell 'tolls' when it sounds one repeated single note.

Nowadays, the tolling of a bell is often used to summon people to church.

It would be used in the past as a sign that someone had died. When people heard the tolling of the local church bell, they would go outside and ask 'for whom the bell tolls?'

> No man is an island
> Entire of itself;
> Every man is a piece of the continent,
> A part of the maine;
> If a clod be washed away by the sea,
> Europe is the less,
> As well as if a promontory were,
> As well as if a manor of thy friends
> Or of thine own were;
> Any man's death diminishes me
> Because I am involved in mankind.
> And therefore never send to know
> For whom the bell tolls;
> It tolls for thee.

Conclusion

We seldom nowadays hear the tolling of a bell to signify disaster or misfortune. Nevertheless, the message of the poem still applies: all of us are involved in the human race – or, as John Donne says, 'in mankind'; when disaster affects others, it reaches us as well.

'Therefore never send to know for whom the bell tolls; it tolls for thee.'

Prayer

Let us pray that we may develop our ability to feel compassion. May we grow towards a deeper awareness of other people – their joys, their fears and their suffering. May we strive to become involved, not just in ourselves, but in the rest of the human race.

Amen

Day 3 ## A Dormitory Suburb

Today's reading is a short poem called 'A Dormitory Suburb'.

A Dormitory Suburb is an expression used to describe an area outside a large town where people have their homes and sleep but don't do anything else very much – they work in the town and very often come into the town for their social life as well.

'Will it rain?'
'Do the rose trees need pruning?'
Oh, infinitesimal trivialities!
Does it matter?
Oh, God, is it important?
Nature, tender the rose trees.

If I stood a starving child before you,
I think you would say:
'Ah, poor thing,'
And go on clipping your hedge.

Jenny Scott

Prayer

May we open our eyes to the problems in the world around us and may we do whatever we can to make other people's lives happier.

May we never become so wrapped up in our own trivial problems that we forget to care about anyone else.

Amen

Day 4 ## Z for Zachariah (1)

Introduction

Today's reading is the first part of a book called *Z for Zachariah* by Robert O'Brien. It takes place in the future after a terrible war and is written in the form of the diary of a girl called Anna. Anna's family are all dead and she now believes that she is the last person left in the world.

May 20th

I am afraid.

Someone is coming.

That is, I think someone is coming, though I am not sure, and I pray that I am wrong. I went into the church and prayed all this morning. I sprinkled water in front of the altar, and put some flowers on it, violets and dogwood.

But there is smoke. For three days there has been smoke, not like the time before. That time, last year, it rose in a great cloud a long way away, and stayed in the sky for two weeks. A forest fire in the dead woods, and then it rained and the smoke stopped. But this time it is a thin column, like a pole, not very high.

And the column has come three times, each time in the late afternoon. At night I cannot see it, and in the morning, it is gone. But each afternoon it comes again, and it is nearer. At first it was behind Claypole Ridge, and I could see only the top of it, the smallest smudge. I thought it was a cloud, except that it was too grey, the wrong colour, and then I thought: there are no clouds anywhere else. I got the binoculars and saw that it was narrow and straight; it was smoke from a small fire. When we used to go in the truck, Claypole Ridge was 15 miles, though it looks closer, and the smoke was coming from behind that.

Behind Claypole Ridge there is Ogdentown, about ten miles further. But there is no one left alive in Ogdentown.

I know, because after the war ended, and all the telephones went dead, my father, my brother Joseph and Cousin David went in the truck to find out what was happening, and the first place they went was Ogdentown. They went early in the morning; Joseph and David were really excited, but Father looked serious.

When they came back it was dark. Mother had been worrying – they took so long – so we were glad to see the truck lights finally coming over Burden Hill, six miles away. When they got out, the boys weren't excited any more. They looked scared, and my father looked sick. Maybe he was beginning to be sick, but mainly I think he was distressed.

My mother looked up at him as he climbed down.

'What did you find?'

He said, 'Bodies. Just dead bodies. They're all dead.'

'All?'

We went inside the house where the lamps were lit, the two boys following, not saying anything. My father sat down.

'Terrible,' he said, and again, 'terrible, terrible. We drove around, looking. We blew the horn. Then we went to the church and rang the bell. You can hear it five miles away. We waited for two hours, but nobody came. I went into a couple of houses – the Johnsons', the Peters' – they were all in there, all dead. There were dead birds all over the streets.

My brother Joseph began to cry. He was 14. I think I had not heard him cry for six years.

May 21st
It is coming closer. Today it was almost on top of the ridge at the crossroads. He has stopped there and is deciding whether or not to come over the ridge. I say *he* because that is what I think of, though it could be *they* or even *she*. But I think it is he. If he decides to follow the highway he will go away, and everything will be all right again. But if he comes to the top of the ridge, he is sure to come down here, because he will see the green leaves. On the other side of the ridge, even on the other side of Burden Hill, there are no leaves; everything is dead.

There are some things I need to explain. One is why I am afraid. Another is why I am writing in this composition book.

I took the book and a supply of ballpoint pens back in February. By then the last radio station had stopped broadcasting. It had been dead for about three or four months. I say *about* and that is the reason I got the book: because I discovered I was forgetting when things happened, and sometimes even *whether* things happened or not. Another reason is that I thought writing in it might be like having someone to talk to, and if I read it back later it would be like someone talking to me.

Sometimes I would put in what the weather was like, if there was a storm or something unusual. I put in when I planted the garden because I thought that would be useful to know the next year. But most of the time I didn't write because one day was just like the day before, and sometimes I thought – what's the use of writing anyway, when nobody is ever going to read it? I was pretty sure I was the only person left in the world.

But now I have something to write about. . . I was wrong. I am not the only person left in the world. I am both excited and afraid.

At first, when all the others went away I hated being alone;

and I watched the road all day and most of the night hoping that a car, *anybody*, would come over the hill from either direction. When I slept I would dream that one came, and drove on past without knowing I was here; then I would wake up and run to the road looking for a tail light disappearing. Then the weeks went by and the radio stations went off, one by one. When the last one went off and stayed off it came to me, finally, that nobody, no car, was ever going to come.

The man on the radio had said that there wasn't any more power. He said some other things, too, that I did not like to hear. And that started me thinking. Suppose a car came over the hill, and I ran out, and whoever was in it got out – suppose he was crazy? Or suppose it was someone mean, or even cruel, and brutal? A murderer? What could I do? The fact is, the man on the radio, towards the end, sounded crazy. He was afraid; there were only a few people left where he was and not much food. He said that men should act with dignity even in the face of death, that no one was better off than any other. He pleaded on the radio and I knew something terrible was happening there. Once he broke down and cried on the radio.

So I decided: if anyone does come, I want to see who it is before I show myself. It is one thing to hope for someone to come when things are civilised, when there are other people around too. But when there is nobody else, then the whole idea changes. This is what I gradually realised. There are worse things than being alone. It was after I thought about that that I began moving my things to the cave.

Conclusion

Anna has seen the worst that people can do to each other. An unnamed government has caused death and destruction to thousands. People in her own country who have been injured, terrified and starving to death have behaved in a way that Anna can hardly bring herself to think about. Knowing this, Anna has to decide whether or not to trust the stranger she sees approaching her farm.

Prayer

Hatred and violence are not just qualities that exist in other people. We all contain the seeds within us of terrible violence and evil as well as the power to do tremendous good.

Let us remember that peace in the world starts and ends with ordinary people like ourselves.

May we seek to develop the powers of good that lie within us.

Amen

Day 5

Z for Zachariah (2)

Introduction

Anna thinks the safest thing is to hide from the stranger that she's seen approaching her farm. But, whilst she's hiding, Anna sees the stranger bathe in a stream which she knows is contaminated with radio-active fallout. She still, however, does not make herself known to him.

May 25th

I suppose it seems wrong to be so afraid. It is just that I don't know what the man will do. I liked most people. I had a lot of friends at school, and a boy friend too. But that was a matter of choice; there were some people I didn't like, and many more that I didn't even know. This man may be the only man left on the earth. I don't know him. Suppose I don't like him? Or worse, suppose he doesn't like me?

For nearly a year I have been here alone. I have hoped and prayed for someone to come, someone to talk to, to work with, and plan for the future of the valley. I dreamed that it would be a man, for then, some time in the future – it is a dream, I know – there might be children in the valley. Yet, now that a man has actually come, I realise that my hopes were too simple. All men are different, but the man on the radio station, fighting to survive, saw people that were desperate and selfish. This man is a stranger, and bigger and stronger than I am. If he is kind, then I am all right. But if he is not – what then? He can do whatever he likes, and I will be a slave the rest of my life. That is why I want to find out, at least as well as I can by watching him, what he is like. . . .

May 26th

I followed the man, staying on my high woods path. I had to work a bit to keep up with him – the path is not as straight as the road; also I had to be careful not to make a noise.

He walked on down the road, heading south towards the far end of the valley. He looked around him as he went; but he did not slow down much until he reached the culvert. At that point the small stream, having flowed into the pond and out again, bears right and is joined by Burden Creek.

He stopped there. I think it dawned on him then for the first time that there were two streams, and that the pond was not formed by Burden Creek. And here, if you look at them closely where they join, the difference between them becomes plain. Even in the last few feet, the small stream has life in it – minnows, tadpoles, water bugs and green moss on the rocks. Burden Creek has none at all, and after they merge, downstream all the way to the gap and out, the water is clear and dead.

I cannot be sure that he noticed all that, but he stared at it for a long time, getting down on his hands. If he did see it he must have begun worrying, and maybe it was then that he started feeling sick. In a short time he was going to get very sick.

About half way back it happened: he stopped, sat down quickly in the middle of the road, and was very sick. He stayed there, retching, leaning to his side on one arm, for several minutes. Then he got up and walked on.

He did that again three times on the way, and after the third time he was barely stumbling along, dragging the rifle. When he reached the tent he crawled in; he has not come out again. He did not make a fire tonight, nor eat any supper. But it may be that in the morning he will be better.

May 27th
The man has not moved.

I know he is sick, but I do not know how sick, and therefore I do not know what to do. It may be that he just doesn't feel very well, and decided to stay in bed.

Or he may be so sick he can't get up. He may even be dying.

Last night I would not have thought that would worry me so much, but this morning it does. It began with a dream I had just before I got up. It was one of those dreams that are more like daydreams; I have them when I am half awake and half asleep . . . I dreamed (or daydreamed) that it was my father in the tent, sick, and then that my whole family were there again, in the house. I felt so joyful it took my breath away, and I woke up.

I lay there realising that it was not true, but also realising something else. I thought I had become used to being alone, and to the idea that I would always be alone, but I was wrong. Now that there was somebody else here, the thought of going back, the thought of the house and the valley being empty again – this time forever, I was sure of that – seemed so terrible I could not bear it.

So, even though the man was a stranger and I was afraid of him, I began worrying about his being sick, and the idea that he might die made me feel quite desperate.

I am writing this partly to get it clear in my head and to help me make up my mind. I think what I will do is wait and watch until late afternoon. Then if he still has not come out of the tent I will go down there while it is still light, very quietly, and see if I can see, without getting too close, how he is. I will take my gun with me.

Conclusion

Anna has enough knowledge and skill in farming to be self-sufficient and yet she still needs other people. She wants companionship but, in order to achieve that, she has to take the risk of trusting someone else and take the risk of getting hurt.

Prayer

We know it is foolish to be too trusting of other people, but may we be prepared to take risks sometimes and give other people a chance to get close to us.

May we be helpful and reliable so that other people can trust in us and find our friendship valuable.

Amen

13 Gowie Corby Plays Chicken
Gene Kemp
(abridged extracts)

Day 1 Gowie Starts School

Introduction

Our readings this week are extracts taken from a book by Gene Kemp called *Gowie Corby Plays Chicken*.

'Corby. Gowie Corby,' shouts a voice. 'Pick up that litter.'

I pick it up, hate, hate. They've started already. Picking on me. Bossing me about. Telling me off. Gowie Corby, Gowie Corby, the theme tune for all that's wrong in this school. All this is ahead of me, lying in store for me, week after week after week, being tidy, trying hard, working, reading, writing, doing Maths . . . .

Coats and shoebags are to go in the cloakroom. I haven't got mine. I can't remember where they are, and I haven't got any plimsolls anyway. I can't be bothered with gym or PE. We're told to get a tray to put our gear into. Gear I have not got, but I grab a tray next to that belonging to Jonathan Johns – call me JJ, he says – glistening and gleaming in full school uniform, brief-case crammed with equipment, pens, pencils, felt tips, rulers, set square, compasses, clip board and bulldog clips, sellotape and paper clips. He bristles with school gear like a hedgehog. Just what is he aiming at? Mastermind, maybe? Not that I care, but it's handy to be near him, 'cos he's always got something you can knock off and it's useful to be able to pinch something of his when the teacher finds you haven't got a pen for the third day running.

So there I am popping my tray next to his in the unit, when he says, right out of the blue, completely unprovoked, I haven't said anything –

'Push off, Corby. Find some place else.'

A new silver papermate is lying on top of the books in his tray, I notice.

'Well, that's nice,' I say gently. 'What's got into you, Jonathan? Rotten holiday?'

He doesn't respond to my friendly greeting.

'Keep your rotten maulers off my things,' he says.

'What unkind words. Don't be like that, Jonathan. When have I ever touched anything of yours?'

'All the time. All the time.'

'You callin' me a thief?'

'Yeh. Yeh. Somethin' like that. Somethin' like that.'

Jonathan always thinks that what he says is so fantastic that he's got to say it twice in case you missed it the first time round. And what he's standin' there sayin' is a bit much, I feel. So –

'You askin' for a knuckle sandwich?' I show him my power-packed bony fist and wave my eight-inch thick-soled boots at him. He's encountered the weight of my right boot before.

'Don't lose your cool, Gowie,' he says, quickly. 'I was only joking. I was only joking.'

With eyes fixed on me as if I was hypnotisin' him, he takes the papermate out of the tray and moves away as if I might bite. (And I might.)

'What I want to know is who's in the team?' asks a gruff voice.

That's Stewart Pitt and he means the football team, of course. He's crazy about football and hopes to be the captain this year. He and I don't get along too well. Most people think he's great. He's known as Stewpot and is a sort of hero to the little kids. I call him Stewpid.

I move to sit by Darren Parker, but Simon Singh gets there first and most of the other seats are taken by now.

'What's the matter? Not found a niche, yet?' asks Sir.

It's always the same. No place for me. Other people have friends. I have enemies. Not that I care. But there is one empty place. The face next to it smiles at me, nervously. I look away fast. No one wants to be smiled at by Heather.

'Hurry up,' says Sir. 'Just sit by Heather. She won't bite, you know.'

Heather pats the chair and smiles again, a truly horrible sight. She must have forgotten a few things in the holidays, like the time I pushed her in the school goldfish pond. I lower myself into the chair, keeping as far away as possible. Given a straight choice, I'd rather sit by a slug. Why on earth should I end up sitting by Heather? Bloomin' unfair. In a gloom at being at school in the first place and being next to Heather in the second, I push my hands into my jeans pocket – we aren't supposed to wear jeans at school – and discover some chewing gum, antique but welcome.

'Put that gum in the bin,' says Sir, without looking up from the register. He must have eyes in the top of his head, under his hair. Life is going to be very tedious this year, I can see.

Conclusion

Most of the children who read this book find themselves quite liking Gowie Corby. They think it might be fun to have a boy like Gowie in their class.

One thing you might have noticed, though, is that there is only Heather who actually wants to sit next to Gowie. The other children don't trust him – they don't mind watching him being horrible to other people but they're afraid of Gowie being horrible to them. He's not the kind of person any of them want to have as a friend.

Prayer

May we learn to value friendship. May we be open and honest and trustworthy so that other people are never afraid of getting close to us and need never be afraid of us hurting them.

Amen

Day 2 | ## The Chase

In the afternoon the weather is really hot, the way it always is when you go back to school, after it's rained non-stop for the summer holidays. We play football and I score a goal, mainly because everyone except Stewpid is playing so badly that it's difficult to miss . . . .

As I change, a beam of sunshine, full of surprise at finding itself in our cloakroom, picks out something silver, the papermate in JJ's pocket, gleaming amid the immaculate school uniform. I give a fearful deadly hiss.

'Jonathan Johns, the hour of your doom is upon you, and you shall DIE . . . DIE . . . DIE . . . AAARRRRHHHHHH!'

He leaps in the air as if ants have just bitten his bum, and I reach out, grab the papermate, and shoot out through the door. Jonathan's still in his football boots, laces trailing, so I have a head start as I rush across the playground to where the crossing lady stands with her lollilop.

Behind me ring out beautiful howls of rage and anger and fury. My heart sings. I find time to turn and wave at him, purple, struggling.

'Give it back you thief,' he bawls after me, but I spurt ahead, knocking over a coupla kids who start bawling and bellyaching as well, but I don't stop to investigate, because after all, I'm doing them a favour, the sooner they learn that life is full of hard knocks the better. Above the angry shouts of the mums I hear another voice and take a quick shufti behind.

'I'll get him for you,' Stewpid is shouting. . . . I barge through the crowd of 'orrible mums, snotty kids and prams that always litter up the gate, and rush across the road, Mrs Moggs, the crossing lady, trying hard to keep up with me on her fat little legs.

'Don't be in that much of a hurry,' she pants. 'You've got all your life ahead of you. I think.'

Down the street opposite, Spring Avenue, and towards the car park, where I head for a silver Ford Granada, so that I can pause and hide a mo, to see how the pursuit is going. And Simon Singh has joined in as well, which means I've got the two best sprinters in the school chasing me. But I can have a lot of fun before they catch up with me, if they ever do. Out of the car park . . . then round the corner and into the High Street, full of fat old housewives and layabouts, past Woolworth's and into Tesco's – perhaps I can lose them among the counters. I peer round a stack of Hovis loaves and see Stewpid just entering the doors with Simon right behind him, no Jonathan though, slow-footed halfwit. I mean to move on silently escaping, but I crash straight into a trolley, pushed by a bloke looking like one of the heavyweights in a James Bond film, so I leap away at speed as he snarls after me and knock over a pile of bean tins. Beanz meanz Bangs and Smashes, deafeningly loud, just missing two old geezers who squawk and screech, and the whole store breaks out in –

'Kids, these days . . .'

' . . . ought to be locked up . . .'

'Out of my way, you stupid old bags!' I yell, and run through the doors, going the wrong way to the multi-storey car park behind. I am starting to puff a bit now so I stop behind a Ford Capri and try to get my breath back.

And a cry goes up.

'Boy! You, there! What are you doing? You're not sup-posed to be here!'

I run on faster, stitch stabbing in my side, now. I feel like packing it in and going home. I'm out of the multi-storey now and still running, though slower. I hope the others have been copped by the attendants. This thought cheers me up, gives me fresh power, so I surge on again past Boots, towards the Library, ready to turn on to the New North Road that takes me back home. But I'm exhausted now, half-dead and looking back, see that Stewpid is gaining on me, has halved the distance between us . . . my breath comes in jags, my chest is going to explode. I keep running.

The feet of Stewpid are right behind me now, pounding louder than my heart beats. Somehow I must get up the Li-brary steps, for if I can get in there before they reach me, they won't be able to duff me in. I don't want to be duffed in.

The sun is dazzling, shining through the leaves of the trees all around . . . it shines in my eyes, dazzling . . . burning me up . . . . A hand grasps my shoulder from behind.

'Got you, Corby!' gasps Stewpid.

'Oh, no, you ain't,' I mutter, turning and twisting and thrusting with my right boot.

Stewart falls clumsily down the steps.

And lands splat! on his right elbow.

Conclusion

Running off with Jonathan's pen might sound like a good joke but, as you probably noticed, it isn't Gowie that the others come and help, but Jonathan.

What seems like a fairly harmless joke can have unfortun-ate consequences – as you can see in tomorrow's reading when we find out what happens to Stewart after his fall.

Prayer

May we learn to get on with other people. May we be caring and considerate so that other people trust us and feel proud to have us for friends.

Amen

Day 3 **Hospital Visit**

I am sitting by the side of a hospital bed watching Stewart trying to open a box of chocolates that Sir has brought him from me, if you get it. Stewpid is up on traction, which means his arm is up in the air, so that he can't lie down at all, even to sleep. If he moves it at all – the elbow, that is – it won't set properly, and he'll be no good at football, ever. I haven't seen him since they took him away, screaming his head off, with Jonathan Johns telling everybody gathered round that it was all my fault, bloomin' unfair because I can't help it if Pitt has the kind of bones that break easily, can I?

Afterwards I have to go to the Headmaster and explain to him that running off with the papermate was all a joke and could I help it if people had no sense of humour. . . ?

. . . With Mr Merchant's assistance Stewart opens up the box of chocolates and offers me one with the hand that isn't attached to a pulley and the ceiling. I look round uneasily. For this place really gives me the creeps. I can't stand the smell. Really unhealthy. And all those nurses look like zombies, not that I mind zombies, proper spooky ones that is. I want to get out of here. Dangerous places, hospitals. You might be in here, harmless, visiting somebody, and before you could say Werewolves Unite they'd have you on the operating table, jacking both legs off.

I don't know what to say to Stewpid. I know I'm not saying sorry, because I said that in those letters I wrote, and then I had to copy them out again, because they weren't neat enough, and that's enough sorries for anyone.

'How are the practices going, Sir?' Stewpid asks.

'As well as can be expected without you there. I've made Simon Singh captain and we play Central next week.'

'Is 'e in it?' he says, pointing the finger that's not on traction at me.

'Well, no. Gowie didn't turn up to any of the practices, did you?'

'You play on Saturday mornings, and I ain't givin' up my Saturdays for anyone.'

'Why not, Gowie?'

'I've got better things to do.'

'What better things?'

I shut my gob tight. Why can't he leave me alone? What I do on Saturday mornings is MY business, and he can poke his long conk in some place else. Get knotted, Sir. Let's change the subject.

'How do you go to the bog, all strung up as you are?' I ask the figure on the bed.

He goes a dirty red colour and wriggles about as much as he can considering his condition, and I wonder if he's shy, but then he explodes and I see that it's anger, not modesty.

'I use a bottle and a bed pan, thank you very much, thank you *very*, *very* much, Mister Bloomin' Corby, for getting me stuck in here when the football season's started!'

I shrug my shoulders, for no matter how mad he gets, he can't duff me in, he's stuck in bed, which is his hard cheese.

'You shouldn't have such rotten bones,' I reply.

'Come along, you two,' Sir says, sharp as a needle. 'Let's have reasonable behaviour. Make an effort to get on with one another, at least.'

'No way.'

'Not likely.'

'All right, all right. Calm down or you'll drive me insane. Now both say sorry.'

Long silence.

'BOTH SAY SORRY.'

We both say sorry. Huh.

Stewpid reaches for another choc, remembers me, and shoves the box towards me with his free hand. I manage to knock it on the floor, where the unwrapped chocs go on a neighbourhood tour. A nurse rushes forward tut–tut–tutting, and in the confusion, people bending over and so on, I some-how knock over Stewpid's orange juice, distributing it quite evenly over him, the nurse and the bed, to say nothing of the chocs, which I've never cared for much anyway. Chewing gum's my favourite.

I look at my watch. Nearly time to go. I don't think Sir will bring me again somehow. He'll leave me alone in the end. I know he's got his reputation as a good teacher to keep up, but that doesn't matter to me, I'm different, I'm not like this soft lot down here, my folks came from the North, descended from the Vikings, and I don't want to be liked, I don't want to be good, I don't want to be in the football team, or a useful member of anything, I don't want to know. I don't care.

Conclusion

Gowie says that he doesn't want to be liked. That probably isn't true because all of us want people to like us. What Gowie means probably is that he doesn't expect anybody to like him and, because of that, he tends not to behave in a likable way.

Prayer

We have to learn to value ourselves before we can expect other people to like us.

May we learn to cherish the good that lies within us. Let us try to recognise our faults and seek to overcome them so that we can learn to feel self-respect. May we learn to value ourselves as well as other people.

Amen

Day 4	**The Gang**

Conkers are everywhere at the moment, it's the season. It's fairly boring, especially when JJ announces that he's the CHAMPION, showing off the most ginormous conker ever, polished and shining like his silly face. The playground is covered with string and bits of nuts.

Stewpid is back at school with his arm in plaster, and he is *the* big *HERO* with kids queueing to write their names on his plasterised arm. I say Hi to him and he hardly speaks back which I consider mean. I don't care for that kind of meanness. After all, I haven't done anything to him. He began it all, chasing me. He isn't allowed to play football and has to go back to the hospital for treatment. The team is losing all its matches, Simon Singh is away with flu and Pete Gillett, the goalie, is ill as well. So Sir has another go at getting me to play.

'I won't say that it's for the school, Gowie,' he says, 'for I know that interests you not at all.'

'No, Sir.'

'No, Sir? You mean no, it doesn't interest you, or no, you're not going to play?'

'Both, Sir.'

'I thought I might get you to play for your own sake, because you enjoy the game.'

'I don't.'

'You look as if you do when you're playing.'

'Load of rubbish. Sir,' I add because he's looking a bit explosive.

He twitches a bit.

'Go and sit down. No matter how I try, sometimes you depress me.'

He looks so miserable that for once I don't kick Heather on the way back to my desk. But it's his own fault. Anyone who chooses to be a teacher deserves to have a rotten life.

At playtime Stewpid heaves over. He looks about as friendly as an anaconda with belly-ache from too much goat-swallowing.

'You listen to me, Corby,' he says as if he was a hundred years old and me a little kid. 'You gonna play for the team?'

JJ joins in unasked.

'Don't ask him, Stew. He'll ruin it.'

'It's already ruined at the moment. We're bottom of the league right now. The team needs you, Gowie, and the team comes first with me. Whatever you think JJ.'

His face shines with effort and love of the TEAM. The TEAM comes above everything else. Even though he can't stand the sight of me, he'll do anything to get me to play if he thinks it will help. I don't give a bent penny for his pathetic TEAM.

'Don't bother, either of you. I wouldn't play for the team if they paid me. I've got better things to do.'

And I walk off, leaving them standing there complaining. But Stewpid still follows me. He can't believe I really mean it. 'Look here,' he begins.

'Where?' I ask, peering round.

'Oh, pack it in. This is serious.'

'What's serious?'

'On Saturday we play Brent Hill. We've only got half a side and we need you. Look, you've got to play.'

'No, you look. Go and look for some of *your* friends, the

Stewpot fan club, and ask them to play for your precious team. You're wasting your time with me. I don't want to know.'

His face goes white, then red, and he raises his fist to me as if to hit me, thinks better of it, pushes his nose in the air and his voice down to his boots.

'You are the rottenest, meanest, horriblest kid who ever came here. You've never done nuthin' for nobody in the whole of your mean, miserable life!'

I push off into the bright sunshine, and across the playground. No one follows. The anger goes, no point in being mad, and I remember a tasty bit of gum I've got stashed in the classroom, and I fancy it.

By now it's empty and there, just in front of me, shining like a polished mirror, is JJ's brief-case, brass bits glowing like gold. I open it. Spotless books nestle in a spotless lining, pens, etc., in a separate partition. I look at what he's reading. Yuck.

'That's Jonathan's,' squawks Heather, putting in an unlovely appearance from nowhere.

I reach for the super glue on the shelf, the extra strong kind that sticks wood and so on. I pull off the top – it's almost full, lots of gooey, gorgeous glue. I tilt it over the case.

'You mustn't do that,' blethers Heather, like an old sheep. Typecasting.

At the bottom of the case is Super Conk, the Champion. I pick it out with loving care.

'Wanna bet?' I ask, stamping on the conker with maximum power as I empty, glug, glug, glug, the glue into JJ's pride and joy, and the slurping noise is music, music, music to my ears. The glue covers the books, the pens, everything and I spread it generously around the fastening before I close it up. For ever, maybe? The conker lies shattered in bits on the floor, string still attached.

I whistle into the bright morning, feeling at one with the world.

Conclusion

Gowie is given every opportunity by his teacher and his classmates to join in with the others and make a useful contribution to the school; but every gesture of friendship he rejects.

Jokes and laughter can be a wonderful way of bringing

people together but Gowie's so-called jokes are the sort that cause only anger and unhappiness and make everyone despise him. As you will see in the final reading from *Gowie Corby Plays Chicken* nobody will put up with Gowie's cruel jokes for ever and it's not long before people's patience with him runs out.

Prayer

Let us give thanks for the gift of laughter. May we never misuse this gift by torments, sarcasm and cruel jokes but use laughter to entertain and bring happiness to others.

Amen

Day 5 | **Attack**

On Friday when I breeze in, fairly cheery 'cos it's nearly Saturday, I find a note waiting for me. It says:

'LOOK OUT CORBY YOUR GOING TOO GET WOTS COMING TO YOU.'

Then when we come out of Assembly there's another.

'DEATH TO YOU SCUM.'

I don't find that nice at all, and spend most of the morning watching them all, wondering who sent it. The last one of the day of the day reads:

'WE'VE GOT A GANG ONTO YOU ROTTEN SWINE AND WE'RE GOING TO DUFF YOU UP SO YOU WISH YOU'D NEVER BEEN BORN, SO LOOK OUT YOU BEAST.'

Pathetic.

Some time later, near home-time, I don't find it so pathetic. At the end of a long, draggy, boring Friday afternoon, it's at last time to clear up. Soon, very soon, the classroom empties, only Heather and a coupla girls left, and Darren, who's reading and has forgotten he's supposed to be going home.

'Where is everybody? They disappeared fast,' I say.

The girls' faces go tight and close up. I know that look. It means that someone is being kept out of the know, and it's often been me in the past, and it's me now.

'Somethin's goin' on,' I say to them.

The girls move away, but I stop Heather near the door, seize her right ear and twist it. She squeals. The other two depart as if there are bombs in the classroom.

'Now talk. What's goin' on?'

'Nuthin'.' She whimpers as I twist a little harder and drag her to the cloakroom, to keep out of Merchant's way.

'Talk.'

'They're gonna duff you in.'

'Where?'

'Outside school . . .'

'Who?'

'They'll hurt me if I tell you . . .'

'I'll hurt you worse . . . tell me who's in it.'

'The team mostly.'

'Why?'

'They're fed up with you 'cos you're so horrible. Oh, stop, stop. I'll tell Sir.'

'Where are they now?'

'You usually go to the shop on the corner after school, for some chewing gum . . .'

'Go on . . .'

'They're waiting for you in the alley way at the back of the shop. That's all I know, honest. Let me go, now.'

'Get out.' I push her through the door. She makes me feel sick. I feel sick anyway. Some of the kids in the team are a horrible size. Stewpid is bigger than Mr Merchant. Not that he'll be doin' much with *his* elbow.

I walk slowly into the playground. Most of the kids have gone home by now. What am I to do? Fancy that lot ganging up on me. I must go very carefully. Think . . . think. I'd better go another way home, the long way round.

And Miss Plum walks through the playground carrying two heavy bags, and in a flash I am beside her, smiling a face full of teeth like Tom in a Tom and Jerry cartoon.

'Miss Plum, please let me carry your bags. You look so laden.'

She looks surprised as well. My nice smile is almost splitting my face. She hands over the bags and we walk along side by side. I start to talk to her.

'I expect that you are looking forward to the week-end, Miss Plum. It must be a relief to get away from an awful mob like us.'

'Oh, you're not that bad, really. But you are right in a way. I do enjoy the week-ends.'

'Have you a hobby, Miss? I like to go bird watching when I get the time.'

'Do you indeed, Gowie? Now, that's very interesting.'

On we walk, discussing hobbies, like two old geezers, and

she tells me how nice it is to talk to me like this as sometimes she feels she hasn't got to know me as well as she would have liked. The corner shop comes into view, with JJ's ugly mug peering round it, and jerking back at the sight of me, and I am killing myself with laughter inside as Miss Plum and I walk right past, together. I bet they're mad. I bet they're astonished. I smile at Miss Plum with all my available teeth. She does a cherry. We go right past and down the road and I'm safe. I've mucked up their dirty little plan. Load of morons. On we go, well away from the scene of danger.

'I catch a bus here,' she says. 'Thank you for your company, Gowie.'

She smiles at me as if she really likes me. I could fancy her if she wasn't so old and a teacher.

''Ave a good weekend, Miss.'

I run on till I come to the cul-de-sac where I live . . . I run along, happy with the Friday freedom feel, all the weekend stretching ahead, just for me, nobody saying do this, do that, go here, go there, Gowie Corby. And it's even better because I've outwitted the TEAM, and there should be something good on tele tonight, and I wonder what there is to eat. I get out my key and open the door, and suddenly . . .

Conclusion

You will have to read *Gowie Corby Plays Chicken* for yourselves if you want to know what happens next.

Gowie makes enemies. He can't complain about people not liking him when he's so horrible to them.

Towards the end of the story, Gowie does start to become much nicer – not because of people threatening him, but because he meets somebody with a stronger personality who wants to be his friend.

Prayer

May we try to avoid being cruel and unkind even with those people we find it really hard to like.

May we be generous with our friendship and learn to be forgiving.

Amen

14 Dreams

See also Martin Luther King, page 234.

Day 1

Joseph and His Dreamcoat (1)

Recommended music: for the first three assemblies, music from Joseph and His Amazing Technicolour Dreamcoat CBS MCS 2544, Decca SKL 4973 or the cassette MCFC 2544, would be appropriate.

Day 1 Jacob and Sons; Joseph's Coat; Joseph's Dream; Poor, Poor, Joseph; One More Angel in Heaven
Day 2 Potiphar; Close Every Door; Go, Go, Go, Joseph
Day 3 songs on the second part of the record

Our assemblies this week are about dreams. All of us dream when we're asleep although we can't always remember our dreams afterwards. When we do remember dreams, they often seem like nonsense, but this strange confusion of people, places and happenings is the way our subconscious mind represents many of the important issues in our lives. In our dreams, strange and often unfamiliar characters represent such things as good and evil, sexuality and authority. Myths and fairy stories use the same kind of symbols and one of the world's richest sources of such stories is the Old Testament. Much of it describes the history of the Jewish people but contained in the book of Genesis is a collection of the myths and stories told by the Jews to explain how the world first came into being and how the nation of Israel began.

In the Old Testament, the character of Jacob represents the original state of Israel and Jacob's sons represent the different tribes. If you look at an early map of Palestine, you will see marked on it the different regions which are also the names of Jacob's sons: Reuben, Judah, Benjamin, Dan, Asher, Naphtali, Gad, Zebulon, Levi, Issachar, Simeon and also one of the most famous dreamers of all: Joseph.

The story tells us that Joseph was Jacob's favourite son but he was most unpopular with his brothers. He was extremely handsome and somewhat vain, spending time dressing his hair and showing off in his favourite piece of clothing – the special gift from his father – his famous long-sleeved coat of many colours. As if this wasn't bad enough, what made his brothers even more angry was when Joseph told them about the dreams which he had had.

In one dream, they were all out binding sheaves in the field. Joseph's sheaf stood upright whilst his brothers' formed a circle around it, bowing and scraping to his. 'What's that supposed to mean?' they asked him angrily. 'That you think you're so much better than us?'

Undeterred, Joseph went on and told them his next dream in which not only sheaves of corn but the sun, moon and eleven stars were bowing down to him. Jacob, his father, heard this and exclaimed: 'What's all this? Do you think myself, your step-mother and all 11 brothers are going to bow down before you and serve you?'

The bitterness between Joseph and his brothers grew until one day when Joseph was sent out by his father in search of his brothers and their flocks several days' march away. When they saw Joseph in the distance, Simeon, Gad and Dan cried angrily: 'Behold the dreamer! Come let us slay him and we shall see what will become of his dreams.'

Reuben objected. He argued that to slaughter Joseph with their own hands would make them murderers. Why not leave him in a pit to starve? So when Joseph came, they stripped him of his colourful coat and threw him into a pit.

The brothers sat down to eat and presently saw a group of Ishmaelites approaching. Judah then had an idea: 'Why should we leave Joseph in the pit to starve?' he said. 'We could sell him to the Ishmaelites as a slave and keep the money.'

So Joseph was sold to the Ishmaelites for 20 pieces of silver. The treacherous brothers slaughtered a young goat, dipped Joseph's beautiful coat in its blood and returned to their father.

'Look what we've found,' they said to Jacob showing him the blood-stained coat. 'Do you think it might belong to Joseph?'

Jacob gazed in horror at the coat of his favourite son, then started weeping in dismay. 'Some wild animal has savaged my son,' he cried out. He tore his clothes and mourned for Joseph, refusing to be comforted.

Conclusion

It is easy to understand why Joseph's brothers were jealous of him. Joseph was already having premonitions of his future greatness – he felt that God had important work in store for him to do and his brothers interpreted that as vanity.

The brothers were bound to feel jealous when it was obvious that their father favoured Joseph and the gift of the beautiful, long-sleeved multi-coloured coat was probably the last straw.

All of us know people who are more gifted and clever than ourselves, or more attractive and popular and it's easy for us to feel jealous instead of admiring their gifts and abilities. Joseph was eventually to become one of the most important men in Egypt and his brothers were later very pleased and proud to be associated with him but their jealousy nearly led instead to his destruction.

Prayer

Let us accept the fact that all of us are different. We all have our special abilities as well as having faults. May we work quietly and patiently to remedy our faults rather than seeking to put down anyone who seems to be better than us.

Amen

Day 2

Joseph and His Dreamcoat (2)

Joseph was taken to Egypt and sold as a servant to Potiphar, one of Pharaoh's officers. Joseph worked hard and everything he did for Potiphar was so successful that he was soon made overseer of the household. Things were working out well for Joseph, but with one big problem – Potiphar's wife, Zuleika. She found Joseph very attractive. It may not sound like too great a problem, but for Joseph to have an affair with the wife of his master would be more than his job was worth so Joseph kept refusing all Zuleika's attempts to seduce him.

Zuleika, however, was not easily put off. She thought she had found her ideal opportunity when she was alone with Joseph one day in the house. Passionately, she put her arms around Joseph then grabbed hold of his clothing and tore it off him. Joseph was horrified. He simply turned and fled, leaving his clothing behind.

Zuleika's affection for Joseph turned to humiliation and then anger. She was determined to get her revenge. Holding on to the torn clothing she cried out for the guard. She told the guard that Joseph had entered her room uninvited and tried to make love to her. The torn clothing which he left behind when she called for help was evidence. She told the same story to her husband. Potiphar believed his wife and Joseph was found guilty. Sentence was passed and he was put in prison.

In spite of his unfair treatment Joseph felt that God was still with him. The prison governor looked after him well, and eventually made him his deputy.

Some time later, Pharaoh's chief butler and chief baker were also sent to prison and were placed under Joseph's supervision. Both of them were disturbed by strange dreams which they couldn't understand.

The butler told Joseph that he had dreamed of a three-branched vine. The fruit on the vine grew ripe and the butler saw himself in the dream pressing the grapes into Pharaoh's cup and then giving it him to drink.

Joseph interpreted the dream for him. 'Each of the three branches represent a day. In three days' time, therefore, Pharaoh will forgive you and you will resume your former position as bearer of the royal wine-cup. When this happens,' Joseph said, 'please tell Pharaoh that I'm in prison on a wrongful charge – if someone puts in a good word for me, I may get to be released.'

The butler thanked Joseph and promised to do as he asked.

The baker felt reassured when he heard Joseph's interpretation so he started telling him his dream. 'I was carrying three bread baskets on my head,' he said. 'The top basket held all kinds of bread and cakes for Pharaoh's table. Then a flock of birds flew down and ate them all.'

The baker wished he had never heard Joseph's interpretation. 'In three days' time,' he said, 'you will be beheaded. Pharaoh will have you put to death and your body will be hung on a tree for the kites to eat.'

Three days later it was Pharaoh's birthday which he celebrated with a palace banquet. To mark the event, he decided to restore the chief butler to his former position but, just as Joseph had predicted, the chief baker was beheaded. Joseph hoped that the butler would remember his promise and speak favourably to Pharaoh about his case but, sadly, the butler forgot all about Joseph who stayed in prison for the next two years.

Conclusion

Joseph's dreams led him to believe that there was important work for him to do for God, which would one day make him great. For many years his luck seemed to be against him, but Joseph never gave up his faith in God or in the dreams which he had had so many years before.

Prayer

Today's prayer was written by Saint Benedict.

O Gracious and Holy Father, give us
  Wisdom to perceive thee,
  Diligence to seek thee,
  Patience to wait for thee,
  Eyes to behold thee,
A heart to meditate upon thee,
And a life to proclaim thee;
Through the power of the Spirit of
  Jesus Christ Our Lord.

Amen

 Day 3   **Joseph and His Dreamcoat (3)**

Two years later, Pharaoh dreamed that he was standing by the side of the Nile out of which stepped seven fat and healthy cows. Nearby stood seven thin, emaciated cows who, to Pharaoh's amazement, walked up to the healthy cows and ate them up. After that he dreamed a second dream: this time he saw seven plump ripe ears of corn growing on a single stalk; nearby were seven empty brittle ears which swallowed down the plump ones.

Pharaoh found his dreams disturbing; he couldn't understand what they meant and there was no one who could interpret them for him. Then Pharaoh's butler remembered Joseph who could interpret dreams better than anyone. He recommended Joseph to Pharaoh who ordered him to be released from prison, washed and shaved and set before him. Then Pharaoh told him about the dreams.

'You have two dreams here with the same meaning,' explained Joseph. 'So the message contained is twice as important. The seven fat cows and the seven plump ears of corn represent seven years of plenty. The harvest will be good and there will be more than enough food for everyone. After that will come seven lean and hungry years when a terrible famine will sweep through the land. God is advising you to appoint a reliable viceroy who will buy up plenty of stocks of food during the years of plenty so that your people will not starve during the famine.

Pharaoh was convinced that Joseph had spoken the truth and appointed him viceroy of all Egypt. Joseph set about his task, storing grain and pulses in each of the main cities so that, when the famine came, the Egyptians were prepared. The famine was just as bad as Joseph had predicted and he was able to make plenty of money for Pharaoh by selling corn to neighbouring states that were also affected.

Back in the land of Canaan, Jacob and his family had also fallen on hard times and so Jacob, hearing that there was corn for sale in Egypt, sent his sons there to buy some, leaving the youngest, Benjamin, at home.

When the brothers reached Egypt, Joseph saw that their names were on the list of buyers and ordered them to his palace. He recognised his brothers straightaway but did not tell them who he was. He spoke to them roughly through an interpreter and accused them of being enemy spies.

Anxious to justify themselves, Judah explained that they were a family of 12. 'One of our brothers is dead,' he explained, 'and the youngest has stayed at home with our father.'

Joseph pretended not to believe them. 'I will keep one of you here as hostage,' he said, 'whilst the others can go home and fetch the youngest son to show me that what you say is true.'

The nine brothers went back home with their corn and told Jacob what had happened. Jacob was terrified of harm befalling Benjamin and refused to let him go – he waited in fact until the new supplies of corn had nearly run out, leaving Simeon, the hostage brother, in prison, before he agreed to the brothers going back to Egypt with Benjamin.

Again they presented themselves before Joseph and again he pretended not to recognise them although, when he saw his youngest brother again, he was so overcome that he had to withdraw into a side room and dry his tears before he could carry on. He ordered a huge banquet for his brothers and gave them their supplies; then he ordered his chief steward to hide his silver cup inside Benjamin's sack. The brothers set off home but then Joseph told the steward: 'Go after those men and ask why they have repaid my kindness with stealing my silver cup from me.'

The steward obeyed and Joseph's brothers were astonished. 'We would never dream of stealing anything,' they answered. 'Search us if you will.'

Their sacks were searched and the silver cup discovered in Benjamin's sack.

The horrified brothers returned shamefully to Joseph's palace with poor Benjamin still protesting his innocence. Afraid for their lives, they threw themselves down in front of Joseph begging his forgiveness.

Joseph could contain himself no longer, the plight of his brothers moved him so deeply. 'Is our father truly still alive?' he asked them.

Completely confused, they didn't know what to say.

Joseph beckoned them closer. 'Look at me,' he said. 'I am your brother Joseph whom you sold into slavery. Do not be upset or angry with yourselves. God wanted me here to preserve life from the great famine. Go back and tell Jacob to come here with all your families. You will be given land and crops and food and your descendents will all prosper.' Then Joseph fell on Benjamin's neck and wept and kissed him and embraced each of his brothers in turn.

When Pharaoh heard of the happy reunion he ordered waggons for Joseph's brothers to go home and fetch their households. 'Don't bother about bringing goods with you,' he told them. 'You'll be given everything here that you need.

I will give you the best of the land and you shall eat of the fat of the land.'

Asses were loaded with grain and provisions for the journey and the brothers returned home. Jacob could hardly believe it when they told him that Joseph was still alive. He joyfully went back with them and their families to Egypt. Then Joseph took out his chariot and rode to meet his father. When they saw each other they embraced and wept.

Joseph's dreams had come true: he had achieved great things and his parents and his brothers were bowing down before him but, instead of despising him for his greatness, it was something for which they and their families were thankful for many years to come.

Prayer

Let us give thanks for those people whose skills and abilities have helped us in some way – our parents, our teachers, our friends – all who have helped to make us what we are. May we live to be worthy of their faith in us.

Amen

Day 4   ## He Wishes for the Cloths of Heaven

Introduction

Today's reading is a poem about dreams by the famous Irish poet, William Butler Yeats. We use the word 'dreams' to describe the imaginings we have whilst we're asleep and we use the same word to describe our hopes and aspirations for the future.

Our hopes and dreams are extremely important to us but they are also fragile and very easily broken.

Had I the heavens' embroidered cloths,
Enwrought with golden and silver light.
The blue and the dim and the dark cloths
Of night and light and the half-light,
I would spread the cloths under your feet:
But I, being poor, have only my dreams;
I have spread my dreams under your feet;
Tread softly because you tread on my dreams.

Prayer

May we treat our own dreams and the dreams of others with respect, remembering how easily they can be shattered and broken. When people share their hopes and dreams with us, may we treat them gently no matter how far-fetched they may seem to be.

Amen

Day 5 | **I Have a Dream**

Introduction

Our assemblies began with a man who was famous for his dreams; they finish with another.

Martin Luther King devoted his life to campaigning for the civil rights of black people in the southern states of America until he was killed by an assassin's bullet on 4 April 1968. The following is an extract from his most famous speech:

I have a dream that one day this nation will rise up and live out the true meaning of its creed that all men are created equal. I have a dream that one day on the red hills of Georgia the sons of former slaves and the sons of former slave owners, will be able to sit down together at the table of brotherhood. I have a dream that one day even the State of Mississippi, a state sweltering with the heat of oppression, will be transformed into an oasis of freedom and justice. I have a dream that my four little children will one day live in a nation where they will not be judged by the colour of their skin but by the content of their character. I have a dream today. I have a dream that one day every valley shall be exalted, every hill and mountain shall be made low, the rough places will be made plain and the crooked places will be made straight and the glory of the Lord shall be revealed.

This is our hope. This is the faith that I go back to the south with. With this faith, we will be able to hew out of the mountain of despair, a stone of hope. With this faith we will be able to transform the jangling discords of our nation into a beautiful symphony of brotherhood. With this faith we will be able to work together, to pray together, to struggle together, to go to jail together, to stand up for freedom together, knowing that we will be free one day. This will be the day when all of God's children will be able to sing with new meaning 'My country 'tis of Thee; sweet land of liberty . . . from every mountain side let freedom ring.' And if America is to be a great nation, this must become true.

So let freedom ring from the prodigious hill tops of New Hampshire. Let freedom ring from the mighty mountains of New York. Let freedom ring from the snow-capped Rockies of Colorado. But not only that, let freedom ring from 'Look out Mountain' of Tennessee. Let freedom ring from every hill and molehill of Mississippi, from every mountain side. Let freedom ring.

When we let it ring from every village and every hamlet, from every state and every city, we will be able to speed up that day when all of God's children, black men and white men, Jews and Gentiles, Protestants and Catholics, will be able to join hands and sing in the words of the old negro spiritual 'Free at last, free at last, thank God Almighty we are free at last.'

Conclusion

Although the United States of America is still not free from racial prejudice, laws have been passed granting blacks the same rights and freedoms as whites. The man who assassinated Martin Luther King wanted to try and stop that happening. On King's memorial is a quotation taken from the book of Genesis in the Old Testament – the words of Joseph's brothers when they saw him approaching in the fields: 'They said to one another, Behold here cometh the dreamer. Let us slay him and see what will become of his dreams.'

Martin Luther King's dreams were powerful enough to live on even after he was murdered.

Prayer

May we respect all those who work for peace and freedom. May we each play our part in seeking to wipe away conflict and hatred between those who ought to be living together as brothers and sisters.

Amen

15 | Potential

See also Booker T Washington, page 227,
Vincent van Gogh, page 231.

Day 1   The Word

In the beginning was the Word, and the Word was with God, and the Word was God.

The same was in the beginning with God.

All things were made by him; and without him was not any thing made that was made.

In him was life; and the life was the light of men.

And the light shineth in darkness; and the darkness comprehended it not.

There was a man sent from God, whose name was John.

The same came for a witness, to bear witness of the Light, that all men through him might believe.

He was not that Light, but was sent to bear witness of that Light.

That was the true Light, which lighteth every man that cometh into the world.

He was in the world, and the world was made by him, and the world knew him not.

He came unto his own, and his own received him not.

But as many as received him, to them gave he the power to become the sons of God . . . .

John 1: 1–12 Authorised version

Conclusion

'But as many as received him, to them gave he the power to become the sons of God . . . .'

Some people regard Jesus Christ as a great prophet; some people regard him as a famous historical character; others regard him as the son of God.

No matter what we feel about Jesus Christ, John's message about him is still relevant: he said that if we follow Jesus's way and receive him, then we shall also be given the power to become the sons and daughters of God.

All of us have potential to do great things. Religious belief gives us an extra source of power with which to achieve that potential.

Prayer

'But as many as received him, to them gave he the power to become the sons of God . . . .'

May we learn to discover within ourselves the source of this vast strength and power – the power which Jesus discovered – the power which can enable us to become the sons and daughters of God.

Amen

Day 2

The Frog Prince

I am a frog
I live under a spell
I live at the bottom
Of a green well.

And here I must wait
Until a maiden places me
On her royal pillow
And kisses me
In her father's palace.

The story is familiar
Everybody knows it well
But do other enchanted people feel as nervous
As I do? The stories do not tell.

Ask if they will be happier
When the changes come
As already they are fairly happy
In a frog's doom?

I have been a frog now
For a hundred years
And in all this time
I have not shed many tears.

I am happy. I like the life,
Can swim for many a mile
(When I have hopped to the river)
And am for ever agile.

And the quietness,
Yes, I like to be quiet
I am habituated
To a quiet life.

But always when I think these thoughts
As I sit in my well
Another thought comes to me and says:
It is part of the spell

To be happy
To work up contentment
To make much of being a frog
To fear disenchantment

Says, It will be *heavenly*
To be set free,
Cries, *Heavenly* the girl who disenchants
And the royal times, *heavenly*,
And I think it will be.

Come, then, royal girl and royal times,
Come quickly,
I can be happy until you come
But I cannot be heavenly,
Only disenchanted people
Can be heavenly.

Stevie Smith

Conclusion

Most of us are afraid of really big changes in our lives. We
don't undergo such overnight transformations as the frog
changing into a prince, but changing from children into

adults or finding suddenly that we're expected to take on new ventures and responsibilities can seem just as traumatic.

In the well, the frog was comfortable and safe and he knew where he was. He had to give that up in order to be a prince. He wasn't quite sure what he was letting himself in for but the chances were that it would be considerably more exciting than sitting in the mud at the bottom of a well.

If we're ever going to find life exciting, we have to move on to new and different things and take risks and that means leaving behind us some of the things that we find most safe and comfortable.

Prayer

Let us pray that we may live our lives adventurously. May we open our minds to new possibilities for using our skills and abilities and strive to develop our potential for the benefit of ourselves and other people.

Amen

Day 3

Madame Ernestine Schumann-Heink (1)

Ernestine Schumann-Heink was born into a large Austrian family. Her parents were poor and, as a child, she often went hungry. When she went away to school, her lunch consisted of dry black bread and coffee; and at night she had dry black bread and soup – nothing else. Butter was an unknown luxury to the family. Her mother used to skim the fat of any soup she made and that was used instead of butter.

In order to satisfy her hunger, Ernestine used to run away from school and go to a small menagerie on the outskirts of town where she used to clean out the monkey cages in return for a few slices of bread.

After many years of study, she was finally given the opportunity to sing for the director of the famous Imperial Opera Company in Vienna.

The director, however, told her that she would never make a singer. He said that she had neither the right looks nor the right personality and he advised her to go back home and buy a sewing machine so that she could start to make dresses. 'An opera singer?' he cried. 'Never, never, never!'

Life continued to be difficult for Ernestine. Her marriage

was a failure and, when her husband left her, he left behind many debts which, under the law then, she became responsible for. Because of this, the bailiffs took away all her furniture except her bed and one chair. When she was able to earn some money from her singing, most of it had to be used to pay off her husband's debts.

Ernestine was so short of money that she had to continue singing in public until six hours before the birth of her third child. She was in agony at the time, but she had to sing to earn enough money to feed her children. When winter came, however, she needed to provide fuel for heating as well and became completely despondent when her children cried with hunger and cold. In a state of absolute despair, she decided to kill her children and herself and set off with them for the nearest railway lines.

We shall hear the rest of the story of Madame Ernestine in our next reading.

Prayer

Life comes with no guarantee that it will always be good. Madame Schumann-Heink was very young when she decided that she wanted to kill herself and she had no way of knowing what the future might hold.

Let us pray that whenever we go through times of pain and distress, we will always see light at the end of the tunnel. May we never give way to despair, but carry hope for the future with us always.

Amen

Day 4 | **Madame Ernestine Schumann-Heink (2)**

Introduction

Today's reading continues the story of Madame Ernestine Schumann-Heink, the woman who wanted to be an opera singer but who became so full of despair that she decided to kill herself and her children.

In her own words she tells her story:
'I was hungry and sick and depressed,' she says. 'And I saw no hope for the future. I didn't want my children to endure

what I had gone through; I felt death would be better than that, so I determined to throw myself and my children in front of a train. I had planned it all out. I knew the time the train would pass. The children were crying and clinging to me, stumbling along at my side. I heard the train whistle. I was already near the tracks. I bent down to pull the children close together. I was ready to hurl their bodies and mine in front of the train when suddenly my little girl threw herself in front of me, crying: 'Mamma, I love you! It is so cold, please let us go home!'

'That childish voice brought me to my senses. I grabbed all my children and ran back to our cold, bare room. I fell on my knees and prayed and sobbed my heart out.'

Until that time, just about everything that Ernestine had tried to do in life had ended in failure yet, only a few years after this suicide attempt, she was being offered jobs with the Royal Opera House in Berlin, with Covent Garden in London and with the Metropolitan in New York. She became one of the greatest contralto singers in the world.

She said that one of the secrets of her success as a singer was the fact that she loved people – and religion taught her to love. She read her Bible every day and used to pray every night and morning.

She claimed that the tragedies of her life had helped her singing because they had given her understanding, sympathy and tenderness. Her own sufferings gave her voice a mystical quality which thrilled the hearts of millions.

Many years after she had become world-famous, she sang in the Imperial Opera House in Vienna. When the director congratulated her on her brilliant performance, he said: 'Your face looks familiar. Where have I seen you before?'

Ernestine Schumann-Heink reminded the director where he had seen her before – there on the very same stage. Then she reminded him of his advice to her to go home and buy herself a sewing-machine . . . .

Conclusion

Not all of us can become great opera stars – not all of us would want to be. But we can all become easily demoralised when the plans we make are thwarted.

The first important thing is knowing what you're capable of – it's no use dreaming your whole life of being a famous singer if you're tone deaf and have no sense of rhythm. On the other hand, if you know that you're capable of something, you mustn't allow yourself to give up just because other people do not appreciate your talent straightaway.

Prayer

Let us pray that we may come to know ourselves – to accept our limitations and strive to make use of our talents. May we learn to be patient and persevering when we find the way forward difficult.

Amen

Day 5

George Washington Carver

You may never have heard of an American negro named George Washington Carver, but your diet and many household products have been influenced by him.

His life story reads like a novel. Born a slave, probably during the American Civil War (his birthdate is unknown), he became an orphan whilst still a baby. His whole family disappeared one night and only the infant, George, was found again.

He was a weak, ailing child, never strong enough to work in the fields with the other slaves but he was passionately interested in the world around him. As he himself said: 'My very soul thirsted for education. I literally lived in the woods. I wanted to know every strange stone, flower, insect, bird and beast.'

Whilst slavery existed it was illegal for George to go to school and, even after its abolition, many schools would not accept black pupils. George's desire for education was so great that he travelled around the country on foot until he found a school which would admit him. He paid for his education by washing dishes and scrubbing clothes. Because he was black, his education ended before High School.

For many years after the abolition of slavery, negroes had no chance of a reasonable education but George refused to be beaten. Eventually, well into his twenties, he was admitted to Iowa Agricultural College. This time he paid for his tuition by running a student laundry.

After graduating, he taught at the Tuskegee Institute, a black college near Montgomery Alabama. George Washington

Carver studied plant life closely and his discoveries eventually influenced the eating habits of everyone in the USA. He found ways to produce better crops, discovered hundreds of new ways of using peanuts and it was he who 'discovered' peanut butter. From the sweet potato he produced many new products including the gum used on postage stamps and a way of making flour. He popularised the use of nutritious plants such as water-cress and chicory. Although his discoveries may not sound revolutionary, in his own quiet way George Washington Carver produced great changes and became very famous in scientific circles.

George Washington Carver could easily have become a millionaire but his interest was in his work rather than money; he never took out a patent but gave away his discoveries freely. So uninterested was he in money that he consistently refused to accept an increase in salary and actually forgot to cash his pay cheques for years on end.

At Tuskegee Institute today there is a museum dedicated to his life and work. There you may hear a recording of George Washington Carver reciting his favourite poem:

The Bridge Builder

An old man travelling a lone highway
Came at the evening cold and grey
To a chasm vast and deep and wide.
The old man crossed in the twilight dim;
The sullen stream had no fear for him
But he turned when he got to the other side
And built a bridge to span the tide.

'Old man,' said a pilgrim near,
'You are wasting your strength building here.
Your journey will end at the close of day;
You never again will pass this way.
You've crossed this chasm deep and wide.
Why build this bridge at evening tide?'

The builder lifted his old grey head,
'Good friend, in the path I have come,' he said,
'There follows after me today
A youth whose feet must pass this way.
This chasm that has been naught to me
To that fair-haired youth may a pitfall be.

He too must cross in the twilight dim.
Good friend, I am building that bridge for him.'

Anonymous

Prayer

On the grave of George Washington Carver is written this inscription:
'He could have added fortune to fame but, caring for neither, he found happiness and honour in being helpful to the world.'
May we strive to follow this example.

Amen

16 Assemblies for Easter Week

Day 1 The Great Plague

Many of you will remember, in your younger days, playing the game of Ring o' Roses. Lots of children play this game but few have any idea of the sinister way in which it originated.

The original 'ring of roses' was a small purplish-red circular rash which appeared on the chest of a person suffering from bubonic plague. The plague was brought to London in the early sixteen sixties and quickly began to rage throughout the city. The streets of London were very narrow, the houses were built extremely close together and there was no sanitation in the overcrowded streets. People tipped all their rubbish onto the streets which then became a breeding ground for germs.

The plague was carried by the fleas which live on black rats. When someone's skin had been punctured by a flea bite it was easy for germs to find their way into the bloodstream. When someone caught the plague, death was almost certain. One of the first symptoms would be an imaginary sweetness in the air as though there were beds of flowers nearby. Within 12 to 14 hours, glandular parts of the body would become painfully inflamed; this would be followed by shivering, sickness, headaches, sneezing and feverishness. The patient would die within a few days.

Apothecaries sold all kinds of supposed remedies against the plague but none of them worked. People used to walk around the city with nosegays of flowers in their pockets hoping that the strong scent would ward off the plague – hence the 'pocketful of posies' mentioned in the rhyme. People in those days had little understanding of how diseases were passed on. They would take drinking water from streams in which the clothing of plague victims had been washed. Germs were easily carried in cloth, particularly in woollen goods and through such things as mattresses, bandages and clothing.

One of the most vivid accounts of London during the plague is obtained from the diary of Samuel Pepys who wrote on 7th June 'The hottest day that ever I felt in my life. This day, much against my will, I did in Drury Lane see two or three houses marked with a red cross upon the doors and *Lord, have mercy upon us* writ there; this was a sad sight to me, being the first of this kind to my remembrance I ever saw.'

The red cross became the sign of the plague – a warning to others that a house was under quarantine and no one should enter or leave it. There were so many deaths in London that it was no longer possible for people to be given a proper burial; all that could be done was to make huge pits as mass graves on the outskirts of the city. In the dead of night, carts would rumble round the streets of London with a crier shouting 'Bring out your dead', ringing a handbell to warn passers-by to scurry away from contamination.

In 1666 there was a terrible fire in London. Although the destruction was horrific, it had the effect of burning out and halting the plague. The new city which was built afterwards was one of wider streets, better houses and more hygenic sanitation.

Prayer

Let us give thanks for the sacrifices that have been made by those who have studied the causes of disease and helped to bring about preventions and cures. May we appreciate our own good health and always be willing to do what we can to help those who are ill and need our help and support.

Amen

The Plague Village of Eyam (1)

The village of Eyam lies in the Derbyshire Peak District – a beautiful hamlet of a few hundred people in the midst of the Derbyshire moorland.

One day, in September 1665, a tailor named George Vicars who was living in Eyam, received a parcel of textiles from London. The material seemed rather damp so one of the servants spread it out by the fire to dry. Within a few days George Vicars was taken ill and died. His death was recorded in the parish register by the rector, William Mompesson without anyone having an inkling of the terrible disease which had travelled all the way with George Vicars' textiles from London.

Shortly afterwards, other members of the same family became ill and it was not long before the infection spread from house to house around the village. The villagers became terrified when they realised that all the victims had died with a circular 'ring of roses' on their chests – an unmistakable symptom of the bubonic plague. During the month of September, six people died in the village; in October there were 23. Villagers hoped that the oncoming winter would quickly halt the plague. There were only seven deaths in November and the subsequent winter was very harsh. Eyam lies in an exposed position high on the moors and can be covered in snow for quite long spells; it was thought unlikely that the plague would survive a Derbyshire moorland winter.

Nine people died from the plague in December, five in January and eight in February.

Some of the wealthier inhabitants of the village had packed their belongings and moved elsewhere; for the rest of the villagers however there was no such escape. Refugees from a plague village would hardly be welcome anywhere else; they could lie about where they had come from but, if they already had the disease when they fled, they might infect all the surrounding area. If they stayed where they were, they would probably catch the plague but save the lives of thousands of others from outside the village who might otherwise become infected.

Rector Mompesson called the villagers together and suggested to them that they should make the most difficult sacrifice possible – they should stay where they were in the village. His congregation realised that it was in their hands to decide whether the plague would spread or not. It was a terrible responsibility for them but they agreed to keep themselves in the village.

Arrangements were made for food and other supplies to be left on boundary stones around Eyam. The villagers paid with money which was left in running water or in a mixture of water and vinegar to try and avoid infection. The inhabitants of Eyam stayed together in their village waiting for the plague to do its worst.

Conclusion

Our readings leading up to Easter are about sacrifice. Jesus made the ultimate sacrifice when he gave up his life on the cross. The villagers of Eyam were prepared to sacrifice themselves for the sake of other people who lived outside the village.

Prayer

Most of us will probably never be called upon to make the kind of sacrifice that was made by the villagers of Eyam. May we be prepared to sacrifice our wants and needs sometimes to bring more happiness and joy to others.

Amen

| Day 3 | **The Plague Village of Eyam (2)**

People in the area surrounding Eyam were very much afraid of catching the plague. On one occasion, a carter from a nearby village insisted, against the advice of all his neighbours, on going into Eyam to deliver some wood. He set off as he had planned but, on arriving at Eyam, could find no one to help him unload his cart. Disconsolately, he set about unloading it himself in the drizzle and fog and then trundled back home. A short time afterwards he started sneezing.

His friends and neighbours were afraid; they insisted that the carter stay indoors whilst they sent to the Earl of Devonshire, the local land-owner, to ask his advice. The earl sent his own doctor to examine the carter on the banks of the river Derwent – the doctor on one side of the river and the carter on the other. The doctor must have had very good eyesight, for he soon decided that the man was suffering from a common cold. He was ordered to go back home.

Having decided to isolate themselves, the villagers of Eyam quickly succumbed to the worst of the plague during the summer months. One of the saddest cases was that of the Riley family where the mother brought out and buried seven members of her family one by one. Another tragic death was that of the rector's wife, Catherine Mompesson. The rector and his wife had sent their children away earlier to relatives for safety. The rector had begged his wife to go with them but Catherine refused, feeling that she could be more useful helping her husband in the village. They were walking together one evening when Catherine exclaimed how sweetly the air was smelling. The rector was horrified, knowing an imaginary sweetness in the air to be one of the first symptoms of the plague. His worst fears were quickly realised: Catherine soon became very ill and hers was yet another name for the rector to add to the list of deaths in the parish register. In all, of the 350 people in the village, 259 died of the plague.

As the rector reported in one of his letters: 'The condition of this place hath been so sad that I persuade myself it did exceed History and example; I may truly say our town is become a Golgotha, the place of a Skull. My ears have never heard such doleful lamentations, my nose felt such horrid smells, and my eyes never beheld such ghastly spectacles. Here hath been 76 families visited within my parish, out of which have died 259. Blessed be God, all our fears are over, for none have died here of the infection since the eleventh of October, besides we have not any one person under a present suspicion and all the pest houses have been long empty.'

When at last the plague seemed to be over, to avoid further infection, the remaining villagers burnt their clothes, bedding and furnishings on huge bonfires and completely fumigated houses which had carried the disease.

The people of Eyam had to mourn the deaths of many treasured friends, relatives and neighbours but they knew that their act of heroism and sacrifice had saved the surrounding area from the plague.

Prayer

May we never become so wrapped up in our own greed and self-interest that we miss out on opportunities to be of service to other people. May we come to learn that it is better to give than receive.

Amen

Day 4 ## The Garden of Gethsemane

Today's reading is taken from the New Testament, from the time just before the crucifixion when Jesus was with his friends in the Garden of Gethsemane.

Jesus, it seems, was already aware of the terrible ordeal that he had to face and, in some ways, it seems reassuring to know that even Jesus, when he realised what was before him, felt very much afraid . . . .

Jesus then came with his disciples to a place called Gethsemane. He said to them, 'Sit here while I go over there to pray.' He took with him Peter and the two sons of Zebedee. Anguish and dismay came over him, and he said to them, 'My heart is ready to break with grief. Stop here and stay awake with me.' He went on a little, fell on his face in prayer, and said, 'My Father, if it is possible, let this cup pass me by. Yet not as I will, but as thou wilt.'

He came to the disciples and found them asleep; and he said to Peter, 'What! Could none of you stay awake with me one hour? Stay awake, and pray that you may be spared the test. The spirit is willing, but the flesh is weak.'

He went away a second time, and prayed: 'My father, if it is not possible for this cup to pass me by without my drinking it, thy will be done.'

He came again and found them asleep, for their eyes were heavy. So he left them and went away again: and he prayed the third time, using the same words as before.

Then he came to the disciples and said to them, 'Still sleeping? Still taking your ease? The hour has come! The Son of Man is betrayed to sinful men. Up, let us go forward; the traitor is upon us.'

Matthew 26: 36–46 New English Bible

Conclusion

'The spirit is willing but the flesh is weak' – we do not know whether Jesus said this to reprimand his disciples for falling asleep or whether he was referring to the conflict within himself, or both.

It has been said that the stronger someone's spirit is and the deeper their faith, the more that faith will be tested.

Jesus was called upon to make the ultimate test and sacrifice – that of laying down his life. He himself didn't understand why that had to be done and it was only natural for him to argue against it and to question God's purpose.

Two thousand years later, we can see more clearly why Jesus actually had to die before people would really start to listen to his message.

Prayer

May we look to the example of Jesus Christ when we fail to understand the purpose behind our own suffering.

When we are called upon to sacrifice our self-interests for the good of others, may we do so without resentment and find fulfilment in the service of other people.

Amen

Day 5

The Ballad of the Bread Man

Our reading today is a modernised version of the story of Jesus and of his crucifixion.

Mary stood in the kitchen
Baking a loaf of bread.
An angel flew in through the window.
'We've a job for you,' he said.

'God in his big gold heaven,
Sitting in his big blue chair,
Wanted a mother for his little son.
Suddenly saw you there.'

Mary shook and trembled,
'It isn't true what you say.'
'Don't say that,' said the angel.
'The baby's on its way.'

Joseph was in the workshop
Planing a piece of wood.
'The old man's past it,' the neighbours said.
'That girl's been up to no good.'

'And who was that elegant fellow,'
They said, 'in the shiny gear?'
The things they said about Gabriel
Were hardly fit to hear.

Mary never answered,
Mary never replied.
She kept the information,
Like the baby, safe inside.

It was election winter.
They went to vote in town.
When Mary found her time had come
The hotels let her down.

The baby was born in an annexe
Next to the local pub.
At midnight a delegation
Turned up from the Farmers' Club.

They talked about an explosion
That made a hole in the sky,
Said they'd been sent to the Lamb and Flag
To see God come down from on high.

A few days later a bishop
And a five-star general were seen
With the head of an African country
In a bullet-proof limousine.

'We've come,' they said, 'with tokens
For the little boy to choose.'
Told the tale about war and peace
In the television news.

After them came the soldiers
With rifle and bomb and gun,
Looking for enemies of the state.
The family had packed and gone.

When they got back to the village
The neighbours said, to a man,
'That boy will never be one of us,
Though he does what he blessed well can.'

He went round to all the people
A paper crown on his head.
Here is some bread from my father.
Take, eat, he said.

Nobody seemed very hungry.
Nobody seemed to care.
Nobody saw the god in himself
Quietly standing there.

He finished up in the papers.
He came to a very bad end.
He was charged with bringing the living to life.
No man was that prisoner's friend.

There's only one kind of punishment
To fit that kind of a crime.
They rigged a trial and shot him dead.
They were only just in time.

They lifted the young man by the leg,
They lifted him by the arm,
They locked him in a cathedral.
In case he came to harm.

They stored him safe as water
Under seven rocks.
One Sunday morning he burst out
Like a jack-in-the-box.

Through the town he went walking.
He showed them the holes in his head.
Now do you want any loaves? he cried.
'Not today,' they said.

Charles Causley

Conclusion

It's easy to think of the Crucifixion as something that happened two thousand years ago that needn't concern us much – except for the fact that we have Easter eggs at Easter and a holiday from school.

A modern version of the story helps to bring home to us the suffering of Jesus and the message of love that is still there for us to listen to.

Prayer

May we keep our minds open to the message of Jesus Christ. Even if we find it difficult to identify with him or to accept

him as a living person, let us not close our minds to his suffering and to the message of love which he brought to the
human race.

Amen

17 Love Your Enemies

Love Your Enemies

Introduction

Today's reading is one of the most contentious pieces of writing ever published.

It's something people argue about and have argued about ever since it was first written nearly 2,000 years ago. Some Christians would claim that this passage expresses some of the most fundamental principles of their religion; others would say that it contains ideas which are completely unacceptable to Christians living in modern society.

I say to you, Do not resist one who is evil. But if anyone strikes you on the right cheek, turn to him the other also; and if any one would sue you and take your coat, let him have your cloak as well; and if anyone forces you to go one mile, go with him two miles.

Give to him who begs from you and do not refuse him who would borrow from you.

You have heard that it was said, 'You shall love your neighbour and hate your enemy.'

But I say to you, Love your enemies and pray for those who persecute you, so that you may be sons of your Father who is in heaven; for he makes his sun rise on the evil and on the good; and sends rain on the just and on the unjust.

For if you love those who love you, what reward have you? Do not even the tax collectors do the same?

And if you salute only your brothers, what more are you doing than others? Do not even the Gentiles do the same?

You, therefore, must be perfect, as your heavenly Father is perfect.

Matthew 5: 39—48 Authorised version

Conclusion

Jesus is not saying that there is anything wrong with loving those people who are fond of us, but he's saying that we must love our enemies as well.

If someone, for whatever reason, thinks of you as an enemy, they expect you to behave in a certain way. They expect you to say unpleasant things to them, to 'persecute them', as Jesus says, and perhaps if you're provoked enough, turn round and attack them. When we do this, we confirm people's expectations of us. We become enemies.

If we refuse to be put into the role of enemies, if we can still manage to treat people with respect, even when they seem to hate us, they become very confused. It's very difficult to carry on treating someone as an enemy, when they don't behave like one.

What Jesus Christ realised was that, refusing to be put into the role of someone's enemy, difficult as it might be, can often be the best way of diffusing an explosive situation and of avoiding conflict and aggression.

Prayer

Our prayer today is the one that has become famous as the prayer of Saint Francis of Assisi:

Lord, make me an instrument of Thy peace:
Where there is hatred, let me sow love;
Where there is injury, pardon;
Where there is discord, union;
Where there is doubt, faith;
Where there is despair, hope;
Where there is darkness, light;
Where there is sadness, joy.
O divine Master, grant that I may not so much seek
To be consoled as to console;
To be understood, as to understand;
To be loved, as to love;
For it is in giving that we receive,

It is in pardoning that we are pardoned;
And it is in dying that we are born
To eternal life.

Amen

Day 2

Gandhi (1)

One of the greatest men to put into practice Jesus Christ's teaching that we should love our enemies, was not a Christian but a Hindu – the great Indian leader Mahatma Gandhi.

When Gandhi was a young man, India was part of the British Empire – 'the brightest jewel of the British crown' as the English prime minister, Disraeli described it. The British presence did bring some benefits to India: the British built railways and canals and helped to contain killer diseases such as cholera and typhoid. They also set up schools and universities but, in economic terms, India suffered a great deal from British rule. Raw materials were grown cheaply in India and then exported to Britain to be manufactured. The British thought of the Indians as inferior and treated them as second-class citizens in their own country. The Indians resented this. They wanted the freedom to develop their own industries and to grow food to feed their own people instead of growing products just to be exported to Britain.

Many Indians fought for Britain in the 1914–18 war and there was a strong feeling that Britain should show her gratitude by granting India her independence when the war was over. When this was refused there were angry scenes, particularly in the Punjab where a mob got out of control and murdered four Europeans in Amritsar.

Shortly afterwards a crowd of 10,000 Indian men, women and children gathered in one of the squares of Amritsar. The British military commander, General Dyer told his men to seal off all exits from the square and then ordered them to fire continuously on the crowd for ten minutes. The horror did not finish after that: 500 students and teachers were arrested, men were publicly flogged and women tortured. The atrocities went on for a period of eight weeks after which General Dyer, when he returned to England, instead of being punished or reprimanded, was presented with a jewelled sword inscribed with the words: *Saviour of the Punjab*.

The effect of this incident for most Indians was to destroy once and for all any faith they might have had in the British system of justice. Indians became united in their demands to rule their country for themselves.

Such atrocities in any other occupied country would no doubt have led to violent reprisals but in India the movement for independence was led by a man who preached continually to his people that they must love their enemies and use only non-violent methods in their campaign. Gandhi led his people on marches and on pickets; under his example they began spinning their own cloth and boycotted British ready-made clothes as well as other British goods.

One thing which very much annoyed the Indian people was that only the government was allowed to make and sell salt on which they placed a heavy tax duty. Gandhi announced that he would break the salt laws by taking salt from the sea. He set out on a three-week march; by the time he reached the Arabian sea he had been joined by thousands of his followers. They marched to the sea carrying pots and pans which they filled with sea water, then they lit great fires on the sea shore and boiled the water until only the salt remained.

Gandhi, like many of his followers, was arrested and forced to spend many months at a time in prison but his courage and good spirits never left him. He earned the respect of millions of people and through his efforts India eventually achieved independence in 1947.

Shortly after this, Gandhi was walking to a prayer meeting in the garden of the house in which he was staying in Delhi. A young man suddenly pushed his way through the crowd, bowed in greeting and then drew out a gun and shot him three times. Gandhi died shortly afterwards. The assassin was a fanatical Hindu who disapproved of the way Gandhi had been associating with the rival Muslims.

Nehru, the new Indian prime minister, announced to his people the news that Gandhi was dead. 'Friends and comrades,' he said, 'a light has gone out of our lives and there is darkness everywhere . . . Our beloved Father is dead. The light has gone out I said and yet I was wrong for the light that shone in this country was no ordinary light . . . it will illumine this country . . . and a thousand years later that light will still be seen in this country . . . that light represented the living, the eternal truth, reminding us of the right path, drawing us from error, taking this ancient country to freedom.'

In our next assembly we shall look at Gandhi's life and the ideas on which his teachings were based.

Prayer

Let us give thanks for the lives of those people whose example has lit the pathway to truth. May we learn from the wisdom of others.

Amen

| Day 3 |

Gandhi (2)

Gandhi was born in India in 1869. As a boy, he was small and shy with sticking-out ears. He was always self-conscious and dreaded being teased. At school, he found his lessons difficult and left with very few qualifications. He was then sent to England by his parents to study law.

Gandhi found the British way of life so strange and alien that he kept to himself most of the time and made very few friends. After three years he qualified as a barrister and returned home, but he was much too nervous to speak properly for his clients in court; other barristers made fun of his awkward stammering and, before long, no one would bring him cases to defend. That period of his life was very unhappy; his mother and father had both died; Gandhi married when he was a young boy but his first son died as well and Gandhi started to despair and even think about suicide.

Then, through family connections, he was given the opportunity to take on a legal case in South Africa for a year. Gandhi accepted but found the system of government in South Africa repressive and unjust. The country was ruled by a small percentage of whites who treated the Indian and other coloured and black groups as inferiors.

On one occasion, Gandhi bought a first-class rail ticket but a white passenger objected to sharing a first-class compartment with him and asked the guard to remove him to the luggage van. Gandhi refused to move and finished up being thrown off the train at the next station and having to spend the night there, huddled in a corner shivering in the cold.

The incident infuriated Gandhi. He spent most of the night thinking about the situation. Why should one man despise another just because his skin was a different colour? Gandhi decided that he would do whatever he could in future to help stamp out this evil. He also decided that whatever methods he used would not be violent. The Indian people, he felt, must work hard to earn respect from others; one of the best ways of doing this would be to always behave courteously and pleasantly with those who were persecuting them. He said: 'I object to violence because, when it appears to do good, the good is only temporary; the evil it does is permanent.'

Gandhi decided to stay longer in South Africa. He built up a successful legal practice and his skills as a lawyer improved dramatically as he fought racial prejudice through the courts. However, although Gandhi, as a lawyer, had a great respect for the law, he also felt that it was right on occasions to break it – especially when the government introduced new laws which seemed even more unfair to the Indians. Hindu and Muslim marriages were declared invalid; in the Transvaal, Indians were not allowed to vote and non-whites were even forbidden to walk along the pavements. When Gandhi ignored this one day, someone kicked him into the gutter. Gandhi organised marches and strikes against these laws and, although he and his followers were arrested and imprisoned, their determination only grew stronger. The tactics succeeded: eventually the government had to resign and many of the repressive laws were changed.

Gandhi returned to India in 1915 feeling confident that his ideas were right and that they could now be used to stop persecution of the Indians by the British.

Gandhi's philosophy, which he derived from one of the sacred books of the Hindus, was known as *satyagraha*. *Satya* means truth and *agraha* means strength or firmness. There is no English equivalent of this word, so it has been translated simply as non-violence.

Gandhi derived much of his strength through living a very simple life. He was strictly vegetarian and never ate more than he needed. He urged people to simplify their lives by giving up possessions that they didn't need. People sold their expensive clothes and jewellery and gave the money to his campaign.

Gandhi spent part of the day walking and much time in

prayer and meditation, but he seldom slept for more than three or four hours a night and, even as an old man, he was fit and lively. He refused to wear expensive or fashionable clothes and people in Britain thought he looked very odd when he was invited to Buckingham Palace to meet the queen and he arrived wearing open sandals, bare legs and a loin cloth made of material he had spun himself.

Gandhi's personality had completely changed: from being timid, shy and self-conscious, he became completely unafraid. Whenever there was the threat of violence and bloodshed, he walked among the people fearlessly preaching to them. 'Why are you afraid?' he asked the fighters on the north-west frontier. 'You must be afraid to be carrying guns. Look at me – I have no fear and that is why I am unarmed.'

Satyagraha gave Gandhi the strength from which he drew his courage and capacity for hard work. Many people thought of him as a saint and he certainly seemed able to achieve miracles by breaking down the resistance of his opponents and converting them to his cause rather than treating them as enemies.

In spite of this, Gandhi said: 'I claim to be no more than an average man with less than average ability. I have not the shadow of a doubt that any man or woman can achieve what I have, if he or she would make the same effort and cultivate the same hope and faith.'

Prayer

Let us remember that the world is made up of people like ourselves – people who feel the same joys and pain and fears that we do.

May we always remember this when we start to think of someone as our enemy.

When people show hatred of us, may we behave with tolerance and dignity, refusing to play the role of 'enemies', so that we can turn their hatred into respect and understanding.

Amen

Day 4 **Beach Burial**

El Alamein was a relatively unknown railway station 50 miles away from Alexandria in North Africa. It was known to soldiers before the Second World War as a convenient place to stop for the night because, opposite the railway station, was a beach which was easily accessible and it was refreshing for travellers to stop and bathe in the clear blue waters of the Mediterranean before continuing their journey.

In 1943, El Alamein was the scene of one of the major battles of the Second World War. Between August and the beginning of November, 33,500 men were killed or wounded there. The following poem was written after the battle of El Alamein:

Softly and humbly to the Gulf of Arabs
The convoys of dead sailors come;
At night they sway and wander in the waters far under,
But morning rolls them in the foam.

Between the sob and clubbing of the gunfire
Someone, it seems, has time for this,
To pluck them from the shallows and bury them in
     burrows
And tread the sand upon their nakedness;

And each cross, the driven stake of tidewood,
Bears the last signature of men,
Written with such perplexity, with such bewildered pity,
The words choke as they begin –

'*Unknown seaman*' – the ghostly pencil
Wavers and fades, the purple drips,
The breath of the wet season has washed their inscrip-
     tions
As blue as drowned men's lips,

Dead seamen, gone in search of the same landfall,
Whether as enemies they fought,
Or fought with us, or neither; the sand joins them
     together,
Enlisted on the other front.

Kenneth Slessor

Conclusion

Those who died at El Alamein were enemies, but they were

also sons, brothers, fathers, lovers, uncles, grandsons, friends and workmates.

The men on both sides had many things in common, but it took death to unite them under the sand.

Prayer

Let us pray that we may grow up to fight, not wars, but war.

May we seek to remove the seeds of violence within ourselves and play our part in working for a more just and peaceful world.

Amen

Day 5 **Identification**

Introduction

One of the most distressing experiences that anyone can ever have to go through is to be asked to identify the body of someone that they knew and loved.

When there has been a very bad accident, or an act of terrorism such as a bomb attack, the body may be completely unrecognisable and may have to be identified simply by articles of clothing or other possessions. A case such as this is what today's reading is about:

So you think it's Stephen?
Then I'd best make sure
Be on the safe side as it were.
Ah, there's been a mistake. The hair
you see, it's black, now Stephen's fair . . .
What's that? The explosion?
Of course, burnt black. Silly of me,
I should have known. Then let's get on.

The face, is that the face I ask,
that mask of charred wood?
Blistered, scarred could
that have been a child's face?
The sweater, where intact, looks
in fact all too familiar.
But one must be sure.

The scoutbelt. Yes that's his.
I recognise the studs he hammered in
not a week ago. At the age
when boys get clothes-conscious
now you know. It's almost
certainly Stephen. But one must
be sure. Remove all trace of doubt.
Pull out every splinter of hope.

Pockets. Empty the pockets.
Handkerchief? Could be any schoolboy's.
Dirty enough. Cigarettes?
Oh this can't be Stephen.
I don't allow him to smoke you see.
He wouldn't disobey me. Not his father.
But that's his penknife. That's his alright.
And that's his key on the key-ring
Gran gave him just the other night.
Then this must be him.

I think I know what happened
. . . about the cigarettes.
No doubt he was minding them
for one of the older boys.
Yes that's it.
That's him.
That's our Stephen.

Roger McGough

Conclusion

When we label people by their political ideas, their national-
ity or their religion, it's easy to forget that we're talking
about people who feel just as much fear and pain as we do
and who have families and friends who would grieve for them
in just the same way that ours would.

Many people use violence because they think it is justified
in defending the freedom of their country. It is useful to remember, however, that Jesus Christ lived in an occupied
country and still proclaimed to his people living under
repression: 'Love your enemies and pray for those who persecute you.'

Prayer

Jesus recommended that we pray for those who persecute us.

All of us feel persecuted at some time in our lives.

Let us think, in particular, today of those people who seem to be making life difficult for us.

Let us pray that we may be patient with them and forgiving so that their hostility towards us is disarmed and they become patient and forgiving with us.

Amen

18 The Shape God Wears

Day 1   The Blind Men and the Elephant

It was six men of Hindostan
To learning much inclined,
Who went to see the elephant,
(Though all of them were blind);
That each by observation
Might satisfy his mind.

The first approached the elephant,
And happening to fall
Against his broad and sturdy side,
At once began to bawl,
'Bless me, it seems the elephant
Is very like a wall.'

The second, feeling of his tusk,
Cried, 'Ho! What have we here
So very round and smooth and sharp?
To me 'tis mighty clear
This wonder of an elephant
Is very like a spear.'

The third approached the animal,
And happening to take
The squirming trunk within his hands,
Then boldly up and spake;
'I see,' quoth he, 'the elephant
Is very like a snake.'

The fourth stretched out his eager hand
And felt about the knee,
'What most this mighty beast is like
Is mighty plain,' quoth he;
''Tis clear enough the elephant
Is very like a tree.'

The fifth who chanced to touch the ear
Said, 'Even the blindest man
Can tell what this resembles most;
Deny the fact who can,
This marvel of an elephant
Is very like a fan.'

The sixth no sooner had begun
About the beast to grope
Than, seizing on the swinging tail
That fell within his scope,
'I see,' cried he, 'the elephant
Is very like a rope.'

And so these men of Hindostan
Disputed loud and long,
Each of his own opinion
Exceeding stiff and strong,
Though each was partly in the right,
And all were in the wrong!

John Godfrey Saxe

Conclusion

The mistake made by all the so-called wise men was that none of them realised just how big the elephant was. All of them were able to touch just one part of the elephant and they each made the mistake of assuming that their one part was the whole.

People become aware of God in different ways. Someone who loves music might catch a glimpse of the creative force that they think of as God when they are engrossed in playing or listening to music. Someone else might experience that same sense of awe and wonder through Art, or Dance or in some sport where they have to push themselves physically to their limits.

Other people may see something of God reflected in their

relationships with other people – in love and comradeship. But, however we come to see God, it's important that we don't underestimate how vast His presence is – we musn't assume, when we touch one part, that we are in contact with the whole. And we must remember that other people can see God in different ways from us and still not be mistaken when they tell us what God means to them.

Prayer

May we have the courage to keep our hearts and minds open so that we may be aware of God's presence however He chooses to show Himself to us.

Amen

Day 2 ┃ **The Shape God Wears**

But ask now the beasts, and they shall teach thee; and the fowls of the air, and they shall tell thee. Job 12:7

So questioning, I was bold to dare
The sinewy tiger in his lair.
'Come forth, striped sir, make known to me
What God it was who fashioned thee.'

Out leapt he like a muscled blaze,
Patterned in black and gold he was.
'Jehovah is his name,' he cried,
'Tiger of Tigers, beryl-eyed,

'Flat flanked and sleek, His paws are curled
About the margins of the world.
He stalketh in His jungles grim –
I, even I, am like to Him!'

I sought that moving mountain side,
The elephant, with ears fanned wide,
Treading the forests. 'Sir, tell me
What manner of a God made thee?'

He swirled his trunk about the oak
And wrenched it up before he spoke,
Then answered in a trumpet blast,
'Old Super-Pachyderm, that vast

'Lord of the Elephants, the great
Trampler upon the worm's estate.
Crag-shouldered, terrible is He
Who of His substance fashioned me!'

I scaled the precipice, to seek
The eagle on his drafty peak.
'Tell me, O Gazer at the sun,
The nature of that Mighty One,

'Your Lord.' He turned his crested head
And screamed athwart the wind and said,
'Ancient of Eagles, wild and free
Rider of tempests, He made me!

'His wing is stretched above the thunder,
His claws can rip the hills asunder.
His beak of two hooked knives is made –
Look on His likeness. Be afraid!'

Then turned I to the whorléd snail
Whose house is exquisite and frail,
Most deftly wrought. 'Sir, I would know
What God it was Who shaped thee so.'

Then cried he proudly to my face,
'Eternal snail, God of my race.
The lightning is His silvery track,
He wears the world upon His back.

'He is most beautiful and wise,
He dwelleth in the moisty skies,
In the gray wall at heaven's rim,
And He has made me after Him!'

Then laughed I in superior mirth,
'Attend, ye creatures of the earth,
Misled, mistaken, all undone
And self-deceivers, every one.

'Hear ye, deluded beasts, while I
Explain the shape God wears, and why.
Self-evident the truth's displayed:
He is *my* Father, sirs,' I said,
'And in my image His is made!'

Sara Henderson Hay

Conclusion

It's easy to assume that the writer of this poem is wrong
when she says that God is made in her image. It seems ar-
rogant and conceited to presume, like all the animals did,
that God is made to suit us.

The poem starts to make sense if we think of God like the
elephant which the blind men were trying to understand.
Each of us can only see a part of God – none of us is capable
of understanding the whole. When the eagle tried to imagine
something wonderful and all-powerful, he could only think
of it in terms of a magnificent eagle and when the snail tried
to imagine what God must be like, he could only think of
Him in terms of a magnificent snail. That doesn't mean that
the snail or the eagle must be wrong, just that neither of
them could imagine what it would be like to see things
through the eyes of someone else.

We find this very confusing because we're used to asking
factual questions. And when we ask factual questions, we
expect there to be only one right answer. If we ask, 'What's
8×4 ?' and one person says 93 and someone else 64, someone else 18 and another person says a bunch of bananas, we
know they can't all be right.

Experts on religion all come up with different answers. We
can talk to priests and great religious leaders, we can read
through holy books and find that they all have different
answers to the question: *What is God?*

Prayer

May we learn to be tolerant and understanding of people who
see God in different ways from us, or who cannot see God
at all.

Let us remember that we all have much to learn from
people who have different faiths from ourselves.

Amen

Day 3 **The Muslim Religion**

To be a follower of a particular religion usually means accepting certain teachings and following particular rules and guidelines throughout your daily life.

Customs and teachings vary from one religion to another but there are many things which religions have in common. Today we are going to look briefly at some of the teachings of one of the most popular of the world's religions – the Muslim religion.

Muslims worship one God whom they call Allah. They regard Muhammad, the founder of their religion, as a great prophet but they do not worship him and think of him as the son of God in the same way that Christians think of Jesus. Muhammad was born in the year AD 570 in the city of Mecca in the country which is now called Saudi Arabia. Muhammad had visions of the Angel Gabriel who told him that he was to be a messenger of God and must write down the words of God which he received. These writings are contained in the Qur'an – the holy book of the Muslims.

A good Muslim must follow the five pillars of Islam: firstly, there is the creed which should be spoken in Arabic, the language of the Qur'an. Translated into English it means: 'There is no god but God, Muhammad is the prophet of God.'

The second pillar of Islam is prayer. Muslims think it is very important that they should pray aloud together, particularly during festivals and on a Friday which is their special day for prayer. Muslim men and children pray together at a mosque but the Muslim women usually pray in a separate room at the mosque or pray together at home.

The third pillar is an annual tax called the zakat. Every Muslim is expected to give a fortieth of his savings to the poor. This is a voluntary contribution – not one collected by the authorities. Muslims in Britain usually consider that there are no really poor people living here so they are more likely to send their zakat to the poorer people of India and Pakistan.

The fourth pillar of Islam is fasting. The fasting period begins at the end of the eighth month of the year and lasts for the whole of the month of Ramadan, during which time a Muslim should neither eat nor drink between the hours of sunrise and sunset. Ramadan can fall at different times of the year and fasting can be particularly arduous when it has to be done during the summer when the hours of daylight are longer and when people are more likely to become thirsty. The ending of Ramadan is marked by a great celebration called Id when Muslims visit friends and exchange greetings and gifts.

The fifth pillar of Islam is the pilgrimage to Mecca which all Muslims are expected to make at least once during their lifetime. Pilgrims travel to Mecca from all over the world, many of them arriving in Saudi Arabia by air and then travelling to Mecca by bus. Others may go most of the way by sea or road or even walk. Pilgrims undergo a period of fasting in the holy city and carry out sacrifices and important rituals before returning home.

As well as these five pillars, there are other strictures which Islam places on the lives of its followers: a Muslim should not drink alcohol or eat certain foods, particularly pork or anything made from pork. Muslim women are expected to be modest in their appearance. They should keep their legs and their arms and shoulders covered and also wear a scarf over their heads.

Being a good Muslim means much more than visiting the mosque now and again. The Muslim religion is a way of life.

Not all religions are like that. Sometimes a person can be a follower of a certain religion without his or her friends being aware of it. For some people religion is something to share with others in public, enjoying the feeling of comradeship which is brought about by openly sharing the same values, rituals and beliefs. For other people, religion is something personal and private – when they speak to God, they may prefer to do so alone and even in silence.

There are many ways of reaching God. The most difficult pathway for one person may be the easiest for another.

Prayer

To be a true follower of Islam requires a self-discipline that most of us have never even tried to live up to.

Let us pray that we may learn the art of self-control – when we decide to work on something, may we do so without becoming easily distracted by trivialities. May we come to be proud of our dedication.

Amen

The Society of Friends

Today we are going to look at a very different form of religion from that of the Muslims – a religion with far fewer followers and one which has been in existence for less than 350 years – the Quakers.

The Society of Friends, as the Quakers are more correctly known, was started by George Fox who was born in Leicestershire in 1624. The early Quakers were often persecuted and imprisoned for their radical ideas and many Friends eventually left Britain and went to live abroad, particularly in America where there is still a strong Quaker presence.

Quakers hold their Meeting for Worship in a Meeting House which is a simple building, not a church. They have no altar and no prayers or hymns – instead they meditate or pray in silence until someone feels moved to speak aloud and share their thoughts with the rest of the Meeting.

Quakers do not respect rank or status – they do not believe that one person is any better than another. Consequently, they do not have priests – for they believe that one person is just as capable of reaching God as anyone else.

There is no particular creed or set of beliefs that Quakers have to accept but they do share certain guiding principles.

They believe that there is something good in everyone and that it is wrong to kill or bear arms against someone else – even in wartime. Many Quakers have been imprisoned and persecuted because of their refusal to fight when their country has been at war. Where there are areas of conflict in the world, there will often be Quakers acting as mediators, trying to bring the different sides together. There will also be a Quaker presence at rallies and peace marches, although sometimes members of the Society of Friends will prefer to mount a silent vigil against war rather than joining in a noisy demonstration.

Quakers try to be honest in all their dealings – both in private and in business. They will not usually take an oath in court because they do not believe there should be one standard of truth for the court room and a different standard for the rest of their lives.

Although Quakers have no creed, they have a book of Advices to give them guidance in their everyday affairs. Here are some extracts from it:

Show a loving consideration for all God's creatures. Cherish the beauty and variety of his world.

In your relations with others, exercise imagination, understanding and sympathy. Listen patiently, and seek whatever truth other people's opinions may contain for you. Think it possible that you may be mistaken. In discussion, avoid hurtful and provocative language. . .

Be faithful; be patient; be in earnest to fulfil your service as messengers of truth. Feel the power of God in one another, drawing you together as he draws you to himself.

Prayer

Let us pray that we may listen and learn from the wisdom of others.

May we come to accept the possibility that we may be mistaken in our opinions and that other people's truths may hold deeper meanings for us than we realise.

Amen

Day 5 ## Footsteps

One night a man had a dream. He dreamed he was walking along the beach with the Lord. Across the sky flashed scenes from his life. For each scene, he noticed two sets of footprints in the sand: one belonging to him, and the other to the Lord.

When the last scene of his life flashed before him, he looked back at the footprints in the sand. He noticed that many times along the path of his life there was only one set of footprints. He also noticed that it happened at the very lowest and saddest times in his life.

This really bothered him and he questioned the Lord about it.

'Lord, you said that once I decided to follow you, you'd walk with me all the way. But I have noticed that during the most troublesome times in my life, there is only one set of footprints. I don't understand why, when I needed you most, you would leave me.'

The Lord replied, 'My son, My precious child, I love you and would never leave you. During your times of trial and suffering, when you see only one set of footprints, it was then that I carried you.'

Anonymous

Conclusion

All of us go through some times of sadness in our lives. Having faith doesn't mean that God will take all our problems away, but belief in God can carry us through times when those without faith would have given up in despair.

Prayer

Let us pray that in times of deepest misfortune we may be blessed with Faith that God will carry us through and hope that things will turn out for the better. Let us never forget that the sun still shines – even behind the darkest clouds.

Amen

19 Communication

See also Loneliness, page 240.

Day 1   The Damned

Introduction

This week's assemblies are about communication. Our first reading is from a book called *The Damned* by Linda Hoy. It's about a boy called Chris who's recently joined the peace movement.

I pin a card on the notice board in the form room. The wording's stupid but you have to write something like that to make the kids in our class take notice.

> ### LOOK INSIDE YOUR DRAWERS
> and try to find something to donate to the
> Ryecroft Peace Group Jumble Sale.
> For further info: see Chris Fieldsend

Of course the only person who brings me anything at all is Helen Wheatley. She rushes across at break the next day with a carrier-bag full of Pony Club annuals. 'I saw your notice.' She giggles like a gas-filled gibbon. 'I've brought you some things for the jumble sale.'

She insists on taking every item out of the plastic bag; I wish she'd hurry up and go away. 'Where is the jumble sale?' she asks me.

Oh no! I don't want her turning up. I tell her the name

of the church, knowing full well that it won't mean anything to her.

'Thanks a lot,' I say, scooping up the stuff, ramming it into the bag and revving off before she's got a chance to ask me any more. There are at least eight hundred boys in our school. What's wrong with the other seven hundred and ninety nine? It's nice to be good-looking, but only when it sets me up with girls I fancy – not when it gets Helen Wheatley sticking on to me like a Fuzzy Felt that's lost its box.

A couple of other kids ask me about the jumble sale. I explain to them about the peace group but, although they nod and say, 'Oh yeah,' and 'Great,' you can tell straight-away that they think it's something nice kids like them shouldn't get involved in.

It's like when I told Lee Furgusson on the bus the other week that I'd been to see *The War Game*. 'Is that a film?' he asked me.

'Yes. What did he think it was. A flying ballet?'

'Who was in it?'

There are a thousand and one questions you might reasonably ask of someone who's just been to see a film about the nuclear holocaust, but *who was in it* isn't one of them. I looked at Lee in despair. 'I don't know who was in it,' I told him. 'It's like a documentary. It's about nuclear war.'

Lee looked slightly more enthusiastic then and he started prattling on about some film he'd seen on TV about a nuclear war – one of those disaster movies that were all the rage five or six years ago.

I really felt fed up. It wasn't that I minded listening to Lee re-telling all the plot of this boring film in minute detail, though that was bad enough. It just felt so frustrating, want-ing to share the way I felt with someone and not knowing anybody that I could talk about it with. I listened to Lee telling me how this multi–millionaire (whose name he couldn't remember) had kidnapped this film star (whose name he also couldn't remember) and had threatened to press the button that would blow up the world, if her boy friend (whose name Lee could remember, but I can't) didn't do something completely boring and insignificant that isn't worth remembering anyway.

What happened was that I sat there feeling . . . I was going to say *lonely*, but that's not quite the word I want . . . feeling separate . . . sitting next to Lee Furgusson smiling and nodding at him and feeling as though the two of us were about as close together as neighbouring galaxies.

Sometimes I get this awareness . . . I don't know what else to call it . . . an awareness of being alone. A feeling that I'm on my own, standing on the outside looking at people like a space-invader, an android . . . smiling and nodding at their futile conversations and their minds packed tight with trivia. Making all the right responses I've been programmed to produce and knowing that, however hard I try, I can never become like them; I'll always be apart.

That's one of the things I like so much about the peace movement: a feeling that I'm with other people who think and see the same way that I do. There might be nothing much we can actually do that will stop the world from being blown up. If it does happen one day, though, the tragedy will be that so many people realised it was on the cards and never did anything to try and stop it. I just want my name written down somewhere as one of the people who didn't go gently – as one of those who raged a bit to try and stop it happening.

This is what I'd like written on the plastic bag they wrap me up in:

HERE LIE THE MANGLED, BURNT OUT,
RADIOACTIVE REMAINS OF
CHRIS FIELDSEND
Who didn't take it lying down.

Conclusion

It's easy to talk to people about what we've seen at the cinema – it's harder to talk about things that we're deeply concerned about.

A lot of things are scary the first time – like letting go on a helter-skelter or jumping off a diving board. There's no guarantee we won't get hurt – in fact, the chances are that sometimes we will; but the more we do these things, the less scared we become.

All of us are vulnerable. When we open up and tell people about things that really concern us, we're laying ourselves open to being laughed at or ridiculed. The more we hold back, though, the more vulnerable we become.

All of us desperately need to communicate. And the more we practise really talking to other people, the easier it becomes. We might then turn round and find that *we're* the friendly, open sort of people that everyone else wants to share *their* feelings with.

Prayer

May we have the courage to tell people how we feel and be good, sympathetic listeners so that others will want to talk to us.

May we be sure to always keep the confidence of those who are trusting enough to share their anxieties with us.

Amen

| Day 2 |

Speak of Talking

Introduction

Our reading today is from *The Prophet* by Kahlil Gibran.

And then a scholar said, Speak of Talking.
And he answered, saying:
You talk when you cease to be at peace with your thoughts;
And when you can no longer dwell in the solitude of your heart you live in your lips, and sound is a diversion and a pastime.
And in much of your talking, thinking is half-murdered.
For thought is a bird of space, that in a cage of words may indeed unfold its wings but cannot fly.

There are those among you who seek the talkative through fear of being alone. . . .
And there are those who talk, and without knowledge or forethought reveal a truth which they themselves do not understand.
And there are those who have the truth within them, but they tell it not in words. . . .

When you meet your friend on the roadside or in the market-place, let the spirit in you move your lips and direct your tongue.
Let the voice within your voice speak to the ear of his ear;
For his soul will keep the truth of your heart as the taste of the wine is remembered.
When the colour is forgotten and the vessel is no more.

Conclusion

'In much of your talking, thinking is half-murdered.' Sometimes we talk instead of thinking. We talk before we've decided what to say and before we've thought through what the effects of our words are likely to be.

'There are those who have the Truth within them but tell it not in words.' Other forms of communication can sometimes be more important than words: a smile, putting your hand on someone's shoulder, nodding sympathetically when they speak – all these can be more meaningful than long strings of words.

Prayer

Communication, like any other skill, needs to be learned, practised and can always be improved upon.

Let us pray that we will overcome our shyness and our fear about communicating our thoughts to other people.

When we meet our friends on the roadside or in the market-place, may the spirit within us move our lips and direct our tongues.

Amen

Day 3 The Trouble with Donovan Croft (1)

Introduction

Our next assembly on the theme of *Communication* is an extract taken from *The Trouble with Donovan Croft* by Bernard Ashley.

It tells the story of Keith Chapman whose parents decide to foster a West Indian boy called Donovan Croft.

Keith looks forward to Donovan's arrival, hoping that the two will become good friends. Donovan, however, has just been through such a distressing time at home that he's completely unable to communicate. He just refuses to speak to anyone.

Keith worries about what will happen when he takes Donovan to school on the first day of term.

The open register lay on the desk in front of Mr Henry together with his matching red and black fountain pens. . . . 'It's a simple system,' Mr Henry explained, 'and an efficient one. You merely remember your own number and call it out in order. But I only allow three seconds for waking up. If you waste my time I waste yours, and you remain behind at the end of the day for extra work. All clear? Right, now the numbers.'

The class sat up, eyes unblinking, ears cocked like hunting dogs' in case they should miss the vital number.

'Andrews, Leonard, number one.'

Andrews, Leonard, smirked. He was used to being Len, Leonard, Andrews or Leonard Andrews. But he had never been back to front before.

'Arthurs, Mark, number two.' Another smirk. 'Bamrah, Ranjit, number three.'

Mr Henry sounded the unfamiliar name out slowly, like a child with a hard book. Ranjit Singh Bamrah gave a toothy grin. 'Bamrah' was the family name normally reserved for marriage purposes – but there were too many Singhs and he had to be fitted to the English pattern somehow.

'Bell, Dennis, number four.' Mr Henry looked up with a heavy twinkle and added, 'Or should that be 'Bell, Ding-Dong, number four'?'

The class, including Dennis, laughed. It wouldn't be the last time Dennis had to laugh at one variation or another of that same joke. He had great sympathy for Mrs Pressnose.

'Chapman, Keith, number five. Croft, Donovan, number six. Delmonte, Gino, number seven . . .'

The names and the numbers were read through to the end. So far, so good. But with Donovan's name coming so close to the head of the list Keith knew that trouble could not be far away.

Donovan was sitting in his desk like a prisoner in court, head slightly bowed and hands held neatly in his lap. From behind, Keith could imagine how blank the expression was on his face. It was all he had seen since the black boy arrived. He showed not the slightest interest in anyone or anything. His eyes were glazed as if he were hypnotised and his mouth remained firmly closed. All Keith's attempts to get some answer from him, all Keith's parents attempts, all the children's attempts, had met with the same stone wall of silence. But Keith reckoned it couldn't last for much longer. Sooner or later Donovan would have to answer old Henry, and talk to him in class, or there would be an almighty row. This register business would be the first trial. Donovan might just as well be sensible and start now by calling out his number. It wasn't much to ask.

While Mr Henry was sorting out the pronunciation of a girl's name at the end of the list, Keith slid forward on his chair so that his feet were within kicking range of Donovan's ankles . . . . 'Say your number!' he hissed economically. 'Say your . . . .'

'Is that lad talking over there?' boomed Mr Henry, swivelling in his chair to face Keith. Cut short and caught squarely, Keith's face filled with a deep red as rapidly as a character in a cartoon film.

Mr Henry fixed Keith with a beady eye. He spoke almost without moving his lips.

'One lesson to learn in my class, laddie, is that when I am speaking you are silent, and when I am silent you are still silent,' he cautioned. 'That is, unless specific permission is given to the contrary. Is that clear?'

'Yes sir,' answered Keith.

'Right, then you lad will remember what I have told you and we shall continue by having a first run-through of the register. You all know your numbers. You all know where your numbers come.' A pause. 'Or perhaps if you don't you'd better revisit the infant school for a few days. Now, all sit up straight and be ready to begin on the word of command.'

He looked round to check that the troops were ready. They were.

'Right. Andrews, off you go, lad. Number . . .?'

'One,' called Len Andrews.

'Two,' followed Mark Arthurs.

The roll began at a cracking pace. Keith watched Mr Henry closely. He was bent low over his register marking in the squares with a new wooden pencil, in case of mistakes. He was not looking up as the numbers were called. Keith knew he shouldn't have to because there were no absentees.

'Three,' called Ranjit Bamrah.

'Four,' Dennis Bell followed.

Now it was Keith's turn.

'Five,' he called, his heart thumping and a choking feeling rising in his throat. There was a second's pause. Would Donovan be sensible and call out his number? It would be better for him if he did. There was an awful silence, perhaps more apparent to Keith than to anyone else. It went on. Obviously, Donovan was not going to speak.

Keith took a deep breath.

'Six,' he called, deepening his voice and clipping the word short.

'Seven,' sang out Gino Delmonte.

Keith looked up. Mr Henry was still concentrating on the register in front of him as the boys continued to go through the list. Keith breathed a temporary sigh of relief. Trouble had been averted, and he was pleased about that, but he knew very well this couldn't go on for ever. He looked again at Donovan, who hadn't moved an inch in the last ten minutes. He wouldn't be left so unaffected for long.

The roll-call was eventually completed. Mr Henry looked up, beaming.

'Well, that wasn't too bad for the dry run,' he said. 'But I shall be using my pen this afternoon, so on your toes, on your toes.'

His eyes shot over to the left corner of the room as Dave Smith slowly levered his arm into the air.

'Yes, laddie, what is it?'

'Please, sir. . . .'

'Stand up, boy, stand up when you're speaking to me or to the class. It's common courtesy.'

Dave got slowly to his feet, his eyes avoiding Keith's hot stare.

'Yes?'

'Please, sir, Chapman called out Croft's number.'

Nearly everyone else had noticed Keith's impersonation as well, and there was a nasty silence as everyone waited to see what Mr Henry would do.

The teacher looked down at his register, then across at the row of desks containing Keith and Donovan. It seemed a year before he answered. His face gave nothing away, impending anger or likely leniency.

'Ah, some confusion. Well, it seems to have sorted itself out. They're both here and they both have a mark.'

He got up and walked round to the front of his desk, picking up a blackboard pointer as he went. Then he leaned back against his desk, the pointer horizontal between both hands, and cautioned his squad.

'But I want a good run this afternoon,' he said. 'I'll be watching very carefully for mistakes. Watching very carefully . . . .'

Conclusion

Keith's parents had told the school about Donovan's problems, but the message never reached Mr Henry. Without this message, Mr Henry had little hope of understanding Donovan's behaviour.

Explaining a difficult situation, particularly to someone in authority, can take a lot of courage; but we can't expect people to be sympathetic when they don't understand what the problem is.

Prayer

May we have the courage to try and explain our problems to those people who can help us.

When we have friends who find it particularly hard to express themselves, may we be always willing to do what we can to help

Amen

Day 4 **The Trouble with Donovan Croft (2)**

'All right,' said Mr Henry. 'Up straight and concentrate.'

He held his red pen poised above the long column in the register.

'Andrews?'

Len Andrews began the ritual. 'One.'

'Two.'

'Three.'

The first three boys called their numbers. Then they turned in their seats to get a good view of Donovan and Keith. Like safe spectators at a motor race they were waiting for misfortune to hit someone else. Quick glances at Mr Henry told them that he had not looked up yet, but Keith guessed he was not as engrossed in the register as he pretended.

'Four,' called Dennis Bell, and another thick red line was stroked across a printed square in the book.

Now it was Keith's turn. Mr Henry glanced up from beneath his full grey eyebrows and stared intently at him.

'Five, sir,' called Keith.

His words hung in the silence which followed and they echoed in the bare room. Now everyone was waiting for

Donovan. He neither moved nor spoke. It was as if his body was present but his mind was elsewhere. In the silence Mr Henry glanced back to his register and inked in Keith's mark. Keith's heart pounded faster. This was it. He hadn't meant to try, but without thinking of the consequences Keith took a wild half chance. Swiftly raising his hand to cover his mouth, he called Donovan's number.

'Six.'

It was a daft thing to do. He could never get away with it. There was an immediate stir in the room, but Dave Smith was the first to give the disturbance a clear voice.

'Please, sir, that was Chapman!' he shouted in triumph from his seat in the corner.

'It wasn't, sir,' Keith began denying hotly, but Mr Henry was already on his feet. In four angry strides he marched down the aisle and stood over Keith.

'I don't know what stupid and insolent game you two are playing,' he shouted at Keith and Donovan, 'but I am not having this sort of behaviour in my class.'

His voice was fast and thin with real anger, as distinct from the slow thunder of his usual acted outrage.

'Stand up!' he commanded Keith.

Keith did so. Mr Henry backed a pace to stand towering over Donovan.

'Stand up, boy!' he repeated.

Donovan slowly got up and stood looking sullenly forward through half-closed lids, the picture of what Mr Henry called dumb insolence, his old army term for a man who made clear what he was thinking without saying a word.

'If you idiots think you can get away with this sort of out-rageous behaviour in my class you are very much mistaken!' shouted Mr Henry. 'How dare you! How dare you!' he demanded, his hands on his hips, bending forward at the waist. 'What's your name?' he shouted at Keith.

'Chapman, sir.'

'Chapman,' Mr Henry repeated, as if the name was something he had found stinking under his shoe.

He twisted back to Donovan. 'And what's your name?' he shouted.

For a second or so the only sound to be heard was that of Mr Henry noisily replacing his spent breath. Donovan said nothing but remained looking sullenly forward.

'I said, "What's your name?"' shouted Mr Henry, his voice rising a tone higher.

There was still no reply.

'You!' screamed Mr Henry, pushing Donovan's shoulder and almost rocking him off balance. 'What is your name?'

'Please, sir, it's Croft, sir,' said Keith from behind the silent Donovan. 'Please, sir, he can't–'

'I know it's Croft,' cut in Mr Henry, turning and spitting words over Keith. 'You mind your own business!' He swung back at Donovan. 'You, Croft,' his voice screamed even higher, 'What is your name?'

As he spoke he punctuated each of the last four words with sharp blows to Donovan's shoulder, rocking him harder each time until with the final shout Donovan stumbled back across his chair.

As he regained his balance, his face still closed and secret and his dead eyes staring ahead, Mr Henry pushed himself round in front of the desk and stared with bulging eyes into Donovan's face. His chest heaved as he gulped oxygen into his system.

'Tell me!' he shrieked, any grip he had had on his temper now slipping completely from him, totally out of control. 'Tell me your name!'

As he raged, he slapped Donovan hard across the face with the palm of his hand.

'Tell me, you stupid black idiot!'

The words stamped themselves indelibly in 36 minds as Donovan stood there saying nothing. But the hot tears which rolled down his cheeks told their own story of pain and misery.

'Get out! Get outside the door!' screeched Mr Henry in a last high-pitched attack. 'I'm not having it. I am not having it.'

His voice dropped an octave. He suddenly seemed to regain control of himself as Donovan walked slowly out of his place, down the aisle, and out of the class-room door.

'Sit down, Chapman,' he said, his face scarlet. 'You've not heard the last of this. You've not heard anything like the last of this.'

Conclusion

Mr Henry may have thought he was making Donovan look foolish but, when people lose control of themselves like that, they are the ones who look stupid.

Mr Henry was deliberately trying to make Donovan feel

small, hurt and upset but, later on in the story, it is Mr Henry who finishes up feeling most upset and embarrassed at what he's done.

Prayer

Let us give thanks for the precious gift of speech. May we use our words to comfort and console and give pleasure and happiness to others – never deliberately to make someone else feel hurt and upset.

May we avoid saying to other people things we would hate them to say to us.

Amen

Day 5 | **Howlers**

It's often difficult to say what we mean and it can be even more difficult for some of us when we have to write it down.

Some people, when they are answering questions in tests and examinations, try so hard to impress that they finish up writing sentences which don't make any sense at all. Other people, who don't know the answers, sometimes try to make it look as though they do.

Here are a few examples:

- Parallel lines are lines which get nearer together as they get further apart.
- Tarzan is a short name for the American flag. Its full name is Tarzan stripes.
- The inhabitants of Moscow are called mosquitoes.
- The inhabitants of Paris are called Parisites.
- The population of California is getting a bit too thick.
- In France even the pheasants drink wine.
- *Question*: Name six animals to be found in the Arctic. *Answer*: Three bears and three seals.
- A cuckoo is a bird what lays other birds' eggs in its nest.
- A hostage has long legs, a long neck and nice feathers.
- Barbarians are little balls they put in bicycles to make the wheels run smooth.
- A fort is a place to put men soldiers in and a fortress is a place to put women soldiers in.

■ The footballers certainly worked as a team, weaving and unweaving their combinations.

And, just to prove that it is not only pupils who make mistakes:

— ■ 'Please Sir, Excuse Freddy's absence from school. I had a baby. It wasn't his fault . . .'

— ■ 'Dear Sir, Kindly excuse Jimmy's absence from school yesterday. He fell in the river. By doing same, you will oblige.'

There is no bullying in the school – but it's got to be stopped.

Conclusion

What all these people failed to do, of course, was read through their work afterwards, imagining that they were the person reading it.

The secret of good communication is to put yourself into the minds of your audience – to anticipate how you would react if you were reading what you are about to write, or listening to what you are about to say.

Prayer

May we learn to think before we speak and before we write.

May our teachers be blessed with understanding and may they be tolerant and sympathetic towards those pupils who find it hard to explain what they mean.

Amen

May Our God bless us and all people everywhere and fill our hearts with peace and goodwill to our fellows.

20 Democracy – Assemblies Suitable for Election Week

See also Class Assemblies on Apartheid, page 237, and Martin Luther King, page 234.

Day 1	**The Frogs Who Wanted a King**

The frogs were living happy as could be
    In a wet marsh to which they all were suited;
From every sort of trouble they were free,
    And all night long they croaked, and honked, and hooted.
But one fine day a bull-frog said, 'The thing
We never had and *must* have is a king.'

So all the frogs immediately prayed:
    'Great Jove,' they chorused from their swampy border,
'Send us a king and he will be obeyed,
    A king to bring a rule of Law and Order.'
Jove heard and chuckled. That night in their home
There fell a large and most impressive stone.

The swamp was silent; nothing breathed. At first
    The badly frightened frogs did never *once* stir;
But gradually some neared and even durst
    To touch, aye, even dance upon, the monster.
Whereat they croaked again, 'Great Jove, oh hear!
Send us a *living* king, a king to fear!'

Once more Jove smiled, and sent them down a Stork.
    'Long live – !' they croaked. But 'ere they framed the
                               sentence,
The Stork bent down and, scorning knife or fork,

Swallowed them all, with no time for repentance!
The moral's this: No matter what your lot,
It might be worse. Be glad with what you've got.

Joseph Lauren

Conclusion

The frogs wanted a leader – someone to look up to; someone, they said, that they could fear.

The stork seemed like a suitable leader in that it was big, powerful and strong and, probably, quite clever. But it didn't have the interest of the frogs at heart.

There have been occasions throughout history when people have chosen leaders because they seemed powerful and strong but this quest for power has led to the destruction of those who voted for them. The story of the frogs and the king isn't as silly as it first appears.

We might ask ourselves why the frogs wanted a king in the first place when they seemed perfectly capable of looking after themselves. Perhaps they wanted someone else to make decisions for them and to stop them having to think things out for themselves – someone else to blame when things went wrong.

In a democracy we don't choose someone else to do the thinking for us. We have to think things out for ourselves and choose the leaders whose policies we agree with and whose ideas will be best for our town or for our country.

Prayer

In our own lives, may we choose our friends carefully. May we not allow ourselves to be influenced too readily by people who seem powerful and strong but who do not have our best interests at heart.

Amen

| Day 2 | ## Auschwitz

On 27 January 1945, at the end of the Second World War, the Soviet army entered what had become, under the Germans, the largest cemetery on earth – the concentration camp at Auschwitz in Poland. Approximately two million men,

women and children had been killed there – most of them in huge gas chambers built to look like showers. Sometimes as many as two thousand people would be gassed in half an hour. Teeth and hair were removed from the corpses and fleshy parts of the bodies were hacked off for rendering down to make soap. Then the bodies were cremated in huge ovens. At the end of the war, seven tons of human hair was discovered at Auschwitz waiting to be sold as stuffing for mattresses and cushions.

Auschwitz was only one concentration camp amongst many. The people who were sent there were the handicapped, the mentally ill, people who opposed Hitler's fascist regime and, most particularly, Jewish people whom Hitler had persuaded the Germans to think of as their enemies.

It was not until after the concentration camps were liberated that the rest of the world learned about the atrocities which had taken place; when they found out they were horrified. In particular, they couldn't understand how the German people had allowed such atrocities to happen. The majority of Germans must have had some idea of what had been happening – many of them knew of families of Jews who had died or simply disappeared or else they knew of handicapped children who had been sent away and exterminated. Why hadn't they done more to try and stop it? Why hadn't the churches done anything? Hitler had made his hatred of the Jews clear in his election programme and yet good, Christian people had still voted for him. How could they?

Hitler killed himself at the end of the war but many of his officers were brought to trial in Nuremberg at an international court. People thought that such men must be brutal, sadistic thugs to have carried out so many murders and yet the majority of those on trial were pleasant family men who were fond of animals, who loved their children and who even went to church. They had not actually enjoyed watching so many people suffer but regarded it as a necessary part of their job. Because they were told by the government that it was right to murder the Jews and the handicapped, they had never really questioned it – they never thought for themselves about what was right or wrong but simply did as they were told. Their defence was that, as soldiers, it was their duty to obey orders. The court rejected their excuses and most of them were found guilty and sentenced to death or imprisonment.

The conclusions of the Nuremberg international court showed that, in a democracy, all of us are responsible for what is done by our government. It was not just Hitler or the Gestapo who were responsible for the death of the Jews but the rest of the German people who voted Hitler into power; they who knew what was happening and never raised any objections.

We normally associate obedience – doing as we're told – with being good. We say that children are good when they obey their parents or their teachers. It is important, however, that we do not go through life like sheep – always doing as we're told – even when we know that we are causing harm to ourselves or anyone else.

Prayer

May we learn to respect those in authority who have our best interests or the interests of our communities at heart. May we learn to judge whether someone's leadership is good or bad and have the courage to withdraw from those who are doing evil.

Amen

Day 3

Pastor Niemoeller

Introduction

When we learn about the horrors that happened in concentration camps, it is easy for us to feel anger at those who should have spoken out against such atrocities and never did; but speaking out against injustice is not always as easy as it sounds. Today's reading is by a priest called Pastor Niemoeller who was himself a victim of the Nazis in Germany.

First they came for the Jews
and I did not speak out
because I was not a Jew.

Then they came for the communists
and I did not speak out
because I was not a communist.

Then they came for the trade unionists
and I did not speak out
because I was not a trade unionist.

Then they came for me –
and there was no one left
to speak out for me.

Conclusion

If you are with a group of friends who are tormenting or
bullying someone it takes a bit of courage to tell them they
ought to stop. It is easy just to say, 'Oh, leave them alone'
but if it carries on you need to do more than that.

It is often possible to criticise someone's actions without
criticising them as a person – you can make it clear that you
like and respect a person but are still unhappy about a particular thing that they're doing.

A great deal of harm is done in the world not because of
evil people but because of nice, well-meaning people who
have simply kept silent when they should have spoken out.

Prayer

Let us remember in our prayers today prisoners of conscience – those who are in prison all over the world whose
only crime has been to speak out against the injustice of their
government. May we have the courage to speak out against
the wrongs we see around us.

Amen

Day 4   ## The Landscape

When I asked him why he had come,
he said, 'I have come to repaint the landscape.'
'I am rather fond of these old colours,' I said.
But he shook his head. 'Everything must be repainted.'
I watched him mix the new colours on his palate.
There was midnight black and fiery red.
'But they are such simple colours!'
'The simplest,' he said.

I watched him set up his easel.
It towered above us in the sky.
'How long will all this take?' I said.
'Seconds,' he said. 'Split seconds, less.'
And then his brush swept the horizon,
obscuring the outline of the hills.
The sky was midnight black,
the earth was fiery red.
He turned to me, his face as grey as lead.
'Why did you let me do that?' he said.
'You could have stopped me,
you saw the colours, black and red,
you stood and watched me mix them.'
'I am an ordinary man,' I said.
'I do not paint landscapes.'
'But it was your landscape,' he said,
'and now your sky is midnight black
and your earth is fiery red,
and our faces are grey, as grey as lead.'

Stephen Plaice

Conclusion

Information and technology are increasing at such an alarming rate that none of us can keep up; we have to rely on the advice of experts in areas we know nothing about; we can't all be lawyers, architects or surgeons – we have to trust those who are to get on with their jobs properly.

That does not mean, however, that we do not have to make moral decisions and we do not have responsibility for our own lives.

We do not expect lawyers to make laws – our governments decide which laws should be made and it's the job of lawyers to see that they're carried out.

We would not expect a surgeon to decide whether or not a woman should have an abortion – that's a moral and personal decision for a woman to make for herself.

We pay architects to design our towns for us but it is our responsibility as citizens to make it clear how we want them to be planned.

'*I am an ordinary man,*' *I said.*
'*I do not paint landscapes.*'
'*But it was your landscape . . .*'
If we *should* wake up one morning and find that our land-

scape has been wiped out whilst we have been sleeping, we can not then claim, too late, that the landscape never had anything to do with us.

Prayer

Let us give thanks for those who have fought and worked for our right to have a say in the government of our city, our county and our country. May we do those people justice by thinking carefully about issues that concern us, finding out the facts and, when we are able to vote, doing so with responsibility and thought.

Amen

| Day 5 | **Voting** |

It was strange really
that the swallows returned on polling day –
two of them
chasing each other
perhaps in play or combat
above the old school polling station.
I went in
voted as usual:
'Billie Haigh
married – one child –
six years on council',
then coming out
I noticed a curious pattern in the sky –
two strands of cirrus
forming a cross.
Maybe, I thought,
one of the Gods has voted –
drawing his mark up there on heaven's blue.
But what has he voted for? –
Something to do with tax reform,
or a fall in the cost of postage? –
or just that year by year
and age by age
swallows return.

Ian Emberson

Prayer

Let us give thanks for the joy and beauty of our world – for the yearly renewal of life, for the miracle of returning swallows – for the richness and variety of our planet.

Let *us* pray that, year by year, the world will continue to be renewed and that, age by age, the swallows will always return.

Amen

21 When You Are Old

The Assemblies on Days Four and Five would be appropriate in the event of the death of someone at school.

Day 1 When You Are Old

Introduction

Today's reading is a poem written by the famous Irish poet, William Butler Yeats. It's a poem about old age – written to an older woman when she is looking back upon her youth.

When you are old and grey and full of sleep,
And nodding by the fire, take down this book,
And slowly read, and dream of the soft look
Your eyes had once, and of their shadows deep;

How many loved your moments of glad grace,
And loved your beauty with love false or true,
But one man loved the pilgrim soul in you,
And loved the sorrows of your changing face;

And bending down beside the glowing bars,
Murmur, a little sadly, how Love fled
And paced upon the mountains overhead
And hid his face amid a crowd of stars.

Prayer

Let us remember that life is short. May we strive to do what good we can so that, when we become old, we shall be able to look back upon our youth with no regrets.

May the Spirit of Our God direct our thoughts

Amen

and help us to learn of him with honest hearts now
+ always
Amen

Beatitudes for the Aged

Introduction

Our reading today is about some of the problems that are experienced by many elderly people.

> Blessed are they who understand
> My faltering step and palsied hand.
> Blessed are they who know my ears today
> Must strain to catch the things they say.
> Blessed are they who seem to know
> My eyes are dim and wits are slow.
> Blessed are they who look away
> When coffee was spilt on the table today.
> Blessed are they with a cheery smile,
> Who stop to chat for a little while.
> Blessed are they who never say
> 'You've told that story twice today.'
> Blessed are they who know the way
> To bring back memories of yesterday.
> Blessed are they who make it known
> I'm loved, respected, and not alone.
> Blessed are they who ease the days
> On my journey home in loving ways.

Anonymous

Prayer

Let us give thanks for our parents and our grandparents and remember to treat them with respect. May we have the patience to listen to elderly people when they want to talk to us. Let us ask their advice whenever we can and show our appreciation of them.

Amen

The Long Walk

Introduction

Today's reading is an abridged version of a short story called *The Long Walk*. The writer, George Layton, is writing about his childhood memories and, in this story, he tells how he enjoyed his grandad taking him out for walks.

'Where are we going, Grandad, where are you taking us?'

He looked at me. His eyes were watering a bit and he wiped them with a dark blue hanky he always had in his top pocket.

'We're going on a walk – a special walk.'

He was almost whispering, as if he didn't want me mum to hear, bending down with his whiskery face next to mine.

'Where are we going, Grandad . . . ?'

'You'll see son, when we get there.'

He looked a bit sad for a minute, but then he smiled and put on his flat cap.

'C'mon son, let's get going.'

My mum gave us each a pack of sandwiches and off we went. We must have looked a funny sight walking down the road together me and my grandad. Him dressed in his flat cap and thick overcoat and clogs. Me in my maroon wind-cheater and short grey trousers . . . .

'Are we walking all the way, Grandad?' He took such big strides that I was half-walking and half-running.

'No son, we'll get a trackless first to get out a bit.'

By 'trackless' he meant a bus, and I'd heard him say it so often that I never wondered why he said trackless.

'I'll show you where I used to go when I was a lad.'

We didn't have to wait long before a bus came, and we went upstairs and sat right at the front. Grandad was out of breath when we sat down.

'Are you all right, Grandad?'

'Oh aye son. You get a better view up here.'

. . . Soon we were going through the 'posh part' where the snobs lived. This was on the other side of the park.

The conductor came round for our fares.

'One and t'lad to the basin.'

I'd never heard of the basin before. After my grandad had paid our fares I asked him what it was.

'What's the basin, Grandad?'

'That's where we start our walk.'

'What basin is it? Why is it called "basin"?'

'The canal basin – it's where the canal starts. You'll see.'

. . . While we were going down the stairs, I held tight onto my grandad. Not because I thought I might fall, but I was scared for him. He looked as though he was going to go straight from the top to the bottom.

'Are you all right, Grandad? Don't fall.'

He just told me not to be frightened and to hold on tight.

'That's right. You hold onto me son – you'll be all right – don't be frightened.'

We both got off the bus, and I watched it drive away. I didn't know where we were, but it was very quiet.

'It's nice here, isn't it Grandad?'

'This is where my dad was born – your great-grandad.'

It was a lovely place. There weren't many shops and there didn't seem to be many people either. By the bus stop was a big stone thing full of water.

'Hey, Grandad, is that where the horses used to drink?'

'That's right, son. I used to hold my grandad's horse there while it was drinking.'

I couldn't see anything like a basin.

I wondered where it was.

'Where's the basin, Grandad?'

'We've got to walk there. C'mon.'

We went away from the main street, into a side street, past all these little houses. I don't think any cars ever went down this street 'cos there was washing strung out right across the road – all the way down the street. The sun was shining – not hot – but just nice. When we got further down the street, I saw that it was a cul-de-sac.

'Hey, Grandad, it's a dead-end. We must've come the wrong way.'

Grandad just smiled.

'Do you think I'm that old, that I can't remember the way? Here, look.'

He took my hand and showed me the way. Just before the last house in the road was a tiny snicket. It was so narrow that we had to go through behind each other. I wouldn't have even noticed this snicket if my grandad hadn't shown it to me.

'Go on son, through there.'

It was very dark and all you could see was a little speck of light at the other end, so you can tell how long it was.

'You go first, Grandad.'

'No, after you, son.'

I didn't want to go first.

'No, you'd better go first, Grandad, 'cos you know the way, don't you?'

He laughed and put his hand in his pocket and brought out a few boiled sweets.

'Here you are. These are for the journey. Off we go for the last time.'

I was just going to ask him what he meant, but he carried on talking.

'I mean it'll soon be winter, won't it. Come on.'

And off we went through the dark passage. Grandad told me that when he was a kid they used to call it the Black Hole of Calcutta. Soon we reached the other end and it was quite strange 'cos it was like going through a door into the country. We ended up at the top of some steps – high above the canal basin, and you could see for miles. I could only see one barge though, in the basin. We went down the steps. There were 115 steps – I counted them. Grandad was going down slowly so I was at the bottom before him.

'Grandad, there are 115 steps there, I counted them. C'mon let's look at that barge.'

I ran over to have a look at it and Grandad followed me.

'It's like a house isn't it, Grandad?'

'It is a house. Someone lives there. C'mon, let's sit here and have our sandwiches.'

And we did.

The sun was very big and round, though it wasn't very hot, and the leaves on the trees were golden, and the reflection in the water made the canal look golden. There was nobody else about, and all the noises that you never noticed usually, suddenly sounded special, different. Like the siren that let the workers know it was dinner-time.

When we'd finished our sandwiches we walked along the canal . . . and soon we came to a village. My Grandad said we'd catch a bus home from there, but first he wanted to show me something, and he took hold of my hand. I didn't have a clue where he was taking me, but I got a shock when we ended up in the grave-yard. It had gone cold now. I wanted to go home.

'C'mon, Grandad, let's go home now.'

But he didn't seem to be listening properly.

'In a minute son, I just want to show you summat.'

And hand in hand we walked among the grave-stones.

'There you are, son, there's my plot. That's where I'll be laid to rest.'

I didn't know what to say.

'When, Grandad?'

'Soon.'

He smiled and looked very happy and he bent down and pulled out a couple of weeds. It was a very neat plot.

'C'mon son, we'd best get going now.'

When I told my mum that night that Grandad was going to die soon, she got very cross and told me not to talk like that.

'He's as fit as a fiddle is your grandad. Don't you talk like that.'

It happened three days later – at dinner-time. It came as a great shock to everybody, except of course to me and Grandad.

Conclusion

The writer of this story accepted that his grandad was old and that he would die soon. This doesn't mean that he didn't love his grandad because obviously they were very fond of each other.

Many people, like the boy's mother, are afraid of talking about death – they just try not to think about it. But then, when it does happen to someone they love, they find the sudden shock and sense of loss probably much more difficult to cope with.

Prayer

We shall pass through this world but once. If, therefore, there be any kindness we can show or any good thing we can do, let us do it now; may we not defer it or neglect it, for we shall not pass this way again.

Amen

Day 4   **Why Bad Things Happen to Good People**

Introduction

Today's reading is an extract from a book called *Why Bad Things Happen to Good People* by a Jewish rabbi called Harold Kushner.

In his book, Kushner explains his point of view that it is quite wrong of people to assume that it's God's will for someone to die at a particular time. He explains that God does not cause us to have an accident, nor does he send us terrible diseases nor withhold miraculous cures from us.

I don't know why people are mortal and fated to die, and

I don't know why people die at the time and in the way they do. Perhaps we can try to understand it by picturing what the world would be like if people lived forever.

In Homer's *Odyssey*, there is a passage in which Ulysses meets Calypso, a sea princess and child of the gods. Calypso, a divine being, is immortal. She will never die. She is fascinated by Ulysses, never having met a mortal before. As we read on, we come to realise that Calypso envies Ulysses because he will not live forever. His life becomes more full of meaning, his every decision is more significant, precisely because his time is limited, and what he chooses to do with it represents a real choice.

In Jonathan Swift's fantasy, *Gulliver's Travels*, it happened once or twice in a generation that a child was born with a circular red spot on its forehead, signifying that it would never die. Gulliver imagines those children to be the most fortunate people imaginable . . . . But as he comes to meet them, he realises that they are in fact the most miserable and pitiable of creatures. They grow old and feeble. Their friends . . . die off. At the age of 80, their property is taken from them and given to their children, who would otherwise never inherit from them. Their bodies contract various ailments . . . and they can never look forward to being released from the pain of living.

Homer shows us the immortal being envying us for being mortal. Swift teaches us to pity the person who can not die. He wants us to realise that living with the knowledge that we will die may be frightening and tragic, but knowing we will never die would be unbearable . . . .

If people lived forever and never died, one of two things would have to happen. Either the world would become impossibly crowded, or else people would avoid having children to avoid that crowding. Humanity would be deprived of that sense of a fresh start . . . which the birth of a child represents. In a world where people lived forever, we would probably never have been born.

But . . . we have to acknowledge that it is one thing to explain that mortality in general is good for people in general. It is something else again to try to tell someone who has lost a parent, a wife or a child, that death is good. We don't dare try to do that. It would be cruel and thoughtless. All we can say to someone at a time like that is that vulnerability to death is one of the given conditions of life. We can't explain it any more than we can explain life itself. We can't control it, or sometimes even postpone it. All we can do is try to rise beyond the question *why did it happen?* and begin to ask the question: *what do I do now that it has happened?*

Prayer

Let us pray for the strength to enable us to come to terms with sorrow.

When we have to face tragedy in life, may we use it to deepen our understanding so that, through it, we may grow in patience, acceptance and humility.

Amen

Day 5

Joy and Sorrow

Today's reading is from *The Prophet* by Kahlil Gibran.

Then a woman said, Speak to us of Joy and Sorrow.

And he answered:

The deeper that sorrow carves into your being, the more joy you can contain.

When you are joyous, look deep into your heart and you shall find it is only that which has given you sorrow that is giving you joy.

When you are sorrowful, look again in your heart, and you shall see that in truth you are weeping for that which has been your delight . . .

Your pain is the breaking of the shell that encloses your understanding.

Even as the stone of the fruit must break, that its heart may stand in the sun, so must you know pain.

And could you keep your heart in wonder at the daily miracles of life . . . you would accept the seasons of your heart, even as you have always accepted the seasons that pass over your fields.

And you would watch with serenity through the winters of your grief.

Much of your pain is self-chosen.

It is the bitter potion by which the physician within you heals your sick self.

Therefore, trust the physician, and drink his remedy in silence and tranquility . . . .

Kahlil Gibran

Conclusion

We accept, as Gibran says, 'The seasons that pass over our fields' because we know we can rely on the fact that after winter there will always be spring and summer again. What Gibran calls the 'seasons of our hearts' are more difficult to accept. We sometimes feel as though life is one long winter – we can't see the light at the end of the tunnel.

There is often a purpose in our unhappiness even though, at the time, we can't understand what the purpose is. Learning to understand ourselves can be a painful experience but something we have to do before we can share our thoughts and ourselves with others. We feel angry and disappointed when we fail at something – something we have been trying to learn or a relationship we've worked at; but we may fail because that thing isn't right for us – there may be something or someone much better waiting for us later on.

Prayer

Pain, says Gibran, is the bitter potion by which the physician inside us heals our sick selves.

May we have the courage to trust the physician and to drink his remedy in silence and tranquility.

Amen

Day 1 | To Everything There Is a Season

Our assemblies this week are centred on the theme of Time. The first reading is from the Old Testament, from the book of Ecclesiastes:

> The thing that hath been, it is that which shall be; and that which is done is that which shall be done; and there is no new thing under the sun. . .
>
> To everything there is a season, and a time to every purpose under the heaven.
>
> A time to be born and a time to die; a time to plant and a time to pluck up that which is planted.
>
> A time to kill and a time to heal; a time to break down and a time to build up.
>
> A time to weep and a time to laugh; a time to mourn and a time to dance.
>
> A time to get and a time to lose; a time to keep and a time to cast away.
>
> A time to rend and a time to sew; a time to keep silence and a time to speak.
>
> That which hath been, is now; and that which is to be hath already been; and God requireth that which is past.
>
> All go unto one place; all are of the dust, and all turn to dust again.
>
> Wherefore I perceive that there is nothing better than that a man should rejoice in his own works; for that is his portion; for who shall bring him to see what shall be after him?

Ecclesiastes 1: 9; 3: 1–8, 15, 20, 22 Authorised version

Conclusion

When we go through bad times, it's easy to be impatient and feel that nothing can ever improve. Life doesn't come with a guarantee that things will always be easy.

Someone once said that 'the world is a wheel and will all come round all right.' We have to go through good times and through bad, through 'times to laugh' as well as through 'times to cry'. We have to learn to be patient and take consolation in the fact that things usually do turn out right for us in the end.

Prayer

Today's prayer is a translation of a Frankfurt prayer from the 16th century.

The Scripture says: 'There is a time for silence and a time for speech'. Lord, teach us the silence of humility, the silence of wisdom, the silence of love, the silence of perfection, the silence that speaks without words, the silence of faith.

Lord, teach us to silence our own hearts that we may listen to the gentle movements of the Holy Spirit within us and sense the depths which are of God.

Amen

Day 2   **Lord, I Have Time**

I went out, Lord.
Men were coming out.
They were coming and going,
Walking and running.
Everything was rushing: cars, lorries, the street, the whole town.

Goodbye Sir, excuse me, I haven't time.
I'll come back, I can't wait; I haven't time.
I must end this letter – I haven't time.
I'd love to help you but I haven't time.
I can't think, I can't read, I'm swamped, I haven't time.
I'd like to pray, but I haven't time.

You understand, Lord, they simply haven't the time.
The child is playing, he hasn't time right now. . .

Later on. . .
The schoolboy has his homework to do, he hasn't
time . . .
Later on . . .
The young man at his sports, he hasn't time . . .
Later on. . .
The young married man has his new house, he has to fix
it up, he hasn't time. . .
Later on . . .
The grandparents have their grandchildren, they haven't
time . . . Later on . . .
They are dying, they have no . . .
Too late! They have no more time!

And so all men run after time, Lord.
They pass through life running – hurried, jostled,
overburdened, frantic
and they never get there. They haven't time, in spite
of all their efforts.
Lord, you must have made a mistake in your calculations.
The hours are too short,
The days are too short,
Our iives are too short.

You who are beyond time, Lord, you smile to see us
fighting it.
And you know what you are doing.
You make no mistakes in your distribution of time to men.
You give each one time to do what you want him to do.

But we must not lose time
waste time,
kill time,
For time is a gift that does not keep.

Lord, I have all the time that you give me.
The years of my life,
The days of my years,
The hours of my days,
They are all mine.
Mine to fill, quietly, calmly,
But to fill completely, up to the brim,
To offer them to you, that of their insipid water
You may make a rich wine such as you once made in Cana
of Galilee.

I am not asking you, Lord, for time to do this and then
    that
But your grace to do conscientiously in the time that
    you give me,
What you want me to do.

Michel Quoist

Prayer

Let us try to make sure that we use our time for things that
are important. May we never be so busy that we don't find
time to stop and think what life is about. Let us make time
to consider what we want to do with our lives.

Lord, give us your grace to do conscientiously in the time
that you give us, what you want us to do.

Amen

Day 3 | **An Old Irish Prayer**

Take time to work –
it is the price of success.
Take time to think –
it is the source of power.
Take time to play –
it is the secret of perpetual youth.
Take time to read –
it is the foundation of wisdom.
Take time to be friendly –
it is the road to happiness.
Take time to dream –
it is hitching your wagon to a star.
Take time to love and be loved –
it is the privilege of the Gods.
Take time to look around –
the day is too short to be selfish.
Take time to laugh –
it is the music of the soul.

Prayer

May we learn to order our lives in such a way that we always
leave time for the things that are important. May we never

be too busy to care for others and may we always leave a little time for being kind and gentle to ourselves.

Amen

Day 4   **Leisure**

What is this life if, full of care,
We have no time to stand and stare?

No time to stand beneath the boughs
And stare as long as sheep or cows.

No time to see, when woods we pass,
Where squirrels hide their nuts in grass.

No time to see, in broad daylight,
Streams full of stars, like skies at night.

No time to turn at Beauty's glance,
And watch her feet, how they can dance.

No time to wait till her mouth can
Enrich that smile her eyes began.

A poor life this if, full of care,
We have no time to stand and stare.

W H Davies

Prayer

May we find time to appreciate the beauty of the world around us. May we find time for stillness and for peace – even in a crowded room – even on a crowded day.

Amen

Rising Five

(For the last day of term)

Introduction

If you were asked what was important about this week, most of you would probably not mention anything that's actually happened to you; you'd probably say that this is the week when you break up for the school holidays.

If you can remember as far back as the end of the summer term at your last school, the chances are that you were looking forward to leaving and starting your new school. Now the first years are looking forward to the time when they'll be in the second year; the second years are looking forward to the third year and older pupils are looking forward to leaving school, hoping that they'll get a job or go on to college or university.

Older teenagers often look forward to the time when they can leave home and be independent. Then they look forward to setting up their own home and having children. When parents have very young children, they often look forward to the time when their children will be grown up – when they can have some peace and quiet again. Then they look forward to being grandparents. They look forward to the day when they can retire from work. At last, they think they'll be able to sit back and enjoy life and really start to relax but, when they do, they often realise that the best and the most rewarding years of their lives have already gone. They feel regrets that they've wished away the happiest times of their lives.

And that's what this morning's reading is about – the fact that, if we're not careful, we can find ourselves wishing away the best years of our lives.

The poem is called *Rising Five* and it's by Norman Nicholson. 'Rising Five' is a term used to describe children who are still four but nearly five – children who are just about ready for starting school.

> 'I'm rising five,' he said,
> 'Not four,' and little coils of hair
> Unlicked themselves upon his head.
> His spectacles, brimful of eyes to stare
> At me and the meadow, reflected cones of light
> Above his toffee-buckled cheeks. He'd been alive

Fifty six months or perhaps a week more:
  Not four
But rising five.

Around him in the field the cells of spring
Bubbled and doubled; buds unbuttoned; shoot
And stem shook out the creases from their frills,
And every tree was swilled with green.
It was the season after blossoming,
Before the forming of the fruit:
  not May,
But rising June.
  And in the sky
The dust dissected the tangential light:
  not day,
But rising night;
  not now,
But rising soon.
The new buds push the old leaves from the bough.
We drop our youth behind us like a boy
Throwing away his toffee wrappers. We never see
  the flower,
But only the fruit in the flower; never the fruit,
But only the rot in the fruit. We look for the marriage bed
In the baby's cradle, we look for the grave in the bed:
  not living.
But rising dead.

Norman Nicholson

Prayer

Let us remember that the morning of our lives is short and beautiful. We are only young once.

May we strive never to wish our lives away, but to treasure every moment . . . every experience. We shall not pass this way again. May we live our lives to the full.

Amen

$\boxed{23}$ Subject-based Assemblies

$\boxed{\text{Day 1}}$ ### Geography – Holidays

Preparation

Teachers can use their own holiday slides for this or, alternatively, borrow slides of a beautiful part of any country to be shown in conjunction with appropriate music.

If slides are available of local beauty spots or interesting areas as well, these can be added afterwards. Most of the assembly should consist simply of slides and music.

When we look at pictures or photographs of places that are famous for their beauty, it's easy to sit back and marvel about what a beautiful world we live in.

We don't often think that about our own area – the places we see everyday – but every part of the country has a beauty of its own and a special character which sometimes people from elsewhere discover and appreciate more than we do.

If we see photographs of our own area on a calendar or on film, that will often bring home to us the special character and beauty that has been stuck under our own noses – that we walk past every day without appreciating it.

Prayer

May we open our eyes to the wonder and beauty of our world. May we each try to play our part in keeping the world such a beautiful place.

Amen

Day 2

Geography – Holland

Introductory music with slides of Holland (tulips, windmills, canals etc.) although not essential, would make an interesting beginning to this assembly.

Holland is a small country, less than a third the size of England, with a large population. It is particularly famous for bulbs and flowers. The Dutch are great lovers of plants. Most Dutch houses have very small gardens but people compensate for this by filling their houses and window sills with elaborate displays of plants.

Two fifths of Holland's surface lies below sea level and, for 900 years, the Dutch have struggled to reclaim their land. There is a saying:

'God made the world but the Dutch made Holland.'

The Dutch have made their country twice as big as it used to be by reclaiming land from the sea. Very briefly, this is how it is done:

(An overhead transparency might be used here)

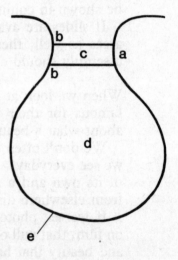

a) A dam is built across the narrowest part of the sea with two walls of heavy clay.

b) The walls are strengthened with stones to stop the sea washing them away.

c) The space between the walls is pumped out and filled with sand.

d) The water is pumped out from here and trenches are built to drain away more water.

e) What is left is a piece of land called a 'polder'.

Changing the physical structure of a country must have seemed an impossible task, but it has been done successfully in Holland by careful planning and by the committed work of many people over a very long period of time.

Tasks which at first may seem impossible can be achieved by people working together, each making his or her own contribution. It's easy to feel that your contribution to your family, school, team or community is not important, but these groups only exist because they have been built up by the work of individuals like yourself. Everybody's contribution is important in helping to make any venture worthwhile and productive.

Prayer

Let us remember that we are all members of communities and that we each have a part to play in building our homes, our schools and towns. May we strive to be cheerful and useful members of all the communities to which we belong.

Amen

Day 3 | **A Geography Lesson**

Introduction

Show some aerial slides with either music or commentary.

Viewing the world from above, from an aeroplane or from the top of a tall building or mountain, is a wonderful sensation. When you fly over the land you can see the world from a fresh perspective as if you had grown new eyes. A city from the air can look wonderful because you can see it almost as a whole in a way that you never can from the ground. Even the most chaotic city viewed in this way seems well-planned and organised and peaceful. Seeing things from this angle helps us to realise what a wonderful world we live in; how much we have done with it and also how insignificant we are.

When the jet sprang into the sky,
it was clear why the city
had developed the way it had,
seeing it scaled six inches to the mile.
There seemed an inevitability
about what on ground had looked haphazard,
unplanned and without style
when the jet sprang into the sky.

When the jet reached ten thousand feet,
it was clear why the country
had cities where rivers ran
and why the valleys were populated.

The logic of geography –
That land and water attracted man –
was clearly delineated
when the jet reached ten thousand feet.

When the jet rose six miles high,
it was clear that the earth was round
and that it had more sea than land.
But it was difficult to understand
that the men on the earth found
causes to hate each other, to build
walls across cities and to kill.
From that height, it was not clear why.

Zulfikar Ghose

Prayer

May we learn to appreciate the beauty of the world in which
we live. May we play our part in preserving the beauty and
order of our world.

Amen

| Day 4 | **Mathematics** |

Using an overhead projector

Will someone give me a four-figure number?   e.g.   7413
(Write the number on the overhead project-
or transparency)
(From this number, the eventual answer to
the sum can be worked out in advance and
concealed. To do this, put a 2 in front of the
first figure – making a five-figure number –
and subtract 2 from this whole sum which
gives, in this case, the answer: 27411)

Can I have another four-figure number?   e.g.   2321

Let me put one down
(Write down the number which, added to
the number given, will make 9999)   i.e.   7678

Can I have another number?   e.g.   4513

Let me put another down
(Again, write down a number which will add
to the number just given to make 9999)   i.e.   5486
Now, let's add all those numbers together   ——————
(Reveal previously-concealed answer)   Total: 27411
        ——————

Magic? No; this was worked out using the laws of Mathematics. Many of the things you may have thought of as 'magic' when you were smaller, turn out to be the application of scientific knowledge – the use of our brains.

The human brain is an amazing object. It is made up of over 12,000 million cells – there are more cells in our brains than there are stars in the Milky Way.

We often talk about particular people being 'brainy' but we all have brains that are amazingly complex and which no one ever uses to the full. The potential of the human brain is enormous.

When we think of people as being 'brainy' what we mean is that they have discovered where their strengths and abilities lie and have set out to make maximum use of their brain power – a vast source of power which all of us have at our disposal.

Prayer

May we strive to make the best use possible of our abilities.

May we use our strength to help the weak, our wealth to help the poor and our brain power to dispel ignorance and prejudice.

Amen

| Day 5 |

Biology – Baby Animals

The best stimulus for this assembly is an incubator full of newly-hatched chicks. If chick-hatching is part of the science syllabus the opportunity of using them for an assembly is almost too good to miss. The incubator should be placed on a table at the front of the hall and a number of chicks taken out and shown by the pupils. A set of slides or a video showing chicks hatching will serve the same purpose but the 'real thing' is obviously preferable.

Alternatively, pupils could be asked to bring other baby animals to school, e.g. baby rabbits, kittens or pups and the assembly adapted accordingly.

Three weeks after a hen's egg has been fertilised and kept at body temperature, a crack appears. During the next hour a whole line of tiny cracks are made as the chick battles to break out of the shell which has provided it with food and shelter during its growth.

Eventually, the chick flops out – wet, bedraggled and unable to walk. Within another couple of hours it is dry, fluffy, walking, eating and making plenty of noise.

Baby animals are very appealing. Most of us at some time have seen young kittens or puppies, rabbits or foals and wanted to take them away with us and care for them. Almost everyone has this feeling which is why pictures of small animals appear on chocolate boxes and birthday cards. The very vulnerability of newly-born animals makes us feel protective. If we didn't have this instinct we wouldn't look after human babies and young children and our race wouldn't have survived as long as it has.

Few of us could be consciously cruel to a new-born animal and yet all of us are cruel and unkind to one another at times. If we can feel compassion for something as insignificant as these chicks, how can we fail to show compassion to one another?

It may be that we forget, or don't realise, that each one of us is almost as vulnerable as a new-born creature – not physically as helpless, but certainly capable of real hurt. We feel under a lot of pressure sometimes to hide our vulnerability. We would probably find that if we were less afraid of admitting our weaknesses to one another, there would be less unkindness, less thoughtlessness and less infliction of pain.

Prayer

May we accept the fact that other people are as vulnerable as we are ourselves and treat them with kindness and consideration.

Amen

24 Plays and Mimes: pupils' own assemblies

Day 1 Maxwell's Silver Hammer

The music is the Beatles' song: 'Maxwell's Silver Hammer' from the LP Abbey Road. Copies of the lyrics would be useful.

Main characters

MAXWELL wears a lab coat under which he sports an extreme example of the latest in teenage fashions.

JOAN Maxwell's girl friend. Needs a lab coat and test tubes. Also comb and mirror.

POLICE comic police of varying heights. Ill-fitting uniforms, truncheons and whistle if available.

TEACHER girl wearing gown and mortar board. Also blackboard and stick of chalk would be useful.

JUDGE wears a black cloak and wig.

CROWD responds to everything Maxwell does, miming horror, acclaim, amusement etc.

Props

Toy hammer or small mallet for Maxwell is the only important item.
2 phones   make-up   mirror   blackboard   test tubes
stethoscopes   truncheons   whistles   benches or chairs

Other jobs for pupils not wishing to appear on stage

wardrobe   make-up   props   sound technician
curtain operator   choreographer

Verse One

Opens with JOAN, stage left, working with test tubes. Enter MAXWELL, stage right – an extrovert character, swaggering in time to music.
Phones JOAN, asking her out.
Could have friends listening in, egging them both on.
JOAN nods – starts getting ready.
MAXWELL crosses to stage left and knocks on imaginary door. When JOAN opens it she is knocked unconscious. Rolls or is carried off stage.

Verse Two

SCHOOLCHILDREN file briskly in time to music to sit on chairs/benches.
TEACHER   begins lessons.
MAXWELL   (lab coat discarded now) disrupts class – fires imaginary pellets, pulls faces, chats up girls etc.
TEACHER mimes telling him off. Dismisses rest of class who file out, then peer at Maxwell through imaginary window.
TEACHER gives MAXWELL lines to write but, when she turns to write on the blackboard, he creeps up behind and knocks her out.

Verse Three

Musical Interlude
POLICE enter. Quick comedy routine with rhythmic leg-bending, truncheon swinging – preferably with one of them out of step.
Spot MAXWELL who is writing on imaginary wall rear-stage. After bumbling police chase, whistle-blowing, truncheon-waving, Maxwell is arrested and brought to court.
CROWD quickly file in and sit down. JUDGE appears stage left.
CROWD chant 'MAXWELL MUST GO FREE' to music.
Judge shakes his head. Meanwhile MAXWELL is creeping up behind him. Judge is knocked unconscious.
Final Music
Needs an organised dance routine which looks improvised
Possibilities include chanting – *Max-well – Clap . . . Clap . . . Clap . . .* from crowd. Or crowd carrying Maxwell around shoulder-high
A well-organised quick dance sequence at the end could include 'dead' characters returning and joining in the formation.

MAXWELL should be centre front stage for the final 'bang bang' when he knocks himself out.

Conclusion

Maxwell is fun to watch, especially as we know that it's all a mime and he isn't actually hurting anyone. People who really behave like that we call vandals or hooligans.

The people who performed this dance/drama had confidence in themselves. You need a lot of confidence to stand and perform on stage in front of an audience – especially an audience composed of your own schoolfriends.

Real hooligans seldom have any confidence. They don't have anything in life that they're good at or can be successful in so, as a last resort, they try to lay claim to fame by frightening little old ladies on their way home at night or by feeling proud to think that their name has been spray-painted on the walls of a public lavatory.

All of us want to have achievements we can be proud of. To do that we need to work at things people will respect – not despise us for.

Prayer

Let us give thanks for the pleasure we derive from music and entertainment.

May we seek from our entertainment a celebration of human life and its achievements.

May we never stoop to the level of having to destroy other people's achievements before we can start to foster belief and confidence in ourselves.

Amen

Day 2 **The Enchanted Shirt**

Speaking parts

18 READERS

KING	COURIER 2
DOCTOR 1	BEGGAR
DOCTOR 2	READER 19 for Conclusion
COURIER 1	READER 20 for Prayer

Mime only

2 PATIENTS	EXECUTIONER
CITIZENS	TWO MEN
DOCTORS	NAGGING WIFE

The number of characters can be varied to suit the size of the class.

(Mime)

READER 1   The Enchanted Shirt by John Hay

READER 2   The King was sick. His cheek was red,   (KING)
And his eye was clear and bright;
He ate and drank with a kingly zest,
And peacefully snored at night

READER 3   But he said he was sick, and a king should
know,   (KING, DOCTOR
And doctors came by the score.   EXECUTIONER)
They did not cure him. He cut off their heads,
And sent to the schools for more

READER 4   At last two famous doctors came,   (Enter
And one was as poor as a rat,   DOCTORS 1 and
He had passed his life in studious toil.   DOCTOR 1
And never found time to grow fat.   comes
                                                           forward.)

READER 5   The other had never looked in a book;   (DOCTOR 2 with
His patients gave him no trouble;   PATIENTS)
If they recovered, they paid him well;
If they died, their heirs paid double.

READER 6   Together they looked at the royal tongue,   (DOCTORS 1 and
As the King on his couch reclined;   2 with KING)
In succession they thumped his august chest,
But no trace of disease could find.

READER 7   The old sage said,   (DOCTOR 1 with
                                                           KING)
DOCTOR 1   'You're as sound as a nut.'

    KING   'Hang him up,'

READER 7   roared the King in a gale –
In a ten-knot gale of royal rage!
The other leech grew a shade pale;   (DOCTOR 2)

READER 8   But he pensively rubbed his sagacious nose,
           And thus his prescription ran –

DOCTOR 2   *The King will be well, if he sleeps one night*
           In the Shirt of a Happy Man.

READER 9   Wide o'er the realm the couriers rode,   (Enter
           And fast their horses ran,   COURIERS, take
           And many they saw, and to many they spoke,   orders from
           But they found no Happy Man.   KING, then
                                                           exit,
                                                           searching.)

EADER 10   They found poor men who would be rich,   (COURIERS and
           And rich who thought they were poor;   CITIZENS)
           And men who twisted their waist in stays,
           And women that shorthose wore.

EADER 11   They saw two men by the roadside sit,   (COURIERS, TWO
           And both bemoaned their lot;   MEN and
           For one had buried his wife, he said,   NAGGING WIFE)
           And the other one had not.

EADER 12   At last they came to a village gate,   (Enter BEGGAR
           A beggar lay whistling there;   doing
           He whistled, and sang, and laughed, and rolled acrobatics.)
           On the grass in the soft June air.

EADER 13   The weary couriers paused and looked   (COURIERS 1
           At the happy and carefree man;   and 2 with
           And one of them said,   BEGGAR)

OURIER 1   'Heaven save you friend,
           You enjoy life whilst you can!

BEGGAR   'Oh yes, fair sirs,'

EADER 14   the rascal laughed,
           And his voice rang free and glad;

BEGGAR   'An idle man has so much to do
           That he never has time to be sad.'

OURIER 2   'This is our man,'

EADER 14   the courier said;

COURIER 2   'Our luck has led us aright;
I will give you a hundred ducats, friend,
For the loan of your shirt tonight.'

READER 15   The merry blackguard lay back on the grass,   (acrobatics
And laughed till his face was black;   from BEGGAR

BEGGAR   'I would do it, God wot,'

READER 15   and he roared with the fun,

BEGGAR   'But I haven't a shirt to my back.'

READER 16   Each day to the King the reports came in   (KING and
Of his unsuccessful spies,   CITIZENS)
And the sad panorama of human woes
Passed daily under his eyes.

READER 17   And he grew ashamed of his useless life,   (KING)
And his maladies hatched in gloom;
He opened his windows and let the air
Of the free heaven into his room.

READER 18   And out he went in the world and worked   (KING and
Through good times and through bad;   CITIZENS)
And the people blessed him, the land was rich
And the King was healthy and glad.   (All characte
return and
applaud KIN

Conclusion

READER 19 The only person in this story who was really happy was the man who seemed to have nothing – not even a shirt to wear.

It's easy to think that everyone else in the world is happier than you. When you have problems, you think that nobody else in the world has ever suffered as much.

But when, like the King, you start to listen to the problems other people have, you may find that, in comparison with everyone else, you're really quite well off.

Prayer

READER 20 Let us remember that true happiness only comes from what we are – not from what we own.

If we allow ourselves to be miserable just because we think we don't own enough, we can find that we are simply wasting our lives away.

May we discover happiness by finding people who need us, work that absorbs us and the peace of mind which so often evades us.

Amen

Day 3 | Booker T Washington: This Is Your Life

A full script is given here for one assembly but the 'TV biography' treatment can be adapted for any similar character.

Costume would be useful but is not essential.

Some of the cast of this assembly are fictitious characters. Others may be added and names changed to suit the size of the class and the sex of the actors. The commentators' part can be shared by as many actors as necessary.

Booker T Washington's words are taken from his autobiography, *Up from Slavery* and *My Life and Work*.

Characters

14 COMMENTATORS
BOOKER T WASHINGTON
ELIZABETH BURROUGHS – *plantation owner's daughter*
GENERAL SAMUEL C ARMSTRONG – *Principal of Hampton College.*
JOHN J JOHNSON ⎫
DELROY SMITH ⎬ *fictional characters*
AUDIENCE *and* GUESTS *at the Opening Ceremony*

COMMENTATOR 1	Ladies and Gentlemen, we are gathered here today for the opening of the magnificent new science block at Tuskegee Institute. But we have another purpose. We know you will be pleased to join us in honouring the founder and principal of this famous institution ... Dr Booker T Washington – This is Your Life. ...

Applause. Booker T Washington strides forward and shakes hands.

COMMENTATOR 2   Dr Washington, your story begins nearly 60 years ago in 1858 in a tumble-down shack where you were born, the son of a slave, on the Burroughs plantation. Do you remember your parents at all?

BOOKER   I never knew my father. I had no surname and I myself chose the name, Washington. I used to be listed on the property inventory simply as 'Booker – value 400 pounds'. My mother's name was Jane. She was wholly ignorant as far as books were concerned. But the lessons she instilled into me during her short period of life will never leave me.

COMMENTATOR 3   Can you remember working on the plantations?

BOOKER   Yes, indeed. As a very young boy I carried cans of water to the slaves in the fields. I also went to the Plantation House to pull the ropes that controlled the fans.

COMMENTATOR 4   Can you remember this voice?

ELIZABETH   (*From off-stage*) Fetch my books, boy. Hurry now.

BOOKER   That has to be one of the Burroughs girls – Elizabeth, maybe?

COMMENTATOR 5   Elizabeth Burroughs, three years your senior, daughter of the owner of the plantation on which you worked.

Elizabeth Burroughs comes forward and shakes hands.

ELIZABETH   In those days Booker used to carry my books and those of my sisters to school. Those were the days of slavery you understand.

COMMENTATOR 6   Did it ever occur to you that this slave was destined to become the learned man he is today?

ELIZABETH   The idea never entered my head. We were brought up to think of slaves as

	beasts of burden – too stupid even to read. I guess we were the ones who were foolish.
BOOKER	From the time I can remember having any thoughts about anything I recall that I had an intense longing to read.
COMMENTATOR 7	State laws of the time made it illegal for a slave to go to school, but in 1865, slavery was abolished. You were nine years old and started work in a salt furnace and then in a coal mine. Our next guest is a companion from those days ....
JOHN J JOHNSON	(*Enters and shakes hands*) Life was tough in those days. We worked hard and long for very little money. Booker had no money; his step-father took it all. He owned one shirt, one pair of britches, no coat, no shoes, no socks. I remember the only thing Booker really wanted was to learn to read. Do you remember your first book?
BOOKER	I remember it very well. I had begged my mother for a book – any book – and one day she got me a second-hand spelling book. That book was really precious to me.
JOHN J JOHNSON	You asked every man in the mine to show you how to read that book, but no-one could.
BOOKER	In the end I managed to teach myself.
COMMENTATOR 8	Your other overriding ambition was to go to school. A school did open nearby but your step-father wouldn't allow you to go.
BOOKER	He didn't want to lose my wages, but he did let me go to evening lessons and I learned quickly. Later on, I was allowed to go to school but, before I set off, I had to go and work in the mine from four until nine o'clock in the morning.

COMMENTATOR 9 When you were 16, you left home and found a High School that would take you. Delroy Smith, one of your fellow students there can still remember you . . .

DELROY SMITH (*Walks forward*) I can remember Booker T Washington as the brightest student in the school. We had to pay for the lessons of course, but Booker persuaded the principal to let him work as school caretaker in order to raise the money. Every evening he swept out the classrooms and did many hours of extra work. In spite of all that, he passed his exams and became a teacher.

COMMENTATOR 10 For two years, Dr Washington, you worked as a village teacher – teaching black children. By now your ambition was to supply really superior education for your people. You went back to school in Washington DC and took a degree. The son of a slave became Dr Washington, highly-qualified and well-respected. You took up a teaching job at a secondary school, but you were still not satisfied.

GENERAL (*From off-stage*) I was most impressed by Booker as a young man, and when a Negro school was proposed at Tuskegee I recommended him.

BOOKER General Armstrong . . . .

COMMENTATOR 11 Your principal at Hamton, the man who recognised your abilities . . .

General Armstrong strides forward and shakes hands.

GENERAL That school wasn't up to much. It was a leaky wooden church and a rickety cabin. There were no desks and only a few pupils but Booker went to work at once.

COMMENTATOR 12 He was how old? 25? That was quite a responsibility.

GENERAL   Sure, but Booker coped with it. He recruited pupils, raised money, bought land. He and his pupils cleared the land and built a three-storey school house. The school grew and Booker T Washington became the inspiration for the rest of Black America.

COMMENTATOR 13   Now, 35 years after the school first started, Tuskagee Institute consists of a 100 buildings, 200 teachers and 1,500 students.

COMMENTATOR 14   As Tuskegee has grown, so has the prestige of its founder. Three American presidents have sought out the help and advice of this man ... Booker T Washington ... This is Your Life!

Applause and congratulations from guests and audience.

Conclusion

Booker T Washington was born into great hardship and repression. He was very fortunate in having both the ability and the determination to become successful. Dr Washington used his success, however, to enable his own people to obtain better education and standards of living. Many young people in the United States owe their education to the pioneering work of men such as Booker T Washington.

Prayer

Lord grant us the serenity to accept those things we cannot change; the courage to change the things we can, and the wisdom to know the difference.

Amen

Day 4   **Vincent Van Gogh**

This assembly can be done as a straight reading with different speakers, or it can be enhanced by the use of dance and/or film slides. In this case, the recording of 'Vincent' by

Don Maclean would be most useful plus slides or film strip of Van Gogh's work which are obtainable from many art galleries or teachers' centres. For the dance work, an artist's palette, either real or made from plywood or cardboard is necessary.

15 READERS

READER 1 Our assembly today is about one of the world's most famous and popular artists, Vincent Van Gogh.

READER 2 Vincent was born in 1853, the son of a clergyman, at Groot-Zundert in Holland.

READER 3 For a time he worked in London and then became a French teacher at a boarding school in Ramsgate.

READER 4 One of his jobs was to collect school fees from the parents who lived at Whitechapel. When he saw the terrible poverty of the area, he returned without collecting the money and was sacked.

READER 5 Van Gogh was a deeply religious person and he became a lay preacher and missionary in a coal-mining district of Belgium before he took up painting.

READER 6 He gave most of his possessions to the poor and slept in a simple wooden hut.

READER 7 He preached and nursed the sick. He worked so hard that he became sick himself and had to give up his mission.

READER 8 Eventually, he devoted himself completely to painting. In the last seven years of his life he painted thousands of pictures but could not sell a single one. He remained desperately poor.

READER 9 Van Gogh had periods of acute depression and madness and was eventually put into a hospital for the insane. In spite of this, however, he still continued painting.

READER 10 Eventually, at the age of 37, Vincent Van Gogh shot himself.

Dance sequence
Small groups of pupils could listen to the song and work out their own sequences.
Other pupils could work out an appropriate order and timing for the slides.
Pictures can be projected onto the screen together with the shadow of the dancer symbolising Van Gogh. The main dancer can 'paint' using the palette and a brush, moving rhythmically – sometimes frenzied, sometimes frozen, sometimes showing despair, and acting out the final suicide. Supporting dancers can surround the artist and work in sequence.

READER 11   Today Van Gogh is one of the world's most popular artists and his work is priceless. You will probably find that you already know and recognise some of his pictures.

READER 12   In Amsterdam there is a huge, multi-million-pound art gallery dedicated to his work. It seems ironical that during his lifetime no one wanted to buy his paintings.

READER 13   Vincent's style of painting was different from any other painters and, as always, people were mistrustful of anything new. They thought that, if Van Gogh didn't paint like the traditional artists, he couldn't paint at all.

READER 14   Many of his contemporaries, in fact, laughed at his work and thought he was stupid. Looking back, it seems as though they were the ones who were stupid for failing to appreciate his talent.

Prayer

READER 15   Let us pray that we may open our minds to new ideas. When we encounter different forms of expression in music, art or writing, or when we listen to people with different points of view, may we try to be open-minded and listen to whatever truths they may hold for us.

Amen

Day 5 **Martin Luther King**

Speaking parts

3 NEWSREADERS, 3 REPORTERS, LOUISE RIVERS, WOMAN 1, WOMAN 2, MAN 1, MAN 2, 3 READERS

Props

2 tapes – TV news music, and Martin Luther King's 'I Have a Dream' speech, desk, microphones (could be dummies)

The assembly begins with a recording (or reading) of Martin Luther King's speech. This is interrupted by 'TV news' music.

NEWSREADER 1   News is just coming in of the murder of civil rights leader, Martin Luther King, in Memphis, Tennessee. Over to our reporter . . .

REPORTER 1   Martin Luther King was shot today on the balcony of this motel. It is assumed that a gunman fired at him from the window of a bathroom in the building opposite. Dr King was dead before he reached hospital. There is no trace of his killer.

NEWSREADER 2   Dr Martin Luther King was born in the South in 1929. He became a minister of religion in Montgomery, Alabama where his work as a civil rights leader began. His death is a tragic blow to both black and white in America. Over to Montgomery.

REPORTER 2   The first news of Martin Luther King's assassination reached Montgomery half an hour ago. By now, everyone seems to have heard and groups of people, many of whom knew Dr King as a minister and friend, are gathering on the streets. Their mood is one of anger and sadness.

(*Approaching a group of people*) Excuse me, madam. Did you know Dr King?

WOMAN 1   Yes, I did. I was involved in the beginning of the movement against segregation here in Montgomery. It was widespread then. Many restaurants, theatres and cinemas had 'Whites Only' notices. Black people were not allowed into such places. In others, some of the poorer seats were set aside for blacks. Even the buses had separate seats for blacks and whites. That's how it started.

MAN 1 One day a Negro woman refused to sit in the seat where she was supposed to and she was sent to prison.

WOMAN 2 It was Dr King who organised the resistance against that. He told us to find a way to stop travelling on the buses.

MAN 2 So we walked to work, or shared cars. Lots of taxi drivers helped by taking people to work for the price of a bus ride. It wasn't easy but we held out for almost a year and the bus company had to give in and that was the end of segregation there.

REPORTER 3 And this was the first of a line of victories for Martin Luther King and the Civil Rights Movement. With me is a friend and associate of Dr King's who will attempt to explain the importance of Dr King's work.

LOUISE RIVERS Dr King organised the black people of America to claim their rights by non-violent means. He had no time for those who urged riots and armed resistance. It is ironic that this man of peace should have died in this way. He led the black people of America in their fights against segregation in schools, shops, restaurants and all public buildings. He set an example to us all. We occupied white seats in those places; we were arrested; we went to jail; we came out and did it again – and again. We did not defend ourselves against our enemies and we were attacked many times – sometimes by the police, but we won through.

REPORTER 2 There have been other attempts on Dr King's life...

LOUISE RIVERS Yes, indeed. He was thrown in jail many times and beaten up. He was stoned and stabbed. His house was bombed. Now he is dead, but his work will go on.

REPORTER 2   From a bitter and mourning Montgomery, Alabama ... back to the studio.

NEWSREADER 3   Martin Luther King's work has resulted in laws forbidding the segregation of blacks and whites in schools and public buildings throughout America. He was widely loved and widely hated. Today that hatred cut him down. Martin Luther King is dead, but his work and his memory will live on in the minds of all who believe in justice and in freedom.

(*The second extract from Martin Luther King's speech could be used here*).

Conclusion

READER 1   The Civil Rights Movement was the organisation which claimed equal treatment for black people in America. The importance of Martin Luther King, its leader, has been recognised with numerous memorials throughout the United States.

READER 2   The motel room where Martin Luther King was staying on that fateful day in Memphis was an unpretentious place. Today, the only thing to distinguish that room is a simple plaque bearing a quotation from the Bible.

READER 3   The quotation refers to Joseph and the dreams which *he* had. It says:
'And they said one to another, "Behold, the dreamer cometh. Let us slay him; and we shall see what will become of his dream".'
You remember what became of Joseph's dream.

Prayer

May we learn to live and work together peacefully. Let us strive to overcome injustice and ignorance wherever we may find them. May we help to play our part in enabling people's dreams of a better, fairer world to turn into reality.

Amen

25 Plays and Mimes: pupils' own assemblies

Day 1 Nelson Mandela

Speaking parts

NELSON MANDELA
WINNIE MANDELA
3 NEWSREADERS
5 SPEAKERS

Recommended music: There are many recordings available of South African freedom songs by groups such as Mayibuye. Also a recording of 'Nelson Mandela' by Specials AKA.

SPEAKER 1   Our assembly begins with some international news from South Africa.

NEWSREADER 1   Soweto anniversary marked by tear gas.

NEWSREADER 2   Police fired tear gas yesterday at black youths who pelted their vehicle with stones. The clashes occurred after an emotional church service to commemorate those who died in the Soweto riots of 1976.

NEWSREADER 1   Abandoned baby coloured, say police.

NEWSREADER 3   Police say that a month-old baby found abandoned yesterday in a field is coloured, but the government has not yet formally classified the child's race. The case focuses attention on South Africa's race classification system. The race assigned to the girl will determine who can adopt her, which school she will be allowed to attend and where she will be allowed to live.

(Recommended music may be played or performed here.)

SPEAKER 1   In many parts of the world, people go to prison, not for committing crimes, but simply because they have different political views from those of their government. One such country is South Africa, a country with which Britain has very close links through history and through commercial ties.

SPEAKER 2   South Africa is a country of over 20 million blacks and only 4½ million whites. Whites are the immigrant population in South Africa, having gone there originally from Great Britain and Holland, but only the whites have political rights. Blacks may not vote or organise themselves and, wherever possible, they are kept separate from whites – they have to live in different areas, attend different schools, be treated at different hospitals, bathe at different beaches etc. And always the facilities they use and the conditions in which they live are inferior to those of the white population. This system of separation and discrimination is called apartheid.

SPEAKER 3   Blacks who object to the system are brutally treated. In 1976, over 1,000 people, mainly school students, were shot dead by police in the town of Soweto during protests about their inferior schooling.

Black leaders who oppose apartheid are sent to prison. White people too who, in some cases, challenge the apartheid system suffer the same fate. David Kitson, a white trade unionist and opponent of apartheid was jailed for 20 years in 1964. There are many others.

SPEAKER 4   The most famous of South Africa's political prisoners however, is Nelson Mandela, black leader of the African National Congress. He has become a symbol of the oppression of his people and of the fate of all the country's prisoners. Nelson Mandela was tried and imprisoned for life in 1963. It is likely that he will remain in jail until he dies. He was charged with seeking to overthrow the apartheid system. At this trial he said this:

NELSON MANDELA   I was made by the law, a criminal, not because of what I have done, but because of what I stood for, because of what I thought ... because of my conscience ... It has not been easy for me ... to separate myself from my wife and children, to say goodbye to the good days when, at the end of a strenuous day at the office, I could look forward to joining my family at the dinner table and, instead, take up the life of a man hunted continuously by the police.

Living separated from those closest to me, in my own country, facing continuously the hazards of detection and arrest ... No man in his right senses would voluntarily choose such a life ... but there comes a time, as it came in my life, when a man is denied the right to live a normal life, when he can only live the life of an outlaw because the government has so decreed ...

I have dedicated myself to this struggle of the African people. I have fought against white domination. I have cherished the ideal of a democratic and free society in which all persons live together in harmony and with equal opportunities. It is an ideal which I hope to live for and to achieve. But if needs be it is an ideal for which I am prepared to die.

SPEAKER 1   Mandela's wife, Winnie, has also suffered long periods of prison detention and house arrest. She has described what detention has meant to her:

WINNIE MANDELA   That midnight knock when all about you is quiet. It means those blinding torches shone through every window of your house before the door is kicked open ... it means your seizure at dawn, dragged away from children screaming and clinging to your skirt, imploring the white men dragging mummy to leave her alone. It means being held in a single cell with the light burning 24 hours so that I lost track of time and was unable to tell whether it was day or night.

Prayer

SPEAKER 5   Let us remember the millions throughout the world who experience tyranny and repression. Let us remember Nelson Mandela and the many thousands of his people who are imprisoned by the apartheid system in South Africa. Let us praise those with the courage to struggle and suffer in the cause of freedom. Let us pledge to learn more about injustice, to tell others of it, and to do what we can to end it.

Amen

Day 2   ## Loneliness

The mimes included here are very simple and demand little acting ability on the part of the class.
Short speaking parts for 13 pupils. (With a smaller class it will be easy for pupils to take more than one part.)
Other pupils can take part in the mime.
Optional music: *Eleanor Rigby* or *The Streets of London*
The mime can be done by one or more groups of pupils depending on the numbers available.

READER 1   (*stage right*)
Alone
An island
Unconnected
Untouched
Isolated.

Single pupil enters from stage left and wanders around the stage.

READER 2	I am safe Independent I cannot be rejected I cannot be hurt.	*Group(s) of pupils enter from both sides. They walk amiably together then stand and chat. One of them is teased playfully.*
READER 3	Yet *they* are together Enjoying each other. They cry and are comforted; They share their laughter. They touch.	*Single pupil walks enviously past groups. Someone is comforted then they laugh and hug each other.*
READER 4	I need others I must make contact They do not see me They do not hear me I increase my efforts	*Single pupil approaches others with faint smile and half-hearted wave. Then walks forward with determination.* *Speaks: 'Hello.'*
READER 1	I'm real. I can talk and laugh I can cry and touch I am not alone.	*Mimes talking to the group. They listen attentively, smile and nod. Someone clasps his/her shoulder. They walk off stage amiably together.*

READER 5   Being on your own is not the same as being lonely. You can be happy on your own. We all

need the space to spend some time with ourselves but we also need other people.

READER 6 Loneliness is wanting to be with other people but not being able to reach them. Or being too afraid of other people in case they might tease you or reject you.

READER 7 There are people who are blind or handicapped or who suffer other terrible disabilities who, nevertheless, live happy lives. But not many lonely people are happy. In fact loneliness and happiness can be opposites.

READER 8 Old people are often lonely. Their friends and relatives may have died and not many other people find time to spare for the elderly. Almost every city and town in the world has many old people living alone and isolated.

Optional music – 'Eleanor Rigby' or 'The Streets of London' – both of which would lend themselves to simple mimes.

READER 9 But it is not just old people who are lonely. All of us can be desperately lonely sometimes and some people of all ages are lonely almost all the time.

READER 10 If ever you are lonely, it will be because, for all kinds of reasons, you lack the confidence to make contact and join in with things that other people are doing. This is true of adults just as much as children.

READER 11 It can be a great effort to talk to people first or to ask to join in with what they are doing because that means facing the possibility of rejection, but it is still well worth it.

READER 12 If you show interest in other people and what they're doing and if you ask them questions about themselves, they'll nearly always be happy to talk to you. Most other people you meet are probably wanting to make friends as well.

READER 13 Remember that all of us are unique. Every person is wonderful in their own way no matter how often they may be told otherwise.

Prayer

Let us make sure that we remember to include in our conversation and activities not just popular people but also those who may be wanting and seeking friends. Let us remember that everyone we meet is unique and has something they can teach us.

Amen

Day 3 | **The Parable of the Lost Sheep**

Preparation

Record or tape – *L'Arlésienne* by Bizet
Reminiscences from pupils about times when they have been lost or when they have lost something important
Costume for sheep – white tights, white jumpers, cotton wool tails
Costume for wolf – cardboard pointed nose or mask, pointed ears, black leotard, tail
Costume for shepherd – dressing gown, walking stick for crook

5 SPEAKERS

SPEAKER 1   Many of us lose all kinds of things: pens, pencils, pieces of paper with important notes on, addresses, homework books, glasses and PE kits.

SPEAKER 2   Almost all of us have lost something important at some time.

Individual reminiscences from pupils about the times when they have lost something important.

SPEAKER 3   It is not unusual for parents to lose their children for a short time. This can be very upsetting for the parents and for the child.

Individual accounts from pupils about the times when they have been lost.

SPEAKER 4   Jesus told a story of a sheep that strayed and was lost.

Enter sheep.

> Palestine was a dangerous place for lost sheep. Wild animals such as wolves lived in the hills.

Brief appearance by wolf, leering or howling at sheep. Sheep run to the speaker for protection.

> In the story, the shepherd left his flock to go and search for the lost sheep.

Dance sequence to 'L'Arlésienne'. During the slow phrases the sheep move with playful and fairly graceful movements on different levels and in different directions. During the quick phrases the wolf moves in a series of diving, lunging and aggressive movements. One of the sheep wanders away from the rest of the flock. The wolf stalks the sheep, or cavorts round it in cartwheels or diving rolls.

SPEAKER 5   A shepherd had 100 sheep. One evening when he counted his flock he realised that one was missing.

Shepherd walks up and down, counting his sheep.

> He counted again. He began to imagine all the dangers his lost sheep might be in. He left his 99 safe sheep and searched all night for the lost one.

Shepherd searches for sheep.

> At last he found it and brought it home rejoicing.

A note on the horn signals the end of the dance phrases and the arrival of the shepherd to drive off or kill the wolf. The music needs to be faded out at this point.

Prayer

Let us be grateful for the love which accepts us with all our faults and which finds us when we are lost.

(Recommended hymn: 'Amazing Grace')

Amen

| Day 4 | **Advertising** |

Characters

12 READERS	SEBASTIAN SLOW – ATHLETE
MAD SCIENTIST	PAINTERS AND DECORATORS
FAMILY	'BEAUTIFUL PERSON'

Plus, pupils reading out their own original ideas to put an advertiser's gloss on local places with no genuine appeal e.g. a run-down recreation ground, the local bus station, a waiting room, the most delapidated part of the school.

READER 1   It took our team of top-level scientists years of careful research to develop the new miracle ingredient, Bio-lavo-halitosis ZL97.

Mad scientist wearing lab coat with test tubes. A small slight accident after the word 'careful' would add interest.

READER 2   Advertisers pretend to present us with the facts but all the time they are appealing to our emotions. This advertisement is directed at our faith in science.

READER 3   This winter you and your family could fall victim to Multiplicosis. To guard against this terrible disease, buy KURALL.

Family coughing, sneezing and fainting. Someone rushes in with KURALL which they inhale and then skip and dance round the stage.

READER 4   This advertisement relies on our fear.

READER 5	Sebastian Slow, star of screen and stadium, says:	*Enter S, wearing towel or bath robe, dressing his hair or splashing on after-shave.*
SEBASTIAN	I always use OLSOX after-shave to make sure no-one gets near me on the track.	
READER 6	Advertisements like this appeal to our admiration of the famous.	
READER 7	Only the most beautiful people use YUKKY shampoo remember the name, everyone: Yukky shampoo.	*Enter pupil in glamorous costume or boy in drag. Shakes hair at audience, combs or brushes it, then shows them YUKKY shampoo.*
READER 4	Advertisements like this appeal to our vanity	
READER 8	Ask your local firm of painters and decorators which paint they use and they will tell you: SPLASHO.	*Enter painting team with overalls, brushes, paste bucket, step ladder. They then paste each other, spilling the bucket, wrapping each other in wallpaper.*
READER 6	This advertisement appeals to our respect for experts.	

READER 9   Advertisements are often populated by people who conform to an image that is completely unreal. The women in magazine advertisements are nearly always young, slim and well-groomed.

READER 10   Truth in advertising is not the same as truth elsewhere. In advertisements for houses: *compact* usually means tiny and cramped; *secluded* means miles from anywhere; *quaint* means very old-fashioned and *in need of renovation* means that the house is falling to pieces.

Some original ideas from pupils to describe a local place in advertising jargon here.

READER 11   Large sums of money are spent advertising things of little importance. Most of the really good things in life are never advertised.

READER 12   Things like friendship, peace and honesty, kindness and trust. These things bring real happiness.

Prayer

We are surrounded by demands for our attention. May we recognise and learn to respond to truth. May we seek out those things which are of lasting importance and are truly worthwhile.

Amen

| Day 5 | **War** |

Characters

LORD	GROUP OF PEOPLE (2 or 3)
GENERAL	SISTER
FELLOW	MOTHER
EMPLOYER	COMMENTATOR
17 SPEAKERS	

Preparation

It would be useful to ask the pupils each to interview anyone they know who has been involved in a war – either in the services or as a civilian. Several pupils could then produce for the assembly an edited account of the interview.

As numbers are so difficult to comprehend, it would also be useful for pupils to find ways of portraying one million. They might start by drawing large dots on pieces of paper and, when they had run out of time, patience and paper, then estimate how long it would take to finish the task. Another way would be to programme a computer to draw a million dots, a million crosses, or a million 'matchstick men'.

For the first part of the assembly, some simple costume would help such as appropriate headgear: a top hat for the lord; a military hat for the general, a woolly hat or cloth cap for the fellow; a bowler hat for the employer; a woman's hat or headscarf for the mother.

SPEAKER 1   What is war, my lord?

LORD   War is empire.

COMMENTATOR   Throughout history, men have waged war to steal land and riches from other people. Whole countries have been taken over by foreign invaders.

SPEAKER 2   What is war, general?

GENERAL   War is heroism.

COMMENTATOR   Throughout history, young men have been expected to prove their bravery by fighting and killing.

SPEAKER 3   What is war, fellow?

FELLOW   War is escape.

COMMENTATOR   One reason why men have been willing to go to war is that they become bored with ordinary life and think that war will be exciting. In the past soldiers were sometimes recruited from prisons and are often still recruited from the unemployed.

SPEAKER 4   What is war, kind employer?

EMPLOYER   War is profit.

COMMENTATOR   Thousands of people are employed in making weapons of war. Millions of pounds are made from their sale.

SPEAKER 5　What is war, people?

PEOPLE　War is the bombs falling on our homes.

COMMENTATOR　In modern warfare, thousands of ordinary civilians are killed. Nobody is safe.

SPEAKER 6　Sister, what is war?

SISTER　War is a telegram.

SPEAKER 7　Mother, what is war?

MOTHER　War is three undiscovered graves.

Adapted from 'Definition' by Lawrence Collinson

SPEAKER 8　Most of us know people who have been involved in war. We gathered information from parents, grandparents, uncles, and neighbours about their memories of war.

Brief reports gathered by the pupils of the Falklands war, Suez, the Blitz, Northern Ireland etc.

SPEAKER 9　Wars often result in destruction, starvation, disease, homelessness and death.

SPEAKER 10　During the Second World War, nearly nine million Jews were put to death by the Germans. In the First World War, eight and a half million people died. Nor is it just 'other countries' who cause unnecessary suffering. The British air raids on Dresden towards the end of the Second World War killed 135,000 people most of whom were civilians and many of them refugees. 325,000 British people were killed in the Second World War but the combined total of dead for the Soviet Union, China and Poland came to 40 million.

SPEAKER 11　It is almost impossible to imagine a million.

Previously prepared display to try and depict a million. If dots appear on a screen at the rate of two per second, it will take approximately five and three quarter days to show a million. The pupils can calculate how long it will take a computer to show a million dots at normal speed.

SPEAKER 12   The world never seems to learn from its mistakes. The Second World War had only just finished when another war started in the tiny country of Vietnam. The war lasted three decades, cost millions of lives, 150 billion dollars and there were more bombs dropped on Vietnam than were dropped in the whole of the Second World War.

SPEAKER 13   Since 1945 there have been wars in:

India	Afghanistan	Namibia
Korea	Jordan	Nicaragua
Guatemala	Zimbabwe	Egypt
Pakistan	Northern Ireland	Syria
Lebanon	Vietnam	Chad
Nigeria	Cuba	Israel
Ethiopia	Indonesia	Iraq
Cambodia	Iran	Angola
Granada	Mozambique	The Falklands
El Salvador		

(Other, more recent conflicts can be added here.) The list is almost endless.

SPEAKER 14   Another world war could destroy countless millions of people. How could it be prevented?

General, Your Tank Is a Powerful Vehicle

SPEAKER 15   General, that tank of yours is some car.
It can wreck a forest, crush a hundred men.
But it has one failing:
It needs a driver.

SPEAKER 16   General, you've got a good bomber there.
It can fly faster than the wind, carry more
than an elephant can.
But it has one failing:
It needs a mechanic.

SPEAKER 17   General, a man is a useful creature.
He can fly and he can kill.
But he has one failing:
He can *think*.

Bertolt Brecht

Prayer

Let us give thought in our prayers today for those who are involved in areas of conflict throughout the world. For those who have been made homeless by war and whose friends and families have been killed. May God bless and give strength to all those who are working for peace.

Amen

Acknowledgements

We are grateful to the following for permission to reproduce copyright material:

Angus & Robertson (UK) Ltd for the poem 'Beach Burial' by Kenneth Slessor from *Poems*; Associated Book Publishers Ltd for the poem 'General, Your Tank is a Powerful Vehicle' by Bertolt Brecht from *Poems 1913–1956* trans. Lee Baxenhall, pub. Methuen, London; Autocover, Farnborough for extracts from 'Insurance Forms'; The Bodley Head for extracts from *The Pinballs* and *The Eighteenth Emergency* both by Betsy Byars; Jonathan Cape Ltd for a slightly abridged version of chapter 1 from *Run for Your Life* by David Line, and the poem 'The Identification' by Roger McGough from *Gig*; Jonathan Cape Ltd & the Executors of the W H Davies Estate for the poem 'Leisure' from *The Complete Poems of W H Davies*; author's agents for the poems 'I am the Great Sun', 'Timothy Winters', 'The Ballad of the Bread Man' by Charles Causley from *Collected Poems*, pub. Macmillan; the author, Lawrence Collinson for his poem 'Definition' from a collection entitled *The Moods of Love*, pub. Overland 1957; the author, Ronald Deadman for his poem 'Carol'; the author, Ian M Emberson for his poem 'Voting'; Eyre & Spottiswoode Ltd, Her Majesty's Printers London for extracts from *Authorised King James Version of the Bible*, which is Crown Copyright in the United Kingdom; Faber & Faber Ltd for extracts from *Gowie Corby Plays Chicken* by Gene Kemp, and the poem 'Rising Five' by Norman Nicholson from *The Pot Geranium*; Gill & Macmillan Ltd for the poems 'Lord I Have Time', 'I Like Youngsters' by Michel Quoist from *Prayers for Life*; Victor Gollancz Ltd for extracts from *The Great Gilly Hopkins* by Katherine Paterson, and *Z for Zachariah* by Robert C O'Brien; William Heinemann Ltd for an extract from the story 'Gaffer Roberts' from *Skulker Wheat* by John Griffin; author's agents on behalf of the Estate of M Louise Haskins for an extract from her poem 'God Knows' from *The Gate of the Year*, pub. Hodder & Stoughton, © 1940 by Minnie Lou Haskins; Hodder & Stoughton Ltd for extracts from *Run, Baby Run* by Nicky Cruz with Jamie

Buckingham, and *A Cup of Water* by Janet Lacey; Hutchinson Publishing Group for the poem 'A Dormitory Suburb' by Jenny Scott from *Say it Aloud* ed. Norman Hidden; Joan Daves for an extract from 'I Have a Dream' speech by Martin Luther King Jr. Copyright © 1963 by Martin Luther King Jr; Longman Group Ltd for the stories 'The Fib', 'The Long Walk' by George Layton from *The Fib & Other Stories: A Northern Childhood*, Longman Knockouts Series, 1976, 1978; Macmillan London & Basingstoke for the poem 'Geography Lesson' by Zulfikar Ghose from *Jets from Orange*; National Council of the Churches of Christ for extracts from the *Revised Standard Version of the Bible*; Oxford University Press for extracts from *The Trouble with Donovan Croft* by Bernard Ashley, © Bernard Ashley 1974; Oxford & Cambridge University Presses for extracts from *New English Bible* 2nd edition, © 1970; Pegasus Press Ltd for the poem 'On the Swag' by R A K Mason from *Collected Poems*; the author, Stephen Plaice for his poem 'The Landscape'; Penguin Books Ltd for extracts from pp. 28–9, 67, 72–3 *Hiroshima* by John Hersey (Penguin Modern Classics 1972). Copyright © John Hersey, 1966; The Samaritans for an extract from a *'Samaritans' Publicity Leaflet*, (THE SAMARITANS: To help the suicidal and despairing Your nearest Branch is in the telephone directory. Administrative office – 17 Uxbridge Road, Slough SL1 1SN, tn. Slough 32713); the author, Revd. Denis Shaw for his poem 'A Peace Movement Called Steve'; James McGibbon Executor to the Stevie Smith Estate for the poem 'The Frog Prince' from *Collected poems of Stevie Smith* (Allen Lane); The Society of Authors on behalf of the Laurence Binyon Estate and Mrs Nicolette Gray for the poem 'For the Fallen (September 1914)' by Laurence Binyon; author's agents on behalf of Sue Townsend for extracts from her *The Secret Diary of Adrian Mole aged 13¾*, pub. Methuen. Copyright © 1982 by Sue Townsend; Western Publishing Company Inc for the poem 'The Fox and the Grapes' and an adaptation of the poem 'The Frogs who Wanted a King' by Louis Untermeyer from *Golden Treasury of Poetry*, © 1959 by Western Publishing Co. Inc; author's agents, Michael B. Yeats and Anne Yeats for the poems 'He Wishes for the Cloths of Heaven' and 'When You Are Old' by W B Yeats from *Collected Poems of W B Yeats*, pub. Macmillan.

We have unfortunately been unable to trace the copyright owners of the poems 'The Shape God Wears' by Sara Henderson Hay, and the poem by Pastor Niemoeller, and would appreciate any information which would enable us to do so.

Linda Hoy would like to thank her friend John Flatley for the use of his assembly on Nelson Mandela.